Building Confidence in Communication

Daniel M. Dunn
Purdue University Calumet

Scott, Foresman and Company
Glenview, Illinois   Boston   London

Acknowledgments are listed on pages 369–370, which constitute a legal extension of the copyright page.

Library of Congress Cataloging-in-Publication Data

Dunn, Daniel (Daniel M.)
Building confidence in communication.

Bibliography: p.
Includes index.
1. Public speaking. 2. Communication—Psychological
aspects. 3. Interpersonal communication. I. Title.
PN4121.D924 1989   808.5   88-26449
ISBN 0-673-39929-X

1 2 3 4 5 6—MVN—94 93 92 91 90 89

Preface

Building Confidence in Communication is an introductory textbook for college students that integrates the principles of interpersonal and public communication. The book is designed for instructors who wish to include the following ideas in their basic course: (1) one's confidence as a communicator can be enhanced by practicing activities that focus on skills associated with effective interpersonal and public communication; (2) interpersonal growth can be enhanced through public speaking; (3) self-esteem can be improved through public speaking; and (4) public speaking is a way of sharing ideas with an audience, not merely performing for an audience.

Although the text is grounded in theory, it stresses the practical application of communication skills. Each chapter includes application activities and special sections for practicing specific skills to improve communication; among other things, these sections are aimed at becoming an effective listener, improving nonverbal communication, coping with defensiveness, and preparing a speech outline. By practicing these skills, students will increase their confidence in both interpersonal and public communication.

STRUCTURE

Building Confidence in Communication is organized into three parts: Part One discusses basic concepts in communication theory, Part Two focuses on interpersonal communication, and Part Three explores public communication.

Part One, "The Communication Process," treats the various elements within the process. Chapter 1 provides an overview of communication, in addition to highlighting the importance of building students' confidence as a communicators. Other chapters in this section cover perception, listening, and both verbal and nonverbal communication.

Part Two, "Interpersonal Communication," begins by discussing ways in which we can increase our understanding of ourselves and our relationships with others. Chapter 7 offers ways to improve the communication climate and includes a discussion on defensive communication. Interviewing is also covered, as is small group communication.

Part Three, "Public Communication," examines the steps involved in delivering an effective public speech. The subjects covered include selecting a topic and analyzing the audience, gathering supporting material, and organizing the speech. Chapter 13 offers ways to deliver an effective speech, and the two final chapters look at the application of public speaking skills to informative and persuasive speeches.

The book takes a building-block approach to becoming a confident communicator. Concepts and skills introduced in the foundation chapters are integrated first in the interpersonal chapters and again later in the public communication chapters. For example, the subject of drawing accurate perceptions of ourselves and others, introduced in Chapter 2, is applied to such interpersonal topics as our behavior within relationships (Chapter 6), why people behave defensively (Chapter 7), the employment interview (Chapter 8), and participation in small-group discussions (Chapter 9); later this subject is also applied to such public communication topics as developing the speech purpose and analyzing your audience (Chapter 10). Reinforcement of these concepts makes it possible for students to practice and apply specific skills in both interpersonal and public communication interactions. Through such practice, their confidence and effectiveness as communicators will steadily increase.

SPECIAL FEATURES

This book offers several special features designed to increase student learning. Each chapter starts with a preview of the topics to be covered and with a list of objectives outlining the chapter's goals. Examples appropriate to both interpersonal and public communication are an integral part of the text, their purpose being to enable students to reach an inderstanding of complex principles and theories. Application activities are strategically placed within each chapter to give students an opportunity to practice what they have just read. Checklists are also included to remind students of the principles discussed in the chapter. Rounding out each chapter is a summary that highlights key points, as well as review questions to give students an opportunity to think about the material presented in the chapter.

Finally, an Instructor's Manual is available that contains test questions and additional activities designed to assist the instructor.

ACKNOWLEDGMENTS

Many people have contributed to the numerous stages of this book. First, I wish to thank my students, who have been a source of inspiration for me over the years, and my teachers at Wayne State University, who taught me the value of good teaching. I am also grateful to Purdue University Calumet for the support that enabled me to initiate and ultimately complete this project. My colleagues in the Department of Communication and Creative Arts deserve a special thanks for their encouragement, support, and friendship throughout this project.

Several people are responsible for the actual production of this book. I wish to thank Joseph Opiela, who always maintained his confidence in the book. Shelley Roth guided the development of the manuscript; her care, sensitivity, and expertise will always be remembered and much appreciated. Barbara Muller and Louise Howe assumed final responsibility for the book, and Kay Bartolo and Martha Hicks-Courant guided the book through the final stages of production. I thank them for their collective expertise.

I am immensely thankful for the help of Elizabeth Paschen, who typed the manuscript at an incredible pace both before and after her normal work schedule. Finally, I am grateful to the following people, who reviewed various drafts of the manuscript: Allan Broadhurst, Cape Cod Community College; Martin H. Brodey, Montgomery College; Ann E. Busse, Northern Illinois University; Jerry Feezel, Kent State University; William Jurma, Texas Christian University; Delores Kelley, Coppin State College; Marilyn Kelly, McLennan Community College; Jim Mamarella, San Antonio College; Sandra Manheimer, Bradley University; Michael Minchew, Mississippi University for Women; Terry Mullin, Portland Community College; John Preas, Westark Community College; William J. Seiler, University of Nebraska; Curt Siemers, Winona State University; Douglas M. Trank, University of Iowa; Mary Trimbo, Vincennes University; and David Wohl, West Virginia State College.

Finally, this book is dedicated to the two most important people in my life: my daughter Laura, who at five is a constant reminder of what is really important in life, and my wife Linda, who offered tremendous support throughout the project, reading, critiquing, and editing. Her encouragement and love throughout the years helped make this book possible.

DMD

Contents

Part One

The Communication Process

1

An Overview of Communication

Learning Objectives

At the conclusion of this chapter you should be able to

1. Define *communication*.

2. Explain the various components of the communication process.

3. Explain the significance of intrapersonal communication to both interpersonal and public communication.

4. Describe the difference between dyadic communication and small-group communication.

The alarm goes off to end a restless night of sleep. Today is the first day of class, a day filled with anxiety for students attending college for the first time, and for returning students as well.

Imagine two students, Nancy and Bob. Nancy has decided to return to college after being away for several years. With her children now attending elementary school full time, she has decided that this would be a good opportunity for her to finish her college education. She is, however, questioning her ability to compete with students several years younger than herself. She desperately wants to succeed; consequently, the fear of failure is intensified.

Nancy arrives at school and is frustrated by the complicated parking situation. Her counselor has placed her in two classes, history and speech communication. She understands why she is taking history and feels she can handle the class. She also understands the importance of a communication class, but she is quite anxious about it. She knows she will have to relate to younger students and wonders if they will accept her. Her counselor told her that students find communication classes rewarding, but she is still very apprehensive.

Bob, for different reasons, is also concerned. He is not sure why he is even going to college. His parents have stressed the importance of a college education for his future, yet he recalls articles that discuss the high number of college-educated people who are unemployed. Given today's economy, he is

3

having difficulty comprehending the value of a college education. Also, part of his anxiety stems from the fact that he did not enjoy high school. For Bob, additional schooling is a questionable choice.

He arrives at school early, but he, too, cannot seem to find a parking space. He has registered for four classes in an effort to fulfill some of his general education requirements. He has to take an introductory communication class that he wishes he could avoid. He had a speech class in high school and hated the experience; he definitely is not looking forward to this class in college.

Both Nancy and Bob are enrolled in the same communication class. Although their backgrounds are different, they bring a similar feeling of apprehension to the class. They happen to sit next to each other and nod as their eyes meet. Bob wonders if he will have enough experience to interact with Nancy, while Nancy feels that she is too old and that Bob will not accept her.

. . . .

"Although humans make sounds with their mouths and occasionally look at each other, there is no solid evidence that they actually communicate with each other."

The instructor finally enters the classroom. The students begin to assess his behavior; he, too, looks around the room as initial impressions are being formed. As he introduces himself to the class, his voice cracks, his eyes dart nervously around the room, and he speaks rapidly. Bob, Nancy, and the instructor have all been participating in the communication process.

NATURE AND COMPONENTS OF THE COMMUNICATION PROCESS

It takes a significant amount of work and energy to communicate effectively with others. One measure of our effectiveness stems from our understanding of ourselves and of others, a subject that is treated at length in the following chapter. Several factors contribute to our effectiveness as communicators, namely, our ability to listen, our verbal communication skills, our nonverbal communication skills, our understanding of our relationships with others, our ability to analyze an audience, and our knowledge of the way to research, prepare, and deliver a public speech. All these topics (and more) are covered in subsequent chapters; however, to pave the way for these discussions, we must understand the nature of the communication process.

Communication is the interdependent process of sending, receiving, and understanding messages. This definition implies that the components of the communication process (discussed later in this section) cannot be examined separately. Rather, the relationship that exists between the sender and the receiver, as well as the environment of the communication event, must be viewed as a whole. According to this perspective, if any of the components or circumstances change (that is, the number of individuals involved in the interaction, the seating arrangements, or the time of day), the communication event is altered.

Communication is an ongoing process; we never stop sending and receiving messages. In fact, we do both simultaneously. For example, when we tell our son's fourth-grade teacher that the boy complains about being bored during class, we also observe the teacher's reaction to what we are saying—we simultaneously send a message *and* receive the teacher's message (that is, his or her concern, or surprise, or apparent lack of concentration on what we are saying).

Even though we may not deliberately or directly communicate with another person, we constantly send out information about ourselves. Our clothing, our behavior toward others (children, spouses, lovers, colleagues, and so on), and the amount of eye contact we establish all communicate information about ourselves. People make inferences about our behavior, just as we interpret what we observe about others.

As you will discover, communication is a dynamic process, a process that changes from one communication setting to the next. Although it is difficult to predict the ways your ideas will be interpreted by others, certain components are always present in the communication process: people, a message, encoding, decoding, the channel, feedback, the context, and noise (see Figure 1.1). Understanding these components will give you both an awareness of the communication process and a working vocabulary to help you formulate and dissect messages.

FIGURE 1.1   The Communication Process

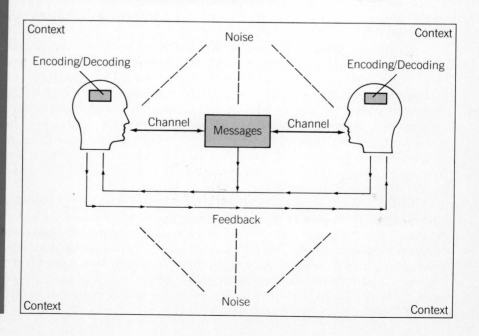

People

People are an integral part of the communication process. Today's technology offers sophisticated telecommunication systems, yet this technology simply facilitates human communication, which includes conversations between individuals, public speeches delivered to an audience, employee interviews, small-group discussions, knowing glances between friends or lovers, and so on. None of these situations is possible without the involvement of people.

Human interaction places the individual in one of two roles—either that of the source or that of the receiver. The **source** is the person who creates and sends a message, whereas the **receiver** is the individual to whom the message is sent. The receiver also sends messages back to the source, so the entire process bounces back and forth. For example, as Joan (the receiver) listens to Karl (the source) recount his experience with a Canadian customs official, she remarks, "How awful!" What she has done, momentarily, is send a message of her own. For that instant Karl becomes the receiver. When people communicate with each other, messages are sent and received simultaneously.

Message

The **message** is the thought, feeling, or action that is sent from the source to the receiver. Messages can be communicated either verbally or nonverbally. Verbal messages are composed of words: "I was so offended by Larry's comments that I thought I was going to scream at him!" Nonverbal messages are composed of gestures, facial expressions, vocal inflection, touch, and so on. Nonverbally, we might communicate our anger at Larry's comments by glaring at him or turning red. The content of our messages can reflect a great deal of preparation or structure (as in public speeches), a casualness (as in a conversation with a good friend), or no forethought at all (as in many of our nonverbal messages).

Encoding

Encoding is the process of putting thoughts, ideas, or feelings into meaningful symbols that another person can understand. **Symbols** represent things—our feelings, names for the objects around us, explanations for behaviors, and so on. We are most familiar with the concept of words (language) as our primary symbol system (more about this in Chapter 4). For example, the words chosen for this message would be easily understood by the receiver: "I'm really glad to see you. I've missed you so much these past two weeks." Nonverbal symbols also convey our messages effectively. A hug, for example, symbolizes an expression of warmth toward another person. In both these examples, the symbols used to convey the message (verbal expression using words, nonverbal expression using a hug) are easily discerned by the receiver.

Decoding

Decoding is the process of interpreting or attaching meaning to another person's message. Communication often breaks down because people decode messages differently. Because of diverse attitudes, knowledge, and past experiences, receivers often interpret messages differently from the way they were intended by the senders.

> An early moment of drama in the 1988 Presidential campaign came during Dan Rather's live interview with George Bush. In that interview Mr. Rather repeatedly questioned the Vice-President about his role in the Iran-*contra* affair, an issue which had received considerable attention during the weeks leading up to the Iowa caucuses. How did the viewing audience interpret Rather's questioning of the Vice-President? A *Newsweek* poll released a few days later showed the public evenly divided over the event: 37% of those polled said Rather did a good, tough job of questioning Bush, while 37% thought he was too aggressive.[1]

The different interpretations here can be explained by the individuals' differing levels of knowledge about the Iran-*contra* affair, by their attitudes toward each man, and by their attitudes toward politicians (in general) or the media (in general). Obviously, the results of the poll indicate that people interpreted (that is, decoded) Rather's message differently.

Channel

The channel is the vehicle by which the message is communicated from the source to the receiver. Familiar channels include the various types of media—television, radio, movies, newspapers, magazines, records, and tapes—letters, reports, and our voices.

Sight and sound are the primary channels we use to communicate with others. We can see people's facial expressions and read the written word. The sound of our voices can travel thousands of miles by telephone, can be recorded on tape, or can be broadcast via radio or television. Another one of our senses—touch—also can act as the channel. We might place our hand on a friend's shoulder to communicate our concern for the loss of a loved one. At such times the use of touch can communicate much more than words.

Feedback

Another important component in the communication process is feedback. Feedback is the receiver's response to the sender's message; it provides information about the way the message is being interpreted. For example, many people reacted to Dan Rather's interview with George Bush by telephoning CBS to voice their anger over the anchorman's conduct.[2]

Often we are unaware of the feedback we send to others. For instance, Ellen may *tell* Jorge that she is interested in hearing about his trip to Cincinnati, but she may be nonverbally communicating her boredom by glancing at the clock or stifling a yawn. In this example, the verbal feedback and the nonverbal feedback differ; Ellen's verbal expression of interest is not supported by her nonverbal yawn. At other times, what we say *is* supported by our nonverbal response. For example, Glen might tell Kevin that he understands Kevin's instructions, and he reinforces this verbal feedback by nodding his head.

As senders we sometimes have difficulty interpreting the feedback we get from a receiver. For instance, we might interpret the feedback from an audience as being negative, when in reality it is positive. Consider the following:

> Cathy is a student who likes to sit in the front row. She feels this helps her stay involved in the class. She never misses class and also enjoys listening to speeches; however, because she finds direct eye contact difficult, she looks down at her class notes frequently. A speaker who chooses to look at Cathy may misinterpret her behavior as a negative response to his or her message.

Cathy's behavior toward the speaker is motivated by her own discomfort, not by her disapproval of the presentation. Now consider another student:

> Jim sits in the front row for a different reason—he hopes to make a positive impression on both his instructor and his peers. He consistently gives speakers nonverbal approval by nodding his head after the presentation of each idea. Occasionally as he nods he is daydreaming about the upcoming weekend.

The preceding examples illustrate the difficulty we can face when attempting to interpret the feedback given by receivers. Because we use feedback to alter our subsequent messages, problems can arise when our interpretations are incorrect. If, for example, the speaker interprets Cathy's lack of eye contact as disapproval of his or her presentation, then his or her future interactions with Cathy might be less than friendly. The importance of interpreting messages accurately is stressed throughout this book.

Context

The conditions surrounding communication with others are referred to as the **context of the interaction.** What types of conditions? The **physical setting** in which the communication occurs can have a substantial impact on communication. Consider the difference between discussing a business proposal with a few clients over lunch at a posh restaurant and discussing the same proposal with the same clients in your firm's conference room. The location influences the degree of formality in the interaction. Such factors as seating arrangements, time of day, degree of privacy, room size, temperature, and lighting affect how people communicate with each other.

A second aspect of context is the **psychological climate** of the interaction. This refers to the attitudes and feelings we have about ourselves and the other people involved in the communication. These feelings can affect how we respond to others. For example,

> Sherry and Kate are both graphic artists. Sherry's previous work assignments with Kate have caused considerable anxiety, because she perceives Kate's comments about her work to be overly critical. Sherry brings these negative feelings about Kate to their next project meeting; as a result, the psychological climate of the meeting is tense.

A positive psychological climate, on the other hand, can contribute immensely to the interaction between people. Consider the following:

> Beth, a student in the basic speech class, is terrified of public speaking. Because her instructor offers encouragement to all the students, Beth gradually feels a genuine warmth develop within the class. After several weeks Beth gains confidence and actually looks forward to coming to class. She notices changes in her classmates as well. As the semester progresses,

Beth's speeches, as well as those of her classmates, show significant improvement.

Chapter 7 includes a more detailed discussion of communication climates, both supportive and defensive.

Noise

Noise, any unintended stimulus that affects the fidelity of a sender's message, disrupts the communication process. Noise can be external or internal, and it can influence our ability to process information. **External noise** includes sounds or visual stimuli that draw our attention away from the intended message. Imagine how difficult it would be to deliver a speech with construction workers drilling outside the classroom; it would be equally difficult for the audience to concentrate on the speaker's message. Similarly, a strange man who walks into the room can distract the audience, especially if he calls attention to himself.

    Internal noise includes our own thoughts or feelings which prevent us from processing a sender's message—such thoughts as our plans for the upcoming weekend, bills that need to be paid and mailed, the fact that we have not had anything to eat since we woke up this morning, the fact that we really dislike the news team on Channel 7, and so on. When we find ourselves concentrating on such stimuli instead of devoting our full attention to the sender's message, we say that noise is interfering with the communication process. In Chapter 3 we will tackle the subject of listening interference in greater detail.

Application Activity

THE COMMUNICATION PROCESS

1. Try to explain your last difficult encounter with someone by using the following terms:

    a. Source   **f.** Channel

    b. Receiver   **g.** Feedback

    c. Message   **h.** Context

    d. Encoding   **i.** Noise

    e. Decoding

2. Evaluate the impact of each of these components on your interaction.

TYPES OF COMMUNICATION

Communication takes place when we interact with one other person, when we interact with a small group, and when we speak to an audience. A special type of communication—intrapersonal communication—is an integral part of any communication event. **Intrapersonal communication** is communication with ourselves; it is an ongoing process that includes such activities as evaluating ourselves and our relationships with others, planning for the future, and doing some internal problem solving. We engage in intrapersonal communication all the time—as we get ready for work or school, during our three-mile jog, as we prepare dinner for ourselves, and before our presentation at a business meeting. The following sections discuss two types of communication: interpersonal communication and public communication.

Intrapersonal communication is a continuous, ongoing process, but it may be most apparent to us as we walk alone on a deserted beach.

Interviews are a more formal kind of interpersonal (dyadic) communication.

Interpersonal Communication

Interpersonal communication is the informal exchange that occurs between two or more people. It usually occurs on two levels: dyads (groups of two) and small groups.

Dyadic communication is the interaction between two people. It can focus on safe topics, such as our day at the office, or on highly sensitive issues, such as our love for a particular person. Dyadic communication tends to be informal, and therefore, it requires little or no preplanning. Interviews are the exception; they are generally formal in nature. (Chapter 8 is devoted to this topic.) Through dyadic communication we can learn a great deal about ourselves and our relationships with others.

Small-group communication includes those interactions with three to eight people present. In most instances, small-group communication is less intimate than dyadic communication and less formal than public speaking. Small-group communication can occur as an informal discussion of such social issues as gun control or shelters for runaway adolescents or serve as a vehicle for problem solving in organizations. Small-group communication is discussed in more detail in Chapter 9.

President Reagan engaging in public communication with the White House press corps.

Public Communication

Public communication involves having an individual share information with a large group; the usual structure has a speaker presenting ideas to an audience. Public communication is more formal
than interpersonal communication; it therefore requires more preparation on the sender's part. Usually, speakers have a limited
amount of time in which to share their ideas; this forces them to
plan and organize what they want to say in advance. Chapters 10 to
15 treat the area of public communication in depth, addressing such
topics as selecting, researching, organizing, and delivering a public
speech.

UNDERSTANDING CONFIDENCE AND ITS RELATIONSHIP TO COMMUNICATION

For many people, the primary goal of a communication course is to
broaden their understanding of the communication process and to
become better at something they have been doing since birth—com-

municating with others. If we reflect for a moment about our communication with others, we realize that some encounters are easier for us than others. For instance, we might feel relaxed talking with a close friend or spouse, but we are self-conscious and nervous when we are introduced to someone new. This anxiety is familiar to all of us—who among us has not been in a situation in which we have felt uncomfortable and wished that we could be more at ease? Confidence. This is what we desire, yet how do we achieve it?

The intent of this book is to help you become a <u>confident, effective communicator</u> by teaching you about the complex nature of communication and by presenting a variety of skills that can help you improve your communication. The application of these skills in both your interpersonal and public communication encounters can transform you into a confident communicator. Consider how this premise operates in another area—tennis, for example:

> Mario is anxious to learn how to play tennis. He follows the sport on television and has a couple of friends who play regularly. After years of interest, he finally decides to take a beginner's course.
>
> The instructor, in addition to demonstrating the appropriate techniques for forehand and backhand returns, for serving the ball, for making lob shots, and so on, explains the strategies involved in the game— where to place return shots, what to anticipate from one's opponent, and how to play to an opponent's weak side.
>
> At first, as Mario practices these skills and attempts to use some of the strategies presented by the instructor, he feels self-conscious about the way he plays and the way he looks. Gradually, however, he begins to feel more relaxed on the court. His strokes come more naturally as his involvement in the game increases.
>
> Mario may never join the ranks of Ivan Lendl or John McEnroe, but he is a more skilled player because he understands what to do and is practicing to become better at it. Mario's confidence is surfacing!

The first part of this chapter discussed the nature and components of the communication process. Building on this foundation, future chapters will explore the numerous aspects of both interpersonal and public communication, including our perceptions of ourselves and others, listening, nonverbal communication, improving the communication climate, selecting speech topics, analyzing the audience, and organizing speeches.

Each chapter presents an explanation of the topic and then suggests specific skills that can be used to improve your effectiveness as a communicator. An increased understanding of the communication process may help you to see the role you (and others) play in that process. For example, after reading Chapter 7 on improving the communication climate, you will be better acquainted with the subject of supportive climates; as a result, you will be better able to see how you can play an active role in creating this type of climate. At the same time, you will be able to recognize when you and others act defensively.

In each chapter both the discussion of the topic and the suggested skills will help you to become an active participant in the communication process. Your involvement in a particular activity, whether it is gathering evidence for a persuasive speech or observing the nonverbal behavior of an interviewer, has a positive effect— it forces you to practice what you have learned. This activity, with its emphasis on *doing,* can help replace feelings of self-consciousness with feelings of self-confidence. Confidence—with it you will become a more effective communicator.

SUMMARY

Communication is the interdependent process of sending, receiving, and understanding messages. Although it is an ongoing, dynamic process that changes from one communication setting to the next, there are certain components that are always present: people, a message, encoding, decoding, the channel, feedback, the context, and noise.

Communication can take place when we interact with one other person, when we interact with a small group, and when we speak to an audience. In all these situations intrapersonal communication (communication with ourselves) can be expected. Interpersonal communication is the informal exchange that occurs between two or more people; the interaction between two people is called dyadic communication, whereas an interaction involving three to eight people is called small-group communication. A final type of communication, public communication, involves having an individual share information with a large group.

The last section of this introductory chapter included a discussion of confidence and its relationship to communication. First encounters with new people and public speaking are two common causes of anxiety, yet there are ways for us to become better, more effective communicators. Throughout this book specific techniques for improving our communication will accompany the discussions of each communication topic.

REVIEW QUESTIONS   *m.T · mid Term*

1. Define *communication*. M.T ·
2. Explain the difference between encoding and decoding.
3. How can people use nonverbal communication to give a sender feedback? M.T·
4. Explain how the physical setting and the psychological climate can affect our communication with others.
5. Differentiate between external and internal noise. M.T.
6. Describe how intrapersonal communication affects our inter-personal and public communication. M T ;

All speech is design to influence the thoughts and attitude of others.

Small group
① stranger
② acquaintance
③ friend.

NOTES

1. Jonathan Alter, "The Great TV Shout-Out," *Newsweek*, February 8, 1988, p. 20.

2. *Ibid.*

ADDITIONAL READINGS
An asterisk indicates an advanced reading.

*Arnold, C. C., and Frandsen, K. D. "Conceptions of Rhetoric and Communication." In C. C. Arnold and J. W. Bowers (Eds.), *Handbook of Rhetorical and Communication Theory*. Boston: Allyn & Bacon, 1984. Pp. 3–50.
    This chapter provides a thorough discussion of several communication concepts and includes an impressive list of references.

*Littlejohn, S. W. *Theories of Human Communication*, 2d Ed. Belmont, Calif.: Wadsworth, 1983.
    Chapter 2 includes a summary of important communication theories.

Rogers, C. R. *On Becoming a Person*. Boston: Houghton Mifflin, 1961.
    For those interested in improving their communication with others, this is a sensitively written book.

2

Perception

Learning Objectives

At the conclusion of this chapter you should be able to

1. Describe the three steps involved in processing information.

2. Explain the two components of self-concept. *Self Esteem* *Self image*

3. Explain how feedback from others helps shape our self-concept.

4. Discuss two factors that influence our perception of others. *more than two*

5. Describe two forms of stereotyping: "allness" and "halo and horns."

6. Explain the importance of developing accurate perceptions of ourselves and others.

After watching the 1986 Academy Awards, Marilyn is eager to see *Platoon*, winner of four Oscars, including that of best picture. She remembers reading about the film in *Newsweek*, and she recalls David Ansen's remark: "After nine years of waiting, Stone has made one of the rare Hollywood movies that matter."[1]

Marilyn sees *Platoon* a week later. She is so overpowered by the film that she wants to read what other noted film critics have to say about it. The reviews she finds at her public library surprise her—there is no consensus of opinion; instead, the comments range from all-out praise to severe criticism. Vincent Canby, film critic for *The New York Times*, expresses his opinion this way: "Now, nearly 12 years after the fall of Saigon and nearly 20 years after the particular time it recalls, comes Oliver Stone's *Platoon*, the best fiction film yet made about the fighting in Vietnam. Here's an exceptionally good, serious, foot-soldier's view of the war that, in spite of its sense of desolation, could well inspire the fantasies of some future generation of American soldiers."[2]

The comments of Pauline Kael, film critic for *The New Yorker*, are vastly different: "Stone tries for bigger effects than he earns. When he doesn't destroy things with the voice-over banalities or a square line of dialogue, he may do it with a florid gesture, such as having the Christus, Sergeant Elias, run away from the Vietcong who are firing at him, run toward a departing helicopter, which is his only chance for life, and lift his arms to Heaven. There are too many scenes where you think, it's a bit much. The movie crowds you; it doesn't give you room to have an honest emotion."[3]

These critics saw the same film, yet they had strikingly different reactions to it. *Question:* What might account for this difference of opinion? *Answer:* Perception. **Perception** is the process of assigning meaning to stimuli. The way we select stimuli from the environment, organize them, and eventually interpret their meaning plays an important role in the way we communicate in relationships and in public-speaking situations. In this chapter we shall learn more about the process of perception, how we perceive ourselves, and how we perceive others. Finally, we shall look at some strategies for developing accurate perceptions about ourselves and others.

THE PROCESS OF PERCEPTION

In the example that began this chapter we read two different reactions to the movie *Platoon*. What caused the two movie critics to look at the film so differently? In order to answer this question, we must consider the critics' past experiences and views—these might account for their perceptions of the movie. For example, Pauline Kael's negative comments may stem from an earlier opinion of writer/director Oliver Stone. In fact, she alludes to his questionable talents elsewhere in her review:

We can surmise that Stone became a grunt in Vietnam to "become a man" and to become a writer. As *Platoon*, a coming-of-age film, demonstrates, he went through his rite of passage, but as *Platoon* also demonstrates, he became a very bad writer—a hype artist. Actually, he had already proved this in his crude scripts for *Midnight Express* and *Scarface*. (He was also co-writer of *Conan the Barbarian, Year of the Dragon*, and *Eight Million Ways to Die*.) Stone has an action writer's special, dubious flair: his scripts have drive—they ram their way forward, jacking up the melodrama to an insane pitch.[4]

From these comments we can see that Ms. Kael did not enter the theater auditorium as an objective critic.

The point is, *none* of us perceives the world objectively. Our perception of each new situation is tempered by our preconceived ideas, our current physiological and psychological states, our interest or attention, and our goals. Understanding that each of us operates from such a base, we can now shift our attention to the way we select, organize, and interpret the stimuli in our environment—that is, the process of perception.

Selective Attention

We are constantly bombarded by stimuli. Since we cannot respond to all the information we are exposed to, we are forced to exercise a degree of selectivity. The process of determining what we pay attention to and what we ignore is called **selective attention.** Of the two dozen "stories" broadcast on the local evening news, we are likely to respond to only a few; this is an example of selective attention. How we select stimuli from our environment is a uniquely personal phenomenon that depends on our interests and needs.

One important factor in selecting stimuli is our level of interest in it. We are often drawn to topics that directly affect us. For instance, we would probably pay particular attention to student gossip regarding a tuition increase because such a change would have an immediate impact on us. Similarly, the more intriguing we find a topic, the more likely we will be motivated to select it and focus our attention on it. For instance, if Lisa is very interested in political communication, she is likely to listen to her instructor's lecture on Reagan's years in the White House. The content of the instructor's lecture stimulates Lisa's interest enough to make her want to listen to the instructor's ideas. On the other hand, if Charles has very little interest in government, it will take more than the content of the instructor's lecture to keep him involved. Other factors, such as Charles's desire to earn a high grade, might encourage him to pay attention to the lecture.

Needs, physical or emotional desires that grow out of circumstances in our immediate environment, also motivate us to select and assign meaning to certain stimuli, as reflected in the preceding example of Charles. Consider this following example as well: If our secondhand car completely "dies," we suddenly find ourselves paying particular attention to newspaper and television advertisements for good "buys." Our need for reliable transportation motivates us to look for a new vehicle.

Needs are triggered by all sorts of circumstances—hunger, security, longing to be part of a group, desire for recognition, self-fulfillment. Abraham Maslow's hierarchy of needs, discussed more thoroughly in Chapter 10, can be used as a framework for understanding needs shared by all of us. We are especially sensitive to those stimuli in our environment which we perceive have the potential to satisfy our needs. For example, until we purchase another used car, we will continue to read the ads in the local newspaper. After the purchase, however, we no longer have either the need or interest to scan the classified section of the paper (assuming, of course, that the car we bought is satisfactory).

Organization

Before we can begin to interpret the stimuli we have selected from our environment, we must be able to place them in a structure that allows us to make sense of them. **Organization** is simply another phase of the perception process; in other words, we perceive that certain items belong together, and therefore, we tend to organize them that way. Consider the organization found in any grocery store. We expect that all brands of cereal will be stocked in the same aisle, and nearly without exception, they are. How frustrated we would be if this were not the case—we would need to wander from aisle to aisle in search of our favorite brand. Similarly, stimuli can be organized into patterns that make sense. Three elements of organization aid this process: similarity, proximity, and closure.

Stimuli that resemble one another are commonly grouped together. Their **similarity** dictates that they be treated in this way (see Figure 2.1). The description of a grocery store's organization just mentioned demonstrates the idea of similarity. So too does the organization of a library's book collection. Specifically, cookbooks are shelved in one section, biographies in another, photography books in another, and so on. The arrangement is by subject; therefore, books about similar topics are likely to be cataloged and shelved in the same area.

Stimuli also can be organized according to their **proximity**, or closeness to one another (see Figure 2.2). When we group two events together because of the closeness of their occurrence, we are applying the principle of proximity. For example, we can probably recall someone talking about the significance of a particular event because it happened "right after my grandfather died" or "the night my daughter was born." We also might recall when a newspaper account of an automobile accident caught our attention because the accident happened next to the high school we attended. Such associations help to organize the stimuli we have selected from our environment.

FIGURE 2.1 Example of Similarity

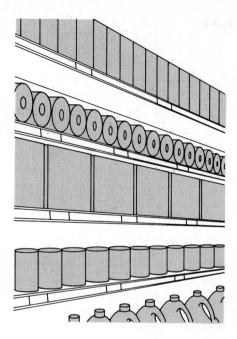

Finally, the element of **closure** contributes to the way we organize stimuli. That is, when we are familiar with an idea or topic, we tend to "fill in the gaps" when pieces are missing (see Figure 2.3). In formulating an opinion about someone, for example, we sometimes make assumptions based on our observations. For instance, if we see an elegantly dressed woman step out of a shiny Mercedes, we assume that this person is wealthy. Closure also af-

FIGURE 2.2 Example of Proximity

Eight shoes or four pairs

FIGURE 2.3   Example of Closure

fects how we listen to a speaker. Sometimes we inadvertently fill in a speaker's words before he or she actually articulates them; we are so familiar with a phrase that we know what the speaker will say even though he or she has not completed the thought. For instance, many of us could complete a reference to Patrick Henry's famous words, "Give me liberty, ..."

A number of potential problems can develop as we attempt to organize information as described so far. For example, referring to people's similarities can lead to stereotyping, a concept discussed at length later in this chapter. With closure, our inclination to "fill in the gaps" or "fill in the missing words" might actually cause us to make false assumptions about a person or that person's message. For example, a football team, down by two touchdowns at the half, might expect to hear a "canned" speech from the coach in the locker room. What might happen if the coach took a different tack in trying to inspire the players to go for a victory in the second half? Some of those players might have already tuned the coach out because they think they "know what the coach is going to say," and therefore, they may miss his message. Finally, because individuals perceive things differently, the way they organize information is likely to be widely varied too. The uniqueness of our perception can result in a breakdown in communication/understanding between people. This phenomenon is discussed more thoroughly in the next subsection.

Interpretation

It is during the interpretation phase of the perception process that we communicate our perceptions to others. Several factors affect how we interpret what we have perceived, including our past ex-

Modern art lends itself to many, varied interpretations. Here, two patrons discuss a painting at the Blum Gallery in New York.

. . . .

periences, our moods, our attitudes, and our physiological well-being. Of these, past experiences and attitudes have the most influence.

Our past experiences play a fundamental role in the way we interpret information, especially since it can determine how we look at both the present and the future. Joan, hearing the weatherman announce that a snowstorm is beginning to hit the city, decides to phone the baby sitter to let her know that both Joan and her husband will probably reach home later than usual because of slow traffic. Joan's past experience driving in snow enables her to anticipate these conditions.

Unlike the positive effect of Joan's past experience in the preceding example, clinging to the past can create problems for an individual who cannot seem to let go of a negative experience. Consider this example:

Nancy is scheduled to have an interview with a local engineering firm. She is quite nervous, in part because it has been four years since her last interviewing experience. She landed a job after receiving her engineering degree, but she still recalls one miserable interview in which she fumbled her responses and did not get the job she wanted most.

Although she comes to this interview with four years of experience, she cannot seem to shake her fear of repeating her previous performance. These thoughts prevent her from interpreting the present interview more positively.

Past experience often shapes our attitude about a particular subject. Certainly Nancy's case is an example of this phenomenon. **Attitude,** a predetermined position regarding a person, event, concept, or object, affects the way we interpret data. For instance, our attitude toward a speaker can determine the way we respond to that person's speech. If we like the speaker's voice or admire his or her confidence, we may interpret the presentation as more powerful. Likewise, our attitude toward the speaker's topic may play a significant role in the way we assess its treatment. Someone who works for Greenpeace, for instance, is likely to be critical of a speech that praises the whaling industry, even if the speech is well organized and well presented.

Our attitude concerning a stimulus can change with time. This transformation occurs when we reinterpret the meaning of information because of changed circumstances. Consider the following example:

Alison's attitude toward cocaine use is ambivalent. *unsettle uncertain*
She has never experienced a desire to experiment with cocaine, but she knows and accepts the fact that several of her acquaintances occasionally get high.

Alison's casual attitude does an about-face, however, when her best friend becomes dependent on "crack." As she witnesses Stacie's behavior change dramatically during the next three months, Alison becomes a staunch supporter of local efforts to crack down on drugs.

Altered circumstances forced Alison to reinterpret her ideas on this subject. Figure 2.4 presents an overview of the process of perception.

FIGURE 2.4   The Process of Perception

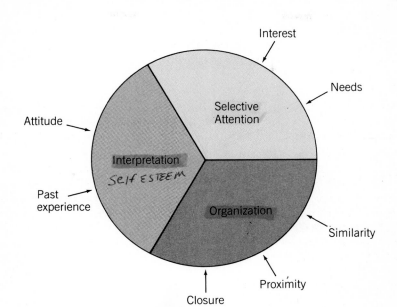

PERCEPTION OF OURSELVES

Our discussion so far has focused on the process of perception. We have learned that perception is highly selective and that it affects the way we organize and interpret the stimuli in our environment. How does this process of perception relate to the way we see ourselves?

Central to the way we perceive the world is the way we see ourselves. Our perception of ourselves dictates the way we send and receive messages. **Self-concept** is our total perception of ourselves, or how we picture ourselves in a very broad sense. To analyze our self-concept, we should consider two major components: self-image and self-esteem.

Self-image is the way we define ourselves. This definition generally reflects how we look at ourselves in relation to our job or career goals, our family relationships, our interests, and so on. Deena describes herself this way: "I am a nursing student at AAA College. I have two more years of course work before I graduate. At that time, I plan to get a full-time job, move out of my parents' home, and get a place of my own."

A second variable of self-concept is self-esteem. **Self-esteem** is our measure of self-worth; as such, it is the evaluative dimension of our self-concept. For example, because Deena believes that nursing is a noble profession, she values her decision to pursue a nursing degree. Deena's positive feelings about herself help to elevate her self-concept. The evaluative function allows us to assess the way we feel.

While not actually a part of our self-concept, the feedback we receive from others significantly affects our self-concept. Moreover, it is the way we perceive that feedback that will have the greatest impact on our self-concept. For instance, if we receive large doses of positive feedback from our family, we are likely to perceive ourselves in a positive light. This, in turn, affects the way we present ourselves to others.

Self-concept is a complex phenomenon that has significant implications for communication. Its key role in the communication process can be attributed to the fact that much of the way we interact with others stems from our self-concept. Perhaps an example will clarify this point:

Our self-concept is the product of our self-image and our self-esteem.

As an attorney, Victor considers himself to be a specialist in the area of wills and estates. His self-confidence is reflected in his communication with those clients who seek his professional help in such matters; however, when Victor agrees to handle a divorce settlement, his communication with his client is less effective. This can be attributed to his decreased feeling of confidence in the area of divorce law.

The way in which we send and receive messages, then, is affected by our own beliefs about ourselves.

Since we all have different experiences, knowledge, and attitudes, we possess different strengths and weaknesses that provide the basis for our unique self-concept. Our self-concept is also situational; that is, there are certain situations in which we feel comfortable with the role that we play, while other situations present a greater challenge for us. The preceding example of Victor is a case in point. Here is another: I feel comfortable teaching a basic communication class, but I find it very threatening to take my car into the garage for service. This is a result of my level of competence in one area and lack of confidence in another.

Because we all have different strengths and weaknesses, it is important not to judge others according to our own positive and negative points. Two factors that affect our self-concept are the self-fulfilling prophecy and significant others. Both are discussed in the following section.

Application Activity

SELF-CONCEPT

1. Describe your self-concept using the following categories:

    a. Your role within your family

    b. Your career goals

    c. Your relationship with your school peers

    d. Your personality traits

    e. Your physical traits

2. Evaluate your self-concept in each of the preceding categories.

3. How does your self-image differ from your self-esteem?

Self-Fulfilling Prophecy

In a **self-fulfilling prophecy,** our behavior matches someone else's expectations. For example, when an individual perceives us to be a certain way, he or she begins to treat us according to that preconceived notion, and eventually we act out or fulfill the way we are being perceived. The following example demonstrates how the self-fulfilling prophecy operates:

> John comes from a highly critical home environment. His parents have difficulty expressing positive feelings toward him, which reinforces his feelings of inadequacy. Moreover, they constantly push him to take on new challenges. The same theme is reinforced on the job; John's boss frequently gives him challenging assignments, but in the same breath communicates his doubts about John's ability to complete the tasks.
>
> As John begins to internalize the image that others have of him, his confidence diminishes. Inevita-

Application Activity

SELF-FULFILLING PROPHECY

Kathy is the supervisor of the Accounting Department of Midwest Electronic's Minneapolis Division. Avery has just been transferred to her unit. In reviewing Avery's personnel file, Kathy discovers that Avery has a history of difficulty in communicating with his supervisors. Although prior supervisors commented favorably about his capabilities as a CPA, they also noted his inability to take directions. Other members of the company also have discussed Avery's reputation with Kathy. She is nervous about supervising Avery because she anticipates having a difficult time.

1. How might the self-fulfilling prophecy operate in future interactions between Kathy and Avery?

2. Has the self-fulfilling prophecy ever operated in any of your relationships? Describe how it affected your communication within the relationship.

bly, his behavior reflects that loss of self-esteem. He stops sharing his ideas with others and reevaluates his goals for the future. His communication becomes guarded; he avoids interaction with others.

Although usually thought of in negative terms, the self-fulfilling prophecy also can have a positive effect on our self-concept. This happens when we are exposed to positive feedback from others. Such feedback suggests that we are capable, talented, and admired. If this feedback is reinforced over a period of time, we naturally begin to believe it.

Significant Others

The development of our self-concept is also influenced by **significant others,** those individuals to whom we are emotionally close and whom we allow to influence our lives. We often feel that it is necessary to gain acceptance from these people because we think their approval will enhance our self-concept. At times we place greater importance on the opinions and advice of our significant others than we do on ourselves:

> During high school, Marty envisioned himself becoming a great chef. He even gathered information about various cooking schools, both in the United States and abroad; however, instead of filling out applications for these schools, Marty mailed applications to several liberal arts colleges and universities. The reason? Marty's father wanted him to become a doctor, and Marty eventually decided not to disappoint his dad.

Foot Note

Families and peers are two groups of significant others that have a strong effect on the development of our self-concept.

Families During our childhood and adolescence we are in constant contact with family members. Consequently, parents play an overwhelming role in the development of our self-concept. As youngsters, we are dependent on our parents; this relationship is likely to change as we grow older and begin to challenge and question our parents' judgments and values.

In some cases, family influence can be devastating to our self-concept. If we grow up in a home where little warmth and love are demonstrated, we may believe that we are not lovable; if our par-

Our parents are significant others who play an overwhelming role in the development of our self-concept.

. . . .

ents scream and shout to vent their frustrations, we may grow up thinking we are the cause of their problems.

Of course, the opposite also can occur. We may grow up in a family environment that is overprotective, one in which individuals are not given the opportunity to explore and take risks. Parents often want to protect their children from the outside world; hence their love is overly possessive. The children, in turn, may feel guilty when they do not want to return the smothering affection shown by their parents. In both these family environments the feedback received from the parents is likely to have a negative impact on the self-concepts of the children involved.

Under ideal circumstances, our families can represent a highly constructive influence on the development of our self-concept. When our home life is warm and the environment is conducive to expressing and sharing feelings, our self-concept is positive. Further, when problems arise and the necessary time is taken to discuss them openly, this also can have a positive impact on our self-concept.

Peers Peers, another group of significant others, also can profoundly influence our self-concept. Some people go out of their way to gain the acceptance of their peers in order to boost their own self-concept; however, we sometimes let our peers play a disproportionate role in our lives because we feel it is vital to be accepted as part of the group.

A by-product of peer pressure can be the exhibition of counter-productive behavior. For example, a young teenager might join a violent street gang in order to be accepted by his or her peers. In this case, the peer pressure is potentially detrimental to the teen's self-concept, because he or she will look to others for self-esteem. In fact, the tension he or she feels from a diminished self-concept may motivate him or her to seek a group that shares his or her insecurities.

On the other hand, peers, like families, can be a positive force in shaping self-concept. Associations with people who are capable of providing support and positive feedback help to boost self-esteem. For example, a friend may encourage you to apply for a job by giving you a "pep" talk: "Your experience as a welder gives you an edge over the other candidates. What better qualification is there for selling and demonstrating how welding equipment works than the experience you have acquired during the last four years?"

PERCEPTION OF OTHERS

The same factors (discussed earlier) that apply to the process of perception also apply to our perceptions of others. In other words, certain aspects of another person either draw our attention or are ignored depending on our own interests and needs. We sort out these facts and then make an effort to interpret them based on our past experience and attitudes. During the process, we develop a perception of this person that subsequently affects our communication with him or her.

Whether our perception of another person is generally positive (he or she is friendly, attractive, talented, knowledgeable, kind, and so on), negative (he or she is overbearing, critical, stubborn, stupid, grouchy, and so on), or neutral (he or she is okay), we react to that perception. It is this reaction that affects our communication with the person. In this section we shall look at two factors that affect our perception of others: power and stereotyping.

Power

When we perceive that a person has **power**—control, authority, or influence over others—our perception dictates how we will communicate with that person. The significance of power rests with one person's ability to influence another's behavior. In either interpersonal or public-speaking situations, the person's perceived power motivates others to communicate or behave in a specific way. For example, because certain professional athletes are admired by thousands of children (a position of power), organizations believe that children will pay close attention to what these athletes say; hence on television we hear them telling kids to stay off drugs or to get a high-school education.

Adults also react positively to those people they consider role models or mentors. For example, consider the following:

> Kate is completing an internship at a public relations firm where Sharon is her boss. She has observed how Sharon takes charge of an advertising campaign and is amazed at Sharon's many talents—her ability to conceptualize the entire campaign, her skillful interactions with clients, her directions to the production staff, and so on. Kate's perception of Sharon's abilities is overwhelmingly positive. She responds to Sharon's positive impact by frequently praising Sharon's ideas and organizational skills.

Both these examples illustrate positive influences of power. How might we react to power we perceive as intimidating or threatening? Consider the following:

> Mary supervises all the student pages at the library. For months she has contemplated asking the personnel administrator to authorize hiring two additional pages, but she has avoided scheduling an appointment because she is intimidated by the woman's brusque personality. When Mary finally arranges to talk with Janet, she spends the next several hours mapping out her strategy for the session. The next day Mary's communication with Janet is very deliberate, a reflection of her discomfort.

Others have attempted to explain how we communicate with persons perceived to have power. John R. P. French, Jr., and Ber-

TABLE 2.1 Types of Social Power

TYPE	DEFINITION	EXAMPLE
Reward power	One's perceived ability to reward another.	Bill believes Cathy can give him a raise.
Coercive power	One's perceived ability to control another person's behavior through negative reinforcement and intimidation	Bill believes Cathy will fire him if he fails to meet his sales quota.
Legitimate power	The perceived power derived from one's position of authority	Cathy has legitimate power over Bill as his supervisor.
Referent power	The perceived power derived from one's feelings of identification with another	Bill identifies with Cathy because she represents a role model for him.
Expert power	The perceived power derived from one's superior knowledge in a particular field	Bill admires Cathy because of her superior knowledge and experience as a sales manager.

[handwritten annotations: "LONG AS PAIN CAST"; "IF ALLOWCE"; "(Foot Note)"]

tram Raven conducted research on the relationship between perception and power.[5] In their seminal study, they delineated five types of social power: reward, coercive, legitimate, referent, and expert. Table 2.1 summarizes the five types of power and offers an example of each.

Application Activity

PERCEPTION AND POWER

1. Identify an individual for each of the types of social power described in Table 2.1: reward, coercive, legitimate, referent, and expert.

2. Describe the circumstances surrounding your interaction with each of the five individuals identified above.

3. How was your communication affected by each individual's perceived power? Be specific.

Stereotyping

Stereotyping, placing or categorizing people, places, objects, or events into groups based on generalized characteristics, also contributes to the way we perceive others. Although stereotyping helps us "order" stimuli, it can distort reality because it fails to recognize individual differences among people and objects. Our perception of others is commonly the result of "allness" stereotyping or "halo and horns" stereotyping. We shall take a look at each of these practices next.

With **"allness" stereotyping,** we attribute a particular characteristic to a group of people—for the purpose of this discussion, we shall use bankers as our select group. Based on our limited contact with bankers, we generalize that this group is a conservative lot. When we find out that someone we have just met is a banker, we

Attired and coiffed in punk style, this schoolboy seems to be getting mixed reactions from his schoolmates.

then make the assumption (frequently wrong) that this person is also conservative. By superficially categorizing people into groups, we severely diminish the possibility of perceiving the unique differences among people.

The following situation aptly demonstrates the narrow-mindedness that commonly results from "allness" stereotyping:

> It is 1986. Bill has just finished watching a news program featuring the punk rock scene in London, New York, and Los Angeles. He finds the teens' outrageous attire and hairstyles repugnant. He asks himself why people would *purposely* dye their hair orange and wear it in Mohawks or shave their heads altogether! He equates the black leather jackets, heavy jackboots, and safety-pin earrings with violence. The program's analysis that these kids are angry and frustrated with life in suburbia and with parents they cannot communicate with has little impact on him.
>
> Ron's family recently moved into Bill's neighborhood. Bill is shocked by Ron's outward appearance and likens him to the hard-core punk rockers he sees on television. He assumes that Ron will be a menace to the neighborhood and will exhibit violent tendencies. Bill judges Ron without ever interacting with him.

How many times have you heard someone pass judgment on another person without first interacting with that individual? We have all made judgments about a person's behavior by placing that person in a racial, ethnic, social, or sexual group based on too little or inaccurate information. The tendency to place people in a group and make generalizations about their behavior because of their group membership illustrates how "allness" stereotyping can distort reality.

A related form of stereotyping, **"halo and horns" stereotyping,** happens this way: Based on our observations of an individual in a particular situation or setting, we develop either a positive or negative perception about that person; we then allow our initial perception to transfer to other situations. The significance of "halo and horns" stereotyping is that we see an individual in either a consistently positive or consistently negative light, which effectively eliminates the sounder practice of assessing the individual's other characteristics on their own merits. Consider the following:

Sandy is a sales representative for Minolta photo-copiers and microform copiers. Because she has been the region's top salesperson for the past two years, Stan, the company vice president, thinks Sandy should be promoted to regional sales manager. Stan assumes that Sandy's success as a salesperson will transfer to the management arena.

What's wrong with Stan's logic in this example? Is he making an objective assessment of Sandy's potential as a sales manager? Making positive or negative judgments about a person's behavior based on limited information often hinders the communication process.

DEVELOPING ACCURATE PERCEPTIONS OF OURSELVES AND OTHERS

Accurate perceptions of both ourselves and others mean better communication and understanding between individuals, something all of us desire. In previous sections of this chapter we discussed not only the process of perception, but also specific factors that influence our perception of ourselves and our perceptions of others. Some of these factors, such as self-esteem and stereotyping, actually cause us to form inaccurate perceptions. In this final section we shall suggest how to develop accurate perceptions of ourselves and others.

Our perception of ourselves is strongly tied to the notion of self-concept. As defined earlier, *self-esteem* is a reflection of the way we view our worth or value. For instance, our work with the Meals-On-Wheels program raises our self-esteem because we view our efforts as worthwhile. On the other hand, our self-esteem diminishes when we judge ourselves to be clumsy in athletics. What should be apparent to us (but frequently is not) is that our self-concept is situational—our estimate of ourselves varies according to the circumstances of the particular situation. To perceive ourselves accurately, then, we must realistically evaluate our behavior in a given situation and take into account the feedback we receive from others. Our perceptions become blurred when we begin to generalize that we behave or communicate a particular way "all the time." This estimation is usually inaccurate.

Accurate perceptions of others are sometimes hindered by clinging to first impressions and by stereotyping. In order to develop accurate perceptions of others we must avoid relying on first impressions and stereotypes; instead, we should be open to altering our perceptions when new information about a person warrants such a change.

We sometimes form an initial impression of someone and then stick to it. Because many people feel uncomfortable when they first meet someone and therefore may act shy or nervous, a first impression may not be an accurate one. This means that distortion and misunderstanding of the other person's behavior can easily occur. Consider the following:

> Bob's behavior is loud and obnoxious at the party where Cristy first meets him. His crude jokes call a great deal of attention to himself. After several minutes people start to whisper about his inappropriate behavior and try to avoid him. Cristy decides that he is a jerk.
>
> At another party two weeks later, Cristy runs into Bob again. This time he behaves much differently. He is more natural and does not try to "put on a show." Instead, he appears relaxed and is easy to talk to. In fact, Cristy is comfortable enough to ask him why he behaved the way he did at the first party. He tells her that he gets so nervous about meeting and talking to new people that he feels he has to impress everyone.

Luckily, Cristy did not adhere to her initial impression of Bob, whose earlier communication behavior grew out of his own discomfort. It took a second encounter for Cristy to realize that her first impression had, indeed, been unfair. Armed with additional information, she was ready to alter her former perception of Bob.

The public-speaking situation is another area where we must be careful about clinging to first impressions. As people get more confident about making speeches, there are undoubtedly significant changes in the way they present themselves. Consider the case of Natalie:

> Natalie has just been hired as the new director of the local YWCA. Part of her job includes soliciting contributions from various businesses in the community. Her initial fund-raising effort involves talking to officials of the town's largest bank. She is nervous about

Application Activity

FIRST IMPRESSIONS

1. Attempt to answer the following questions about your instructor from your perceptions of the first day of class.

   a. Age   **e.** Religious affiliation

   b. Income   **f.** Political affiliation

   c. Marital status   **g.** Favorite hobby

   d. Type of home   **h.** Favorite television program

2. What caused you to form these impressions?

3. How have these impressions affected your behavior in class?

4. How do first impressions affect the way you communicate with others?

her presentation, and consequently, she does not make a particularly strong impression on the bank trustees. A few of these individuals, however, recognize the importance of the agency's service to the community and subsequently show their support with monetary gifts.

Four months later Natalie is serving on a community task force with two bank officers. In the intervening months she has gained confidence in her new position, which is evidenced by her effective participation on this committee. The bank trustees note the changes in Natalie's public image and dismiss their earlier doubts about her capabilities.

Once again, first impressions proved to be inaccurate.

Stereotypes, much like first impressions, are the result of having either too little or inaccurate information about someone. Based on brief observations and insufficient information, we think we know how another person will behave. Is our perception likely to be accurate? Probably not! For example, it is illogical to think that because Sam is a bachelor, he is also shy. We must get to know him better before we can make such a statement (while it is possible that Sam is shy, there is an equal chance that he is not). Our communication with others depends, to a large degree, on the way we perceive them. When our perceptions are inaccurate, the possibility of misunderstandings between ourselves and others increases.

In the chapters that follow we shall see that perception plays a key role in nearly all aspects of the communication process—in listening, in verbal communication, in nonverbal communication, in our relationships with others, and in public speaking.

SUMMARY

Perception is a dynamic process in which we assign meaning to stimuli. This process involves three critical stages: selective attention, organization, and interpretation.

We first select stimuli from the environment through a process called selective attention. What we pay attention to is generally determined by our interests and needs. Next, we attempt to organize the information we have selected from the environment. To make the stimuli more understandable, we can group them according to similarity or proximity. In addition, the element of closure contributes to the way we organize stimuli. Finally, we are ready to interpret the stimuli. Of the many factors that affect how we interpret what we have perceived, our past experience and attitudes have the most influence.

A key ingredient in the way we perceive the world is the way we see ourselves. Self-concept is the total perception we have of ourselves. It has two components: self-image (the way we define ourselves) and self-esteem (the way we measure our self-worth). Furthermore, the way we perceive feedback from others greatly affects our self-concept. Factors such as the self-fulfilling prophecy and significant others (including families and peers) contribute to the development of our self-concept.

Our perception of others affects how we communicate with them. Factors such as power and stereotyping (including "allness" stereotyping and "halo and horns" stereotyping) play a major role in the way we see other people.

Improving the accuracy of our perceptions requires that we avoid such practices as clinging to first impressions and stereotyping. The degree to which we are successful can be measured by our improved communication with others.

REVIEW QUESTIONS

1. Describe the three stages involved in processing information.
2. How can our past experience influence the way we interpret information?
3. Define the term *self-concept*.
4. Differentiate between self-image and self-esteem.
5. How does the self-fulfilling prophecy affect our self-concept?
6. How can stereotyping distort reality?
7. How can first impressions promote inaccurate perceptions of others?

NOTES

1. David Ansen, "A Ferocious Vietnam Elegy," *Newsweek*, January 5, 1987, p. 57.

2. Vincent Canby, "*Platoon* Finds New Life in the Old War Movie," *The New York Times*, January 11, 1987, Sec. 2, p. H21.

3. Pauline Kael, "The Current Cinema: Little Shocks, Big Shocks," *The New Yorker*, January 12, 1987, p. 95.

4. *Ibid.*, p. 94.

5. John R. P. French, Jr., and Bertram Raven, "The Bases of Social Power," in D. Cartwright and A. Zander (Eds.), *Group Dynamics*, 3d Ed. (New York: Harper & Row, 1968), pp. 259–70.

ADDITIONAL READINGS
An asterisk indicates an advanced reading.

*Berger, C. R. "Social Power and Interpersonal Communication." In M. L. Knapp and G. R. Miller (Eds.), *Handbook of Interpersonal Communication*. Beverly Hills, Calif.: Sage, 1985.

Chapter 10 provides a substantial review of the literature on power.

*Combs, A. W. "Some Observations on Self-Concept Research and Theory." In M. D. Lynch, A. A. Norem-Hebeisen, and K. J. Gergen (Eds.), *Self-Concept: Advances in Theory and Research*. Cambridge, Mass.: Ballinger, 1981.

Chapter 1 provides an excellent discussion of the relationship between self-concept and perception.

Cushman, D. P., and Cahn, D. D., Jr. *Communication in Interpersonal Relationships.* Albany: State University of New York Press, 1985.
   Chapter 2 provides a thought-provoking discussion on the relationship between self-concept and interpersonal communication.

3

Listening

Learning Objectives

At the conclusion of this chapter you should be able to

1. Differentiate between hearing and listening. M↑↑↑
2. Explain how noise interferes with listening.
3. Explain how language interferes with listening.
4. Explain how people interfere with listening.
5. Describe the factors that constitute active listening.
6. Use the skills of questioning, paraphrasing, and support.

One part of the communication process we take for granted is listening. Perhaps the reason for this is the attention so often placed on verbal communication. Mention that you are taking a communication class to someone, and his or her response is apt to be, "Oh, aren't you scared to death to give a speech in front of a class? I dread getting up in front of others!" You would not expect to hear, "Don't you worry about being an effective listener?" While you may chuckle over this illustration, the fact is that listening needs to be taken seriously. In recent years, both the business community and numerous professions have begun to stress the importance of developing good listening skills within their organizations.[1] In fact, listening workshops are commonplace in business and industry today. This effort seems entirely appropriate when we consider how much time we spend each day listening to colleagues, friends, family, television, radio, and so on.

The following dialogue takes place shortly after Bob, Emily, Nancy, and Adam have returned home for a family reunion. They are having dinner together at their parents' home:

Bob: I'm really hungry.

Emily: Bob and I were so glad to get away for the weekend. It's been so hectic at work for the two of us.

Adam: Boy, do I have a headache from the long drive.

Bob: This roast beef is great, Mom.

Mom: Does everyone have enough?

Cartoon Copyright © 1970 by United Feature Syndicate, Inc.

. . . .

Nancy: I'm ready to collapse! What a day!

Dad: Wow, are these potatoes spicy!

While these people are glad to be together, there is little inter-action evident in the preceding dialogue. Each person is tired or absorbed in his or her own thoughts, perhaps a little of both. What-ever the cause, these people are not really listening to each other.

What is the difference between hearing and listening? **Hearing** is one's physical ability to perceive sounds; **listening** is the process of giving thoughtful attention to what we hear. Listening is more complex than hearing because it demands that we concentrate on what others say to us. We sometimes assume that when we send a message, the other party will listen to it and digest its content. If this were true, we would have little concern about whether or not our message was understood.

VARIABLES THAT INTERFERE WITH LISTENING

An important part of being an effective communicator is to develop skills in the area of listening. These skills help us to understand the messages others send and ensure that our responses to these messages are appropriate. Later in this chapter we discuss specific skills for effective listening. First, however, we shall consider a number of variables that can interfere with our ability to listen (see Figure 3.1): noise, language, and our perceptions of ourselves and others. A basic understanding of these obstacles will help us to implement the skills described later in this chapter.

Noise

Noise, any unintended stimulus that affects the fidelity of an intended message, can interfere with our ability to listen because it prohibits us from actually *hearing* the message. Incidents of noise fall into two categories, external and internal noise. **External noise** consists of sounds or visual stimuli that draw our attention away from an intended message. For example, if a road crew is repairing the street directly below the lecture hall where a seminar is underway, the audience may have difficulty hearing the presentation be-

FIGURE 3.1 Variables That Interfere with Listening

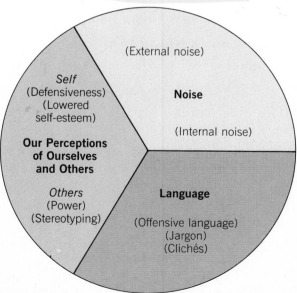

cause of the noisy equipment. Eventually, the audience may give up the struggle and simply quit listening to the message.

In the following example the external noise is a visual distraction:

> Dan comes home from his rounds at the hospital hoping to tell his wife a story about one of the patients. She, however, is absorbed in an episode of *L.A. Law* and is already concentrating on the dialogue in the program. The TV show hinders Linda from listening to her husband.

Internal noise consists of our own thoughts or feelings that prevent us from listening to someone else's message. Perhaps you are thinking about last night's dinner conversation with your aunt—how you ended up storming out of her kitchen because you got so angry with her. By the time you pull yourself out of your reverie, you realize that you have missed several minutes of the anthropology lecture! Now you will be forced to get one of your classmates' notes.

Similarly, internal noise can hinder your interactions or conversations with others. In the following example, Professor Shelley is so absorbed in her own thoughts that she resorts to pat verbal responses in order to appear to be involved in her conversation with Susie. Her preoccupation with her own thoughts makes it impossible for her to detect the "distress signals" Susie is sending:

Susie:	I'm really nervous about this assignment.
Professor:	Oh, there's nothing to be afraid of.
Susie:	I'm not sure that I can do this speech.
Professor:	Oh, don't worry. Just try to be yourself.
Susie:	Yes, but I'm so afraid about being in front of the class.
Professor:	(Her eyes indicate that she's beginning to drift from the conversation.) I'm sure you can get through the assignment, Susie.
Susie:	Can you give me specific suggestions?
Professor:	Well, you know what the book says—just try and practice in front of the mirror. Also, remember that the audience won't be listening to every word you say.
Susie:	(She is more nervous than before, but just wants to leave.) Thank you, Professor.

Professor: (Appears impatient.) I'm sure you will do just fine, Susie. If you have any questions, feel free to get back to me.

Language

Have you ever tried to confront a colleague or friend about an issue that upsets you, but your choice of words only resulted in the other party storming out of the room or yelling back at you? This is an example of language interfering with the listening process. Messages that include words or phrases that offend us, such as ethnic slurs, slanderous comments, profanity, or condescending references, often trigger a negative reaction that actually prevents us from listening to the sender's complete message. For example, you may be in agreement with a speaker's contention that the U.S. Congress should not ratify the INF Treaty with the Soviet Union; however, when the speaker refers to supporters of the treaty as "weak-kneed Commie lovers," you begin to question the speaker's character, based on the tactic chosen to discredit the opposition. A tiny portion of his message ("weak-kneed Commie lovers") offends you; as a result, you discount or pay little attention to the rest of the speech.

Consider these other types of derogatory language; they, too, can stir negative responses and block listening: (1) ethnic slurs—such as "Wops" for persons of Italian descent; (2) profanity—many people are especially sensitive to the use of profanity; consider that some people intentionally avoid reading books or watching movies that include this type of language; and (3) chauvinistic remarks such as "Housecleaning is women's work"—here the phrase "women's work" would undoubtedly turn off many listeners.

In addition to offending listeners, language also can alienate, frustrate, or annoy listeners, and by doing so diminish their ability or desire to listen. For instance, **jargon,** highly specialized words used and understood by specific groups of people, might intimidate or frustrate listeners unfamiliar with the profession or activity associated with such language. Bankers talk about "Fanny-Maes," "balloon versus fixed rates," and "negative amortizations" when describing loans; however, to those who have never applied for a home or business loan, these terms may be intimidating. Feeling like an outsider can affect how we listen: "I'll never be able to understand what they're talking about. Why should I even bother to pay attention?"

Language that is annoying also can interfere with listening. For example, excessive use of **clichés,** worn-out phrases, might prompt listeners to think, "I'm tired of listening to this nonsense. It's boring." In interpersonal contacts with acquaintances, the use of clichés can cause disinterest and set our thoughts racing along a different path. The simple remark "We really should get together some time" can trigger this mental reaction: "We are always saying that to each other, but we never do make any plans. I suppose we should make an effort, at least." In the meantime, your friend has continued making conversation, but you have not been listening.

Some of the variables of language interference described in this section are tied to our perceptions of ourselves and others. These connections will become evident as the subject of perception is addressed.

Our Perceptions of Ourselves and Others

How does our self-perception act as a barrier to listening? In simple terms, if we find the communication setting and/or the message threatening in some way, we may become defensive, which, in turn, causes us to do a poor job of listening. Defensive communication is our response to a threatening interpersonal or public-speaking situation. (The subject of defensive communication is treated in detail in Chapter 7.) These threatening situations can take many forms, but a common factor is that we feel insecure or inadequate. When these feelings surface, they affect our ability to listen. A few examples might help clarify this concept.

Earlier in this chapter the issue of jargon, a form of language interference, was discussed. Nearly all of us have been in situations where others use jargon, whether it is doctors spouting medical terms, lawyers talking "legalese," or actors critiquing a performance in their own special language, and we have felt like an outsider. What sometimes accompanies this feeling of being on the outside is feelings of frustration or intimidation, which may trigger self-doubt or a lowered self-esteem: "I'm not as smart as these doctors. I'll never understand what they're talking about or feel comfortable around them." If we dwell on our lowered self-esteem, we may drift from the conversation or speech and stop listening.

There are also instances when we become defensive because an individual's comments "hit home." These comments threaten us in such a way that we pull back from what has just been said and fail to listen to the rest of the message. Consider the following:

> Instead of giving his regular sermon this Sunday, Reverend Monroe turns his pulpit over to Dr. Eleanor Rodriguez, who has been invited to address the congregation on "The Reasons for the Rise in Teenage Substance Abuse."

One of her points, the lack of time spent by parents with their teenagers, strikes a chord with Paul. He glances at his fourteen-year-old son and realizes how little time the two of them spend together. Paul's reaction is to turn away from the speech; his guilty feelings cause him to stop listening altogether.

The way we perceive others affects our *desire* to listen to them. Simply stated, if our perception of someone is basically a positive one, we are likely to want to listen to that person; a negative perception hampers our desire to listen. Such factors as power and stereotyping (both were discussed in Chapter 2) can assist us in understanding the relationship between our perception of others and listening.

The perceived power held by another person determines the degree to which we listen to that person. For instance, if we respect a professor, we are more likely to listen to him or her and act on his or her advice to pursue an advanced degree. Consider, too, the case of someone perceived as having expert power: Chris Evert-Lloyd is perceived by many to be an authority on the subject of tennis; therefore, when she is asked about the pressures of professional competition and what she does to prepare for her matches, we are likely to pay attention to her responses. People who we perceive as having influence or power have the capacity to motivate us to listen.

As indicated in Chapter 2, stereotyping plays a part in the way we perceive others. If, for example, we have a very narrow view of someone, we may think that we can predict his or her message. Ronald Reagan, for instance, holds the stereotype of being a conservative. As a result, many people avoid listening to his speeches and press conferences because they think they "know exactly what he's going to say." The liberal community may not listen to his messages because it assumes he will see issues from a purely conservative perspective. This perception of Reagan, as a stereotypical conservative, interferes with the way we listen to his messages.

Finally, our perceptions of others can change as a result of the language they use in their messages. If a speaker's choice of words offends or angers us, it can cause us to change our perception of that person, probably to a more negative one. An example used earlier in this chapter illustrates this point; in it the speaker referred to congressmen who favored ratification of the INF Treaty as "weak-kneed Commie lovers." We could understandably find this remark offensive and even alter our perception regarding the speaker's credibility. Further, a shift to a negative perception diminishes both our desire and capacity to listen because we have refocused our attention on the speaker's questionable remarks.

Application Activity

PERCEPTION AND LISTENING

1. Identify an individual with whom you feel uncomfortable.

2. How do you react when this person speaks to you?

3. Evaluate how you listen to this person. Do you interrupt this person? Do you let this person finish his or her thoughts? Why does this happen?

4. Name someone whom you admire.

5. Describe any differences in how you listen to this person and to the individual identified in 1 above.

6. What accounts for the difference in the way you listen?

EFFECTIVE LISTENING

Despite the stumbling blocks to effective listening we have discussed so far—noise, language, and our perceptions of ourselves and others—it *is* possible to become a good listener. What is necessary is an understanding of the factors that contribute to effective listening, accompanied by our commitment to develop the ability to listen effectively. These factors include recognizing the importance of active listening and implementing responsive listening skills.

Active Listening

Active listening is listening with a sense of purpose and involvement. This is in sharp contrast to **passive listening,** in which the only party involved in the message is the sender. Watching television, for example, requires no more of you than that you be a passive listener; there is no need to provide any feedback regarding the message being televised. With active listening, you decide in advance that it is important for you to focus on the sender's message; you therefore make every effort to stay involved in the interaction. On the first day of a new job, for instance, you may be especially alert to your supervisor's comments and instructions; you know your future performance rests on how well you listen. How do you remain focused on the sender's message? These techniques can help: listen with empathy, and listen for the central ideas.

M. T.

Listen with Empathy **Empathy,** the ability to understand what someone else is feeling, involves looking at a situation from the other person's perspective. Empathic listeners strive to take the focus off themselves, to avoid being judgmental, and to display sensitivity to the sender's nonverbal communication. As empathic listeners, our utmost concern is to understand the sender's message, even though our efforts might dictate that we hold in check our own feelings about a topic. Consider the following:

> Your friend Sarah meets with you to talk about her decision to have an abortion. You listen to her explanation and try to imagine yourself in her position. Although you know you could not arrive at the same decision Sarah reaches, your desire to understand her position motivates you to listen attentively to her emotional remarks.

. . . .

Listening with empathy involves taking the focus off ourselves, avoiding being judgmental, and displaying sensitivity to the sender's nonverbal communication.

In this example, your ability to take the focus off yourself enables you to listen carefully to your friend's problem.

Part of empathy involves being **nonjudgmental.** As active listeners, we try to avoid judging the statements of others; instead, we strive to keep an open mind while the other party is speaking (there is always time afterwards to evaluate the entire message). If we mentally criticize what the other person is saying, we risk missing part of the message. Let's look at the following example:

> Edwin personally objects to the entire issue of testing employees for drug use. Currently he is listening to Emilio give a speech that addresses this topic; Edwin is determined to concentrate on the entire message, rather than stopping to judge those points with which he doesn't agree.

By reserving judgment, Edwin can effectively listen to Emilio's entire speech. Edwin does not allow his own personal bias to interfere with his commitment to listen.

Listening with empathy also demands that we pay attention to the sender's nonverbal communication. **Nonverbal communication** is communication without words (this topic is discussed in depth in

Application Activity

LISTENING WITH EMPATHY

1. Select a partner in class.

2. Choose one of the following topics to discuss with your partner:

    a. Should children with AIDS be allowed to attend public schools?

    b. The right of a surrogate mother to maintain custody of her child.

    c. A constitutional amendment that would prohibit all abortions in which the mother's life is not at stake.

3. Evaluate your listening according to the following points:

    a. Did you look at the topic from your partner's perspective?

    b. Was your listening judgmental?

    c. Did you pay attention to your partner's nonverbal communication?

4. How do the preceding points improve your ability to listen?

Chapter 5). Active listeners look for nonverbal messages that support verbal statements. Such efforts help them get to the heart of the sender's message. For example,

> Libby is telling her neighbor about a job interview she has scheduled for tomorrow. Jan can see that Libby is nervous about the interview not only by listening to what she says about the job, but also by the fact that she is talking faster than usual and she keeps jumping up from the kitchen table where they are having a cup of coffee.

By taking into account nonverbal as well as verbal communication, the active listener can construct a more accurate picture of the sender's message.

Listen for the Central Ideas Another way to maintain an active level of listening is to listen for the speaker's central ideas. This goal pushes us forward throughout the entire speech; because we

. . . .

By listening for a speaker's central ideas, we can avoid getting bogged down in and overwhelmed by the details.

Application Activity

LISTENING FOR THE CENTRAL IDEAS

1. Pick a class in which you take extensive notes.

2. During the next lecture, make an effort to listen for the instructor's major points. Record these in your notes, along with any important subpoints.

3. After class, review your notes. Rewrite the major themes.

4. Before the next class, review the major themes to help plant the ideas in your head.

5. How does focusing on overall themes help you to avoid the practice of listening only for details?

are eager to discern the overall message, we listen for "connections" that link the major ideas into a general theme. This activity keeps us focused on the central ideas, rather than allowing us to get bogged down in details.

The extent to which we concentrate on the details of a message, instead of on the major points, can actually interfere with our ability to listen. Consider the following situation:

> Dan decides to attend a beginner's workshop on word processing, primarily because he feels intimidated by the prospect of working with computers. As soon as the instructor begins her introduction, Dan starts taking copious notes. By doing so, he fails to listen for her major ideas, which form the foundation of word processing. At the end of the workshop, Dan's notes are filled with details, yet his understanding of word processing remains sketchy.

Responsive Listening

We have just concluded a section that described active listening and the techniques to accomplish this skill. Are there other skills that can help us to become more effective listeners? There are indeed! Such skills are known collectively as **responsive listening**, which requires that we *interact* with the sender. In other words, as listeners, we provide the sender with feedback about the message by questioning and paraphrasing his or her statements and by offering support that encourages the sender to speak.

Questioning **Questioning** is a communication skill designed to help us understand another person's message (ideas, positions, and feelings). It also keeps us involved in the interaction. Consider the following situation:

> Vivienne Whitehead, a mortgage loan officer at First American Savings and Loan, is the scheduled speaker for this month's library program, "Refinancing Your Home." In her talk she explains the different types of mortgages, that is, fixed rate, adjustable, and FHA, and points out the advantages and disadvantages of each. She also mentions closing costs and other related service fees.
>
> Although you have done your best to stay focused on the topic (you have listened for the central ideas), you are confused by some of the terminology. At the conclusion of the speech you ask Ms. Whitehead a few questions: "How does the lending institution determine the 'points' charged to the buyer?" "Under what circumstances is an adjustable mortgage most advantageous?"

The questions asked in the preceding example help the speaker clarify the information for the listener. In addition, the feedback provided by these questions indicates to the speaker how well the material is understood by the audience.

Paraphrasing **Paraphrasing** means restating another person's message *in our own words*. Paraphrasing forces us to digest the sender's message and then ask for confirmation that we have understood that message. The benefit of this skill is that we receive immediate feedback from the other person—either we have understood or misunderstood the message. This process gives us a better understanding of the sender's message.

Consider the following interaction between Dave and Kevin. Kevin is Dave's supervisor at a large personnel agency. They are meeting to discuss Kevin's recent evaluation of Dave.

Dave: I have a question about this evaluation.

Kevin: O.K. (pause). Is there a problem?

Dave: I don't understand what you mean by this comment, "I am concerned about Dave's attitude." Are you saying that I have an attitude problem?

Kevin: No, not at all. I think you are a very dedicated worker.

Dave: Then are you saying that I take my work too seriously?

Kevin: No. I'm saying that we need to stop spreading you so thin; we need to give you an opportunity to focus more on your work, instead of trying to handle so many other responsibilities.

Dave: So you are saying that the company realizes the stress I've been under and wants to help me reduce that stress?

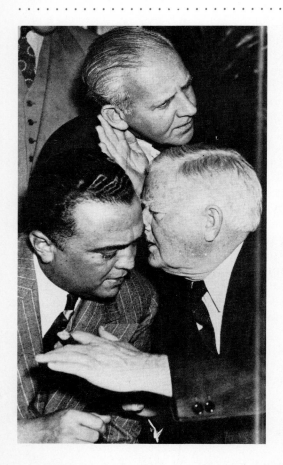

Good listening involves giving thoughtful attention to what we hear. In this photo, Walter Winchell listens carefully while Vice President John Garner whispers to J. Edgar Hoover.

Kevin: Yes. It's the company's responsibility to hire additional employees so that you can work in your area of expertise.

Dave: Gotcha. I had interpreted your comment as a criticism. I'm sure glad I asked you about it. Thanks.

In this interaction, both parties paraphrased the other's questions and concerns. By doing so, they were able to listen more effectively and understand each other better.

Application Activity

QUESTIONING AND PARAPHRASING

Consider the following interaction between Elizabeth and her instructor. Today Elizabeth walks into class ten minutes late after missing the three previous sessions. (During the first day of class the instructor discussed her attendance policy, which this student did not hear because she was absent then, too.) The instructor is extremely disturbed by this latest incident and decides she must speak to Elizabeth about her unacceptable behavior.

Professor: Can I see you after class?
Elizabeth: Yes.
                                (Later)
Professor: You've missed too many classes. If you wish to continue in the course, I'm going to have to start your grade with a B instead of an A.
Elizabeth: (Eyes watering.) Why?
Professor: I made it clear the first day that attendance is mandatory. I consider four absences excessive.
Elizabeth: Well, I'll tell you what I think! I think that's absurd! I should be judged on the quality of my work. If I can accomplish the work, I shouldn't be punished. Besides, where does it say that our grade will be lowered if we miss class?
Professor: (Pointing to the syllabus.) It says right here, *"Attendance is required."*
Elizabeth: Well, that's obvious. Everyone knows that attendance is required—it's expected at a university. But where does it say that our grade will be lowered?

Professor:	I made that announcement in class, probably on a day that you missed. I'm not responsible for the material you miss when you're absent.
Elizabeth:	Your penalty seems a little stiff. I don't think you're being fair.
Professor:	I can understand that you're upset, but I feel strongly about this policy. If you want, you may drop the class.
Elizabeth:	That's not really a choice. I will lose fifty percent of the tuition I paid for this class.
Professor:	I understand your position; however, these are my rules. (Avoids eye contact.)
Elizabeth:	Well, you are not being fair! (She leaves.)

1. How did both the professor and Elizabeth fail to use paraphrasing and questioning to indicate their understanding of each other?

2. Rewrite the dialogue between Elizabeth and the professor using paraphrasing and questioning to improve their interaction.

Being Supportive   **Supportive behavior** is communication designed to assist or encourage speakers to express their feelings. It communicates to them that we are involved in the interaction and that we are making an effort to understand their position. Supportive listeners are involved both verbally and nonverbally. Additionally, they avoid making judgments about the sender's feelings; instead, supportive listeners communicate a sense of caring or empathy. For instance, the remark "I understand why you acted the way you did" lends support to the person who has just finished telling you why they fired an employee. This statement does not judge the other person's actions.

We also can offer support to others through the use of nonverbal communication. Appropriate nonverbal communication demonstrates our involvement in the listening process. One way to show that we care about another person's message is to use direct eye contact. Along with a supportive nod, direct eye contact demonstrates our support and communicates to others that we are listening.

All the responsive listening skills just discussed—questioning, paraphrasing, and being supportive—increase our understanding of another person's message by directly involving us in the communication process. The opportunity to express our understanding communicates to the sender that we have been attentive listeners. Furthermore, as listeners learn through questioning and paraphrasing

TABLE 3.1   Checklist for Effective Listening

✓ Active listening:	Stay involved!
✓ Listen with empathy:	Put yourself in the sender's shoes. Don't judge what he or she says.
✓ Listen for the central ideas:	Don't get bogged down in details.
✓ Responsive listening:	Interact with the sender.
✓ Questioning:	Ask questions when something isn't clear.
✓ Paraphrasing:	Restate the sender's message in your own words.
✓ Being supportive:	Give verbal or nonverbal messages to the sender that communicate a sense of caring.

how effectively they have listened, speakers find out how effectively they have communicated their message. Table 3.1 provides a checklist for effective listening.

Application Activity

SUPPORTIVE LISTENING

Denise, personnel director for Wilson Publishing, supports the merger between her company and Cornell Publishers, Inc. She views the merger as an opportunity for employees to broaden their experience by working on projects in different areas of publishing. Many employees, however, do not share Denise's enthusiasm. One of them, Aaron, stops by her office to talk:

Aaron: Do you have a minute?
Denise: Sure (direct eye contact). Come in.
Aaron: I need to talk to you about the merger.
Denise: It sounds like you're bothered about it. What is it?
Aaron: I think this merger is all wrong.
Denise: What specifically troubles you about it?
Aaron: There's going to be far more paperwork to crank out. I'll be filing separate reports to each company for awhile, and reporting to two bosses, at least for a few months!

Denise:	(Nodding.) I can understand how the prospect of additional paperwork frustrates you. Have you examined ways that you might delegate some of the responsibility?
Aaron:	How can I possibly delegate my work? Ultimately I'm the person who must review everything to make sure it's correct. How do you feel about this whole thing?
Denise:	Well, to be honest with you, I see things differently than you do. I do understand your position, however. Perhaps together we can explore ways to reduce some of your discomfort regarding the merger.

1. Explain how Denise used supportive listening in her discussion with Aaron.

2. How can supportive listening improve communication?

SUMMARY

Listening is the process of giving thoughtful attention to what we hear. It goes beyond hearing, which is our ability to perceive sounds.

Poor listening skills can create a lack of understanding between sender and receiver. Several variables interfere with our ability to listen effectively: noise, both external and internal; language, including words and phrases that offend, alienate, or annoy; and our perceptions of ourselves and others.

Despite the barriers discussed in the first part of this chapter, it is possible to become an effective listener. One way to achieve this is by becoming an active listener, which means listening with a sense of purpose and involvement. In order to do this, we must strive to listen with empathy, which requires that we take the focus off ourselves, avoid being judgmental, and display sensitivity to the sender's nonverbal communication. In addition, we should strive to listen for the speaker's central ideas.

Besides active listening, we can use responsive listening skills to become more effective listeners. This requires that we verbally interact with the sender. These skills include questioning, paraphrasing, and being supportive.

REVIEW QUESTIONS

1. How does external and internal noise interfere with our ability to listen?

(handwritten: To Technical Too simple)

2. Describe three ways in which language can interfere with our ability to listen.

3. What role does defensiveness play in our ability to listen?

4. How can stereotyping contribute to ineffective listening?

5. How can empathy contribute to the effectiveness of our listening? *(handwritten: define ADVISE)*

6. How can the use of questions and paraphrasing lead to improved listening?

NOTE

1. For a straightforward discussion of the importance of listening in business, see Florence I. Wolff et al., *Perceptive Listening* (New York: Holt, Rinehart & Winston, 1983), pp. 221–36.

ADDITIONAL READINGS
An asterisk indicates an advanced reading.

Rogers, C. R. *On Becoming a Person.* Boston: Houghton Mifflin, 1961.
    This book stresses the importance of listening with sensitivity.

*Watson, K. W., and Barker, L. L. "Listening Behavior: Definition and Measurement." In R. N. Bostrom and B. H. Westley (Eds.), *Communication Yearbook 8.* Beverly Hills, Calif.: Sage, 1984. Pp. 178–97.
    This article provides an excellent review of research related to listening behavior.

Wolff, F. I., Marsnik, N. C., Tacey, W. S., and Nichols, R. G. *Perceptive Listening.* New York: Holt, Rinehart & Winston, 1983.
    Chapter 10 stresses the emphasis placed on effective listening by business and industry.

4

Verbal Communication

Learning Objectives

MidTERM

At the conclusion of this chapter you should be able to

1. Discuss the relationships between words, thoughts, and objects.

Demography

2. ✓ Explain how such cultural influences as ethnic background, race, and geographic regions affect the meanings of words.

3. Explain the relationship between perception and language.

Be able to identify

4. ✓ Explain how vague language interferes with understanding.

5. Explain the difference between connotation and denotation.

6. ✓ Explain how technical language can interfere with understanding.

7. ✓ Use descriptive language to improve verbal communication.

8. Use concrete language to improve verbal communication.

9. Use dating to improve verbal communication.

10. ✓ Use indexing to improve verbal communication.

One of the chief ways we express our thoughts, feelings, and attitudes is through verbal communication. Verbal messages are constructed first by selecting words and then by speaking them. Words are **symbols** that represent things—our feelings, names for the objects around us, and explanations for behaviors. Words collected together and understood by a large group form a language. Knowledge of this language makes it possible for us to recognize the symbols (words) others use to send their messages.

Our word choices can make a tremendous difference in how successfully we convey our thoughts and emotions. The more precise and vivid our language is, both in interpersonal and in public-communication settings, the greater impact our messages will have. Consider the following responses Betty gives when asked by her friend Laurie, "What's wrong?"

Response A: Oh, I'm just really depressed.

Response B: John and I are both distraught over the layoff notice he received yesterday from the mill. We just don't know if he'll be able to find a job with comparable pay. We're worried about making ends meet, about what this is going to do to our lives, especially for the kids.

After listening to the second response, Laurie feels great compassion for her friend. Betty's use of precise language in the second response does a better job of communicating her thoughts and concerns.

In public speaking, messages are communicated more effectively when the language is vivid and precise. Ronald Reagan's acceptance address at the 1984 Republican National Convention is a splendid example of how powerful verbal messages can be, especially when the language used creates such imagery:

> . . . Every promise, every opportunity is still golden in this land. And through that golden door our children can walk into tomorrow with the knowledge that no one can be denied the promise that is America.
>
> Her heart is full; her door is still golden, her future bright. She has arms big enough to comfort and strong enough to support. For the strength in her arms is the strength of her people. She will carry on in the '80s unafraid, unashamed and unsurpassed.
>
> In this springtime of hope, some lights seem eternal, America's is.[1]

THE MEANINGS OF WORDS

An important theory that explores the relationship between our thoughts and the words we choose to convey those thoughts was developed by C. K. Ogden and I. A. Richards.[2] They maintain that words are symbols and that these symbols are given meaning when they are placed together to make statements. For example, when we ask someone seated at the same table as us to "pass the salt," that person is likely to respond by picking up the salt shaker and handing it to us. He or she would not in all likelihood toss it down to our end of the table as if it were a football being passed for a touchdown.

According to Ogden and Richards, our thought process is the direct link between the object and the word; consequently, if the word for a particular object is not part of our personal vocabulary, then the word for that object will have no meaning to us. This very thing happens all the time with small children (who are still busy acquiring language). For example, if you were to ask your three-year-old daughter to bring you the dictionary from the kitchen table, she would likely be stumped by your request. You would need to describe and define the term for her, using words that she already understands; that is, "It's the large book that has small holes on one side, by the pages. Each one has a letter of the alphabet on it to help people look up the words they want quickly and easily."

Of course, adults also encounter this type of situation. For instance, Jerry might recognize the word *camcorder*, having heard it before, yet he might have no idea that it refers to a video camera which records both visual images and sounds that can be played back on a television screen via a videocassette recorder (VCR). Because of this, he would not understand his neighbor's statement, "I can't wait to try out the new camcorder I bought last night." Jerry would need to ask Matt for an explanation or try to figure out what Matt is talking about by listening to his subsequent comments. There can be no true understanding of a message if the words that comprise that message are not a part of our symbol system. In this example Jerry did not understand Matt's statement regarding the camcorder because the word *camcorder* was not part of his symbol system (see Figure 4.1).

In our examination of verbal communication we also will discover that our thought process is central to our choice of words.

FIGURE 4.1   Ogden and Richards Model

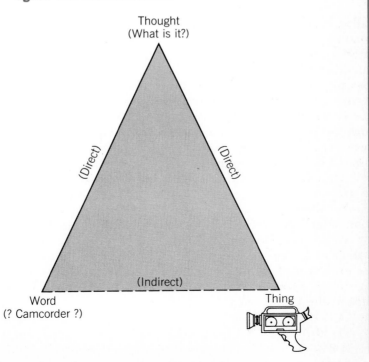

More precisely, our choice of words grows out of our environment, that is, our cultural background, experiences, knowledge, and attitudes. In the next subsection we shall explore how cultural influences and perception affect our choice of words and the ways in which we interpret the words of others.

Cultural Influences and Language

Cultural studies routinely include language as one area of research. By **culture** we mean the customary beliefs and attitudes of a racial, religious, or social group. The customs practiced by a group help shape the language used to communicate with others. Further, the language used by a particular culture has its own set of meanings and often sets the group apart from others. For example, college students desiring membership in a fraternity or sorority quickly learn the language associated with fraternity life—*pledging, rushing, hazing,* and the Greek alphabet are part of the customs practiced by these social groups. Their language makes them part of an inner circle on campus.

The interrelationship between language and culture can be better understood by discussing such factors as ethnic/racial/social groups and geography.

Ethnic/Racial/Social Influence   A country such as the United States is composed of many subcultures. The dozens of groups can be defined as ethnic (Polish-Americans, Italian-Americans, Irish-Americans), racial (blacks, hispanics, Native Americans), and social (fraternities, steel workers, punk rockers). The identities of these groups is in some measure maintained by the language they speak. For instance, one would expect to hear Polish spoken in a neighborhood populated predominantly by first-generation Polish-Americans. Their language binds them together as a group, but at the same time their language can act as an insulator. In order for them to be understood outside the confines of their homes, they need to be able to speak the same language as the majority of the population. If they cannot understand a news program broadcast in English, they must rely on others to translate the information for them.

Some speakers deliberately use language to appeal to a particular group. Stokely Carmichael, for example, attempted to explain the meaning of *Black Power* to different audiences. When describing the meaning of the term to a primarily white audience, he highlighted the sociological implications this way:

Traditionally, for each new ethnic group, the route to social and political integration into America's pluralistic society has been through the organization of their own institutions with which to present their communal needs within the larger society. This is simply stating what the advocates of Black Power are saying. The strident outcry, *particularly* from the liberal community, that has been evoked by this proposal can only be understood by examining the historic relationship between Negro and white power in this country.[3]

The language Carmichael used in his explanation was intentionally analytical, clinical, and academic. He wanted to communicate that Negroes (a deliberate word choice) had to take the same steps as other ethnic groups trying to legitimately establish themselves in this country.

On the other hand, when describing *Black Power* to a primarily black audience, Carmichael adopted a more emotional language style:

Now we've got to talk about this thing called the serious coalition. You know what that's all about? That

· ·

Members of a college fraternity quickly learn the language associated with fraternity life, as well as the customs.

says that black folks and their white liberal friends can get together and overcome. We have to examine our white liberal friends. And I'm going to call names this time around. We've got to examine our white liberal friends who come to Mississippi and march with us and can afford to march because our mothers, who are their maids, are taking care of their house and their children; we got to examine them [applause]. Yeah; I'm going to speak the truth tonight. I'm going to tell you what a white liberal is. You are talking about a white college kid joining hands with a black man in the ghetto, that college kid is fighting for the right to wear a beard and smoke pot, and we fighting for our lives [cheers and applause]. We fighting for our lives [continued applause].[4]

In explaining the term to supporters of the movement, Carmichael used a particular type of language to rally the audience. His language served to keep the members focused as a group, separate from the white liberals he alluded to. The meaning derived from Carmichael's messages to these racially different audiences was vastly different because of his choice of words and his language style.

Geographic Influence   Geographic location often accounts for language differences. For instance, you are probably familiar with the regional variations for carbonated beverages; *soda* is spoken along the East Coast, whereas *pop* is the term used by Midwesterners. The first time Jill heard her cousin order a *soda* while visiting her in Baltimore, she was surprised to see a glass of cola served by the waitress instead of a drink with ice cream in it. Although her understanding of *soda* was something different from her cousin's, obviously the waitress spoke the same language! This simple example of geographic influence demonstrates how easily language affects understanding between communicators. When the meaning of words is different for the parties involved, understanding is not complete.

Perception and Language

Our perceptions are defined by the language we acquire as a result of our cultural background—our education, our family environment, our neighborhood, the geographic area where we grow up, and the social groups we belong to. All these factors shape how we look at the world and at the same time provide us with a language to express what we see as reality.

A theory developed by Edward Sapir and Benjamin Whorf suggests that our perception of reality is dependent on the language system that supports our thought processes.[5] Specifically, our language is the tool by which we assign meaning to events we encounter. We tell the doctor in the hospital emergency room, for example, that we think we broke a finger playing racquetball. She responds by telling us that an X ray will determine whether the injury is a "skeletal, comminuted, or compound fracture." Her medical training accounts for the difference in her perception of the situation. Her language, acquired as part of her medical education, reflects her perception. Her superior knowledge of this subject is reflected by a more sophisticated vocabulary.

Another example of this hypothesis in action follows: Ralph invites his friend Charlie over for a couple of beers. Ralph turns on the television set and begins to watch a baseball game. Although Charlie has no interest in the sport and has never learned much about the game, he watches along with his friend. Charlie makes the following comment midway through the third inning: "Too bad that ball was caught. It almost went into the stands." Ralph responds by saying, "Charlie, that player hit a perfectly executed sacrifice fly which advanced the runner from second to third." Ralph's heightened knowledge about baseball dictates that he describe the "out" this way.

The significance of the Sapir-Whorf hypothesis is that people both perceive and describe events differently, in part because of their language. As communicators, we must realize that the understanding of our verbal messages (and the verbal messages of others) depends on the language system of the listener.

Application Activity

THE MEANING OF WORDS

1. Compare the treatment of a news event in at least two different local newspapers.

2. Find two or three statements that describe the same event in a different light.

3. How can the writers' use of language color our perception of the event?

4. How does our language affect the messages we send?

PROBLEMS WITH LANGUAGE

Language itself is often problematic for communicators. The preceding section pointed out that language is dependent on our perceptions. Additionally, problems of understanding arise because others do not perceive our words in the way we intend for them to be understood. Something that is clear to you, for instance, may be "clear as mud" to someone else. To better explain this idea, three general problems of language will be discussed: vague language, multiple meanings, and technical language.

Vague Language

Vague language is language that lacks directness and specificity; it is void of details. Responses spoken in vague terms can leave the other person wondering what you mean. Consider this interaction between Marge and Pamela at the grocery store:

Marge: When did you get back from your vacation?

Pamela: Last Thursday.

Marge: Did you enjoy it?

Pamela: We were rather disappointed; so were the kids.

Unless Marge pursued her questioning (that is, "What was disappointing about the trip?"), she would probably wonder about her neighbor's vacation. When talking about vague language, two particular problems deserve discussion: abstraction and generalization.

Abstraction   **Abstraction** is the use of broad terms to explain ideas or concepts. For example, if you simply mentioned someone's gen-

. . . .

For Better or For Worse®   **by Lynn Johnston**

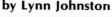

erosity, you would be talking in an abstract sense; to be more definite, you could mention the large donation that person makes annually to the American Cancer Society. Abstraction becomes a problem when the receiver or audience does not comprehend the sender's message because of the language used. Most students, for example, have experienced walking out of a classroom with absolutely no idea of what the instructor was trying to communicate. If he or she had attempted to use more specific language, the ideas might have been better understood.

By its very nature, abstraction also contributes to a false sense of agreement among symbols. Political speakers enjoy addressing such broad concepts as "the promise of the future" or "the American Dream" in their efforts to persuade voters. It might even appear that opposing candidates are saying the same thing because they are using similar abstract language to describe their hope for the country's future. Only when examining their policy speeches do we see the differences in their approaches. This is clearly illustrated in the 1972 Presidential campaigns of George McGovern and Richard Nixon. In that election, both candidates felt they were pursuing the fulfillment of "the American Dream." In their acceptance addresses at their respective conventions, each candidate called on the American people to "come home." At the 1972 Democratic National Convention, George McGovern called on the American people to come home to his vision of America:

> So join with me in this campaign, lend me your strength and your support, give me your voice—and together, we will call America home to the founding ideals that nourished us in the beginning.[6]

Richard Nixon also called on the American people to come home, particularly those Democrats who ascribed to his political vision for the future:

> To those millions who have been driven out of their home in the Democratic Party, we say come home. We say come home not to another party, but we say come home to the great principles we Americans believe in together.[7]

In both these speeches, use of the phrase "come home" is abstract, which gives us a false sense of agreement between the two men. Only by listening closely to remarks made during the campaigns can we get a clearer idea about the different "homes" alluded to in these speeches.

Application Activity

VAGUE LANGUAGE

Use the example of Phillip and his supervisor to answer the following questions:

1. What would your response be to the supervisor's feedback?

2. Can you clearly understand the position taken by the supervisor?

3. Identify the vague language in the preceding dialogue.

4. Rewrite the dialogue between Phillip and his supervisor, eliminating all vague language.

5. How does vague language hinder communication with others?

Generalization   Similar to the problem that occurs when abstract language is used to define concepts is the problem of **generalization**—the use of nonspecific language to describe objects, events, and feelings. It is easier for misunderstandings to occur when others listen to us speak in generalities. Conversely, specific language forces us to be more clearly focused on our subject. Consider the following conversation between Phillip and his supervisor at the hardware store. In it the supervisor's comments lack directness:

Supervisor: I need to talk to you.

Phillip: Sure. About what?

Supervisor: I think you're having a difficult time with your work. I'm not really satisfied with your performance.

Phillip: What do you mean?

Supervisor: It seems to me that you don't enjoy your work.

Phillip: What makes you say that?

Supervisor: I think you need to be friendlier to the customers.

Phillip: How do I do that?

Supervisor: Well, I just think you need to be more outgoing. Spend more time around them.

Phillip: What do you mean—talk to them more?

Supervisor: Well, yes, that would be a start.

Multiple Meanings

If someone you have just met says to you, "I have an interest in the city's downtown renovation project," does he mean that he has a financial interest in the enterprise or that he is concerned about the project's chances of revitalizing an area that he considers his home? In this example, use of the word *interest* is confusing. In order to determine precisely what the speaker meant by *interest,* you would either have to know the individual well enough to realize what he was implying, or you would need to ask him an additional question or two to better understand the comment. Some words have special meanings to individuals; therefore, it is not always easy to discern what someone else's message means. On the other hand, there are many words that have universal meaning—these make it easier for us to communicate with others.

Denotative meaning is the specific reference of a word; it is what we would find if we looked in a dictionary. Denotative meanings are usually shared or understood within a given culture. For instance, most individuals would define *book* as something that is read, and most dictionaries would offer a similar definition for this word.

Multiple meanings occur with denotation on occasion, and these can cause confusion. Take, for example, the word *aggressive.* *Webster's New Collegiate Dictionary* offers the following definitions: "1 a: tending toward or practicing aggression <— behavior> b: marked by combative readiness <an — fighter> 2 a: marked by driving forceful energy or initiative: ENTERPRISING <an — salesman> b: marked by obtrusive energy."[8] After hearing the comment, "Nancy is aggressive," we might wonder which definition of *aggressive* the person had in mind. Is Nancy someone who shows a lot of initiative in her work? Or is Nancy the type of person who displays her aggression by trying to dominate or lash out at others? It is easy to see how we might be confused.

A word's **connotative meaning** is that which is determined by someone's experiences, values, and culture. It is the personalized definition we assign to a word. *Aggressive,* for example, is a word used to describe someone's personality or behavior. This description may mean something entirely different to different people. For instance, a positive connotation for *aggressive* might indicate a person who is enterprising, a go-getter; a negative connotation would indicate one who is overbearing or who tries to dominate others. Our individual experiences determine the way we use and interpret the word *aggressive*.

Technical Language

Technical language, the specialized terms associated with a particular discipline, skill, or career, is another factor that contributes to a lack of understanding between people. Technical language is most effective when used with people who are familiar with the terminology. For example, an attorney would know what a *quasi-contract* is or would readily understand its definition:

> In the civil law, a contractual relation arising out of transactions between the parties which give them mutual rights and obligations, but do not involve a specific and express convention or agreement between them. The lawful and purely voluntary acts of a man, from which there results any obligation whatever to a third person, and sometimes a reciprocal obligation between the parties.[9]

After hearing (or reading) this definition, a layperson is likely to be confused. Other words used in the definition also need defining: *mutual rights, obligations, specific convention.* Rather than grasping the meaning, we would probably need someone to "translate" the technical language, or jargon, into everyday terms.

Technical language, in addition to contributing to increased difficulty in understanding, also can be intimidating. Consider, for example, the anxiety experienced by parents who rush their child to the hospital for an emergency admission. Their anxiety is heightened further when they cannot understand the technical medical terms used by the pediatrician and the emergency room doctor and nurses. They become frightened when they hear the doctor order a "blood culture" and direct the nurses to start an "IV," as well as by mention of the child's dangerously elevated "white count" and possible "septicemia." The language is intimidating, producing more stress. A perceptive physician would recognize the parents' distress and try to alleviate their fears by explaining the child's condition in terms better understood by laypeople. While the language used in the emergency room is undoubtedly an effective way for the medical team to communicate, it can create a higher degree of anxiety for laypeople.

Through the use of technical language, this woman is able to communicate exactly what she wants to her contractor.

· ·

Application Activity

MULTIPLE MEANINGS/TECHNICAL LANGUAGE

1. Select a hobby or area of interest to you that has its own technical language.

2. List five phrases that have specific meanings for this area of interest. For example, potters use such expressions as "throwing," firing," and "feet."

3. For those who are familiar with these expressions, write down the meanings of these words.

4. What might these terms mean to someone who is unfamiliar with the area?

5. What types of problems arise with words that have multiple meanings or that are technical?

IMPROVING VERBAL SKILLS

In the preceding section we identified specific problems concerning language and our communication with others. How do we combat the potential problems associated with abstraction, generalization, multiple meanings, and technical language?

First and foremost, we need to always be aware of the context in which a message is presented. By **context,** we mean the environment or conditions surrounding the communication between two parties. For instance, the responses of two athletes to a sportscaster's question, "What do you think was the key play of the game?" are bound to be tempered by whether or not the players were on the winning or losing side. Knowledge of the circumstances surrounding the interaction gives us a more complete understanding of the message.

In addition, we can learn specific techniques to help diminish language barriers. These techniques include being concrete, being descriptive, dating, and indexing.

Being Descriptive

Descriptive language employs specific words that represent observable behavior or phenomena. Being descriptive directs our communication to actions that are observable, and at the same time it avoids drawing inferences or making judgments about those actions (see Figure 4.2).

For example, consider the difference between these two statements:

Statement A: Heather doesn't look directly at me when we speak.

Statement B: Heather avoids direct eye contact with me because she does not like me.

Statement A is simply an observation made by the individual who is speaking. Statement B goes beyond description; it tries to offer an explanation for Heather's behavior. By doing so, the individual is confronted with a problem addressed earlier in this chapter—making generalizations. In fact, Heather's lack of direct eye contact may be attributed to other factors: perhaps she is shy, or perhaps

FIGURE 4.2   Being Descriptive: Move from the General to the Specific

I have a sweet tooth.

Ice cream is one of my favorite sweets.

I could eat an ice cream sundae every day.

I love hot fudge sundaes made with vanilla ice cream, a mountain of whipped cream, and lots of chopped walnuts.

she actually likes this person and is too nervous to establish direct eye contact.

Being descriptive helps us communicate more clearly and accurately, and it reduces the misunderstandings that occur between people. At the same time, being descriptive can make our speech more interesting. In his keynote address at the 1984 Democratic National Convention, Mario Cuomo created a vastly different picture of the "state of the union" than the positive image advanced by Ronald Reagan during his campaign. Cuomo described his image of the country this way:

> But the hard truth is that not everyone is sharing in this city's splendor and glory.
>
> A shining city is perhaps all the President sees from the portico of the White House and the veranda of his ranch, where everyone seems to be doing well.
>
> But there's another part of the city, the part where some people can't pay their mortgages and most young people can't afford one, where students can't afford the education they need and middle-class parents watch the dreams they hold for their children evaporate.[10]

Cuomo's audience had no problem understanding his message because he mentioned specific ways in which the Reagan administration had failed the American public. The fact that Cuomo did not speak in generalities about the "sad state of the economy" gave the audience a clearer understanding of his message.

Being Concrete

Being concrete, like being descriptive, involves the use of more specific language. While descriptive language often solves misunderstandings that arise from making generalizations, concrete language helps define abstract concepts. **Being concrete** means breaking down or dissecting an abstract concept into parts that are both easier to explain and easier to digest.

"Reaganomics" is an abstract concept that illustrates this point. On an abstract level, this concept represents the economic direction the Reagan administration envisioned for the country. Precisely what does "Reaganomics" mean, though? To better explain the components of this concept, we would want to define (1) *deficit spending,* (2) *supply-side economics,* and (3) *the New Federalism.* For our definition of *supply-side economics,* we could say:

> . . . supply-side economics . . . has come to mean reducing both corporate and individual taxes in order to encourage investment and stimulate the private sector to generate increased employment, productivity, and economic growth, so that . . . the amount of the tax cut, and even more, will be recovered in increased taxes derived from the growth of the economy.[11]

This explanation gives the listener more information about the concept of "Reaganomics." Of course, to increase that understanding even more, we would address the other components as well. Once the individual parts are discussed more thoroughly and specific examples are provided, the listener is better equipped to grasp what was once an abstract concept.

Dating

Dating is the use of a specific time reference to clarify a message. By interjecting a specific date, we make a statement that is based on fact. The following set of statements illustrates the difference between a general comment and one that is more specific as a result of dating:

Russell: I don't get along with my in-laws.

Russell: I didn't get along with my in-laws during our first year of marriage.

The first statement is very general; it does not take into account that the situation may have changed at some point. By dating the second statement, Russell avoids making a generalization about the relationship he has with his in-laws.

Without dating, statements made by one party can cause confusion and/or hard feelings for both parties. Consider this dialogue between Sheila and Jim (dating is not used):

Jim: I just bought a two-bedroom house in Highland.

Sheila: What section of town is the house located in?

Jim: It's just a few blocks west of the downtown area.

Sheila: I've heard that that area of town has a bad flooding problem.

Application Activity

DATING

1. Examine the following statements. Rewrite them using the skill of dating to increase their accuracy.

   a. I can't get along with my boss.
   Dated statement:

   b. Bill never cleans his room.
   Dated statement:

   c. Professor Dunn's classes are always boring.
   Dated statement:

   d. I always have a good meal at the Peking House.
   Dated statement:

   e. The New York Mets are the best baseball team.
   Dated statement:

2. How does the use of dating improve verbal communication?

Jim: You're kidding! The realtor never mentioned that problem to me!

What Sheila failed to do in the preceding exchange was to tell Jim that the flooding problem happened over three years ago. By including this date in her conversation with Jim, Sheila would not be making a misleading statement, and in this case, her comments certainly would not be as upsetting. Dating lends accuracy to our communication with others.

Indexing

Indexing is a technique that takes into account the individual differences among people, objects, and places. The use of indexing helps us to focus on the unique qualities of each person or thing. For example, to say that car salesmen are dishonest would be generalizing or stereotyping. To prevent making such an irresponsible statement,

Application Activity

INDEXING

1. Examine the following statements. Rewrite them using the skill of indexing to increase their accuracy.

a. Fat people are jolly.
Indexed statement:

b. Redheads have hot tempers.
Indexed statement:

c. Basketball players are the finest athletes in the world.
Indexed statement:

d. Your couch is fifteen years old. You need to buy a new one. Michael did.
Indexed statement:

e. People who drive big cars have lots of money.
Indexed statement:

2. Analysis: How can a lack of indexing lead to stereotyping? How does the use of indexing improve verbal communication?

it would be better to say, "The salesman at Downtown Oldsmobile failed to honor the price he quoted me two days ago, but the salesman at Suburban Olds came up with the same figures when I went back to put a deposit on a car." This is a more accurate statement because it points out the individual differences between the salesmen; in this case, one was dishonest, but the other was not. Since language and perception are interconnected, the use of indexing can more accurately reflect our perceptions of people, events, or objects. Table 4.1 offers a checklist for improving verbal skills.

TABLE 4.1   Checklist for Improving Verbal Skills

√ Being descriptive	Use specific words that avoid generalizations.
√ Being concrete	Use specific language to explain an abstract concept.
√ Dating	Use a specific time reference to clarify your message.
√ Indexing	Focus on the unique qualities of each person or thing.

SUMMARY

This chapter explored the role of language in the communication process. Words are symbols which represent such things as our feelings, names for the objects around us, and explanations for behaviors.

C. K. Ogden and I. A. Richards developed a theory to explain the relationship between our thoughts and the words we select to express those thoughts. Cultural influences, including ethnic/racial/social groups and geography, and perception are factors that affect our choice of words and our interpretations of others' words. The Sapir-Whorf hypothesis maintains that our perception of reality is dependent on the language system that supports our thought process.

Problems of understanding sometimes arise because others do not perceive our words as we intend for them to be understood. These problems stem from the use of vague language, including abstraction and generalization, the use of words having multiple meanings, and the use of technical language.

We can improve our verbal communication by using such techniques as being descriptive, being concrete, dating, and indexing.

REVIEW QUESTIONS

1. What is the relationship between the word, the thought, and the thing?
2. Describe how ethnic/racial/social influences and geographic influences affect the meanings of words.
3. What is the relationship between perception and language?
4. Explain the difference between connotation and denotation.
5. Describe two ways that vague language hinders our understanding of messages.
6. Describe four skills to improve your verbal communication.
7. How can dating lead to more accurate verbal communication?
8. How can indexing help you avoid stereotyping?

NOTES

1. Ronald Reagan, "Acceptance Speech," *Vital Speeches of the Day,* September 15, 1984, p. 710.

2. C. K. Ogden and I. A. Richards, *The Meaning of Meaning* (New York: Harcourt, Brace, 1923), p. 11.

3. Stokely Carmichael, "Stokely Carmichael Explains Black Power to a White Audience in Whitewater, Wisconsin," in Robert L. Scott and Wayne Brockriede (Eds.), *The Rhetoric of Black Power* (New York: Harper & Row, 1969), p. 102.

4. Stokely Carmichael, "Stokely Carmichael Explains Black Power to a Black Audience in Detroit," *ibid.*, p. 91.

5. For a further discussion, see Edward Sapir, *Language: An Introduction to the Study of Speech* (New York: Harcourt, Brace & World, 1921), and Benjamin Whorf, *Language, Thought, and Reality* (New York: John Wiley & Sons, 1956).

6. George McGovern, "The Democratic Candidate for President: Acceptance Speech," *Vital Speeches of the Day*, August 1, 1972, p. 612.

7. Richard M. Nixon, "The Republican Candidate for President: Acceptance Speech," *Vital Speeches of the Day*, September 15, 1972, p. 707.

8. *Webster's New Collegiate Dictionary* (Springfield, Mass.: G. & C. Merriam Company, 1980), p. 23.

9. Henry Campbell Black, *Black's Law Dictionary*, 5th Ed. (St. Paul, Minn.: West Publishing Company, 1979), p. 293.

10. Mario Cuomo, "Keynote Address," *Vital Speeches of the Day*, August 15, 1984, p. 646.

11. J. Morton Davis, *Making America Work Again* (New York: Crown Publishers, 1983), p. 287.

ADDITIONAL READINGS
An asterisk indicates an advanced reading.

*Ehninger, D., and Hauser, G. A. "Communication of Values." In C. C. Arnold and J. W. Bowers (Eds.), *Handbook of Rhetorical and Communication Theory*. Boston: Allyn & Bacon, 1984. Pp. 725–728.
> This section summarizes a number of theories concerning the relationship between language and values.

*Littlejohn, S. W. *Theories of Human Communication*, 2d Ed. Belmont, Calif.: Wadsworth, 1983. Pp. 77–86.
> This is an excellent overview of several theories of language.

Newman, E. *On Language*. New York: Warner, 1980.
> A leading personality highlights some of our problems with the English language.

5

Nonverbal Communication

Learning Objectives

At the conclusion of this chapter you should be able to

M.T. (handwritten)

1. *Two Types* (handwritten) ~~Compare~~ and contrast five types of bodily movements.
2. *Recouze* (handwritten) ~~Define~~ four levels of personal space.
3. *describe* (handwritten) ~~Explain~~ the significance of territory in nonverbal communication. *How use in differ situation* (handwritten)
4. ~~Explain~~ *what is* (handwritten) why people react differently to touch. *How is touch used* (handwritten)
5. Explain how clothing can be used to create an image. *want* (handwritten)
6. Explain how paralanguage operates in nonverbal communication.
7. Apply three techniques to improve interpretation of nonverbal messages. *will ask for more than 3* (handwritten)

Kathy and John are sitting in their favorite restaurant discussing their plans for the future. Both of them work for radio stations in the area, but they have been job-hunting for positions at stations with a larger market share. Tonight Kathy tells John about a job offer from a Boston station. John responds by telling Kathy that he understands her eagerness to get a better job and encourages her to pursue the position, yet his face gets flushed and he looks down at his food.

What do you think John's actions communicate to Kathy? Although John verbally expresses his support of Kathy, his nonverbal behavior belies his real feelings of jealousy/disappointment/frustration at not getting the first job offer. In many instances, the messages we send nonverbally more accurately reflect our feelings than those we send verbally. This is true in the case just described.

Nonverbal communication encompasses the broad spectrum of messages we send without verbalizing our thoughts or feelings. Included in this definition are the following: bodily movements, space, touch, clothing, and paralanguage. We communicate nonverbally in our interpersonal relationships, within small groups, and in public-speaking situations. In addition, part of our listening includes nonverbal responses. When we consider the widespread use of nonverbal communication, it becomes evident that this subject warrants further study.

KINESICS

Kinesics is the study of bodily movements. As mentioned at the beginning of this chapter, we communicate a great deal about how we feel in a given situation by our nonverbal actions. Paul Ekman and Wallace V. Friesen developed a classification system that helps us understand our nonverbal communication.[1] Their system identifies the different types of kinesic behaviors: emblems, illustrators, affect displays, regulators, and adaptors (see Table 5.1). A definition and a discussion of each will help us see how bodily movements affect our communication.

Emblems

Emblems, according to Ekman and Friesen, are body motions that take the place of words. For instance, holding up your hand, palm flattened, signals "stop" to someone standing across the room from you. Likewise, a basketball coach motioning "time out" with his hands communicates to a player on the court that he should signal the referee to stop play so that the team can discuss a new strategy. In order for emblems to be an effective form of nonverbal communication, both parties must readily understand the motions being used. A spectator unfamiliar with sports might not understand the "time out" motion used by those involved in the game and therefore might question why the referee officially signaled time out. Emblems also can be used effectively when there are obstacles to verbal communication. The example of the basketball game applies here as well—the coach may signal to a player to call for time out because the crowd is generating too much noise for the coach to be heard by the player.

TABLE 5.1 Body Movements at a Glance

Emblems	Body motions that take the place of words.
Illustrators	Nonverbal symbols that reinforce a verbal message.
Affect displays	Signs of our emotional state.
Regulators	Nonverbal behaviors that attempt to control communication between people.
Adaptors	Nonverbal behaviors that grow out of our discomfort.

Illustrators

Illustrators are nonverbal symbols that reinforce a verbal message. While emblems take the place of a verbal message, illustrators enhance the verbal message. A tight squeeze that accompanies your saying, "I missed you so much these past two weeks," illustrates the sincerity of your verbal message. Similarly, after screaming at your boyfriend or girlfriend, "I never want to see you again," slamming the door further demonstrates your anger. Illustrators must be natural in order to be effective. Consider the effect of slamming a door ten minutes after you have concluded an argument with someone—the effect would be rather hollow. Effective public speakers frequently use illustrators to emphasize their points. For them it is a natural behavior to raise an arm or point a finger when they become passionate or emphatic about their topic.

Affect Displays

Affect displays are nonverbal signs of our emotional state. Giving someone a cold stare, for example, would indicate that we are angry or displeased with them. Conversely, a smile would indicate that we are happy or pleased with our immediate environment. In many cases, we are unaware of the affect displays we use; they tend to be automatic. For instance, Sherry does not realize that she is trembling as she approaches the lectern to deliver her speech, yet her behavior belies the nervousness she is experiencing.

On the other hand, there are times when we deliberately con-

Application Activity

RECOGNIZING ILLUSTRATORS

1. The next time you go to a party do the following:

  a. Observe the behavior of someone who catches your interest.

  b. Note how that person uses illustrators.

  c. Which illustrators did you find most intriguing or appealing?

2. Using the steps outlined above, observe one of your classroom instructors in a public-speaking situation.

3. How do illustrators enhance one's nonverbal communication?

Ever famous for his affect displays, Billy Martin, former New York Yankee manager, indicates his displeasure with a call by kicking dirt at the umpire.

. . . .

trol our affect displays in order to hide our feelings. What does this mean for the person who observes our behavior? Basically, affect displays can be misleading—they do not always portray how we feel. Perhaps an example will clarify this point. We might smile after a prospective employer informs us that we were not selected for the position; despite our disappointment, we do not want to let the other person know how much we had hoped to get the job. Perhaps the situation has made us feel self-conscious; we perceive that our image will suffer, so we behave accordingly. Other factors that influence the way we use affect displays include the upbringing we received from our family (for example, some children are taught to display little emotion in public) and gender expectations (for example, men should always appear strong).

Regulators

Regulators are nonverbal behaviors used to control, or regulate, communication between people. These cues indicate whether or not it is appropriate for the sender to continue his or her message. For instance, if we notice someone smiling at us or nodding his or her head in agreement, we might be encouraged to continue speaking. Catching someone glancing at his or her watch or gazing across the room, however, might indicate that we are not holding the attention of our listeners. As public speakers, we can benefit from reading audience regulators. Often these regulators indicate when adjustments need to be made: whether it is time to move on to the next point or whether we should conclude our speech.

As receivers, we may wish to control the direction or focus of a conversation. One way to achieve this is by using regulators. If we approve of what is being said, we can demonstrate our support by nodding our heads. This communicates to the sender, "Yes, that's right. Please continue." If we wish to change the direction of the communication, we might shake our heads or pound our fists on the table in an attempt to say, "I disagree" or "You're mistaken. Let me tell you how it really is!"

Who uses regulators? Both people with acknowledged influence, such as company executives, parents, or clergymen, and individuals who feel uncomfortable expressing themselves verbally use regulators. They might effectively control a discussion by using such nonverbal cues. For example, a student listening to an instructor lecture about Chaucer's *Canterbury Tales* may be totally disinterested in the subject, but she realizes that it would be unacceptable to tell the instructor how bored she is. Instead, she can effectively communicate her sentiments by thumbing the pages of a book, yawning, or glancing at the clock on the wall. These regulators represent the student's effort to control the instructor's communication.

Application Activity

RECOGNIZING REGULATORS

1. Rent one of your favorite movie classics from your local video store (for example, *Gone with the Wind*). Focus your attention on the interaction between the main characters in the story (that is, Scarlett O'Hara, Rhett Butler, and Ashley Wilkes).

2. How do these characters use regulators to control each other's communication? Note your observations.

3. Share your observations with a partner in class.

4. How did the use of regulators affect the communication between the main characters? Was it an effective means of controlling behavior?

5. At home, observe how members of your family use regulators in their interactions.

6. How does the use of regulators influence communication?

Adaptors

Adaptors are nonverbal behaviors individuals use to adjust to or cope with uncomfortable communication situations. For example, Dean is extremely anxious about his upcoming job interview. What he would really like to do is bound out of his chair, make a mad dash for the elevator, and forget about the whole thing. Instead, he taps his feet nervously on the tile floor, waiting to be called.

Although adaptors are meant to help us through stressful situations, they can pose problems for public speakers. An audience who notices a public speaker wringing his or her hands or twisting a strand of hair can easily be distracted by this behavior; their attention shifts from the speaker's message to watching the nonverbal behavior. Once the speaker is made aware of the problem, he or she can practice controlling the distracting behavior during the delivery. The speaker can work at incorporating natural gestures in the delivery to take the place of adaptors. Repeated efforts should result in the speaker actually feeling more comfortable before the audience and in delivering a more effective speech.

SPACE

What is your reaction when someone you have just been introduced to moves within a few inches of you to begin a conversation? Do you take a step back? If you are feeling uncomfortable, you might wonder, "Why is this person invading my space?" Factors such as your cultural upbringing play a part in how you respond to someone else's communication. **Proxemics** is the study of physical space as it relates to human interaction. This section discusses two types of space: personal space and territory.

Personal Space   18 in to four feet

Personal space is the area that exists between ourselves and others. While we are not always conscious of the amount of personal space

Dancing is a form of expression that involves two people at intimate distance. This couple's pleasure is obvious.

. . . .

we need, our communication behavior is likely to change in response to fluctuations in that space. When we feel that someone has infringed on our personal space, for example, we will likely display defensive behavior. In his book, *The Hidden Dimension*, Edward Hall discusses how people use space to insulate and protect themselves.[2] He identifies four distances that correlate with the levels of space that people need in various communication settings. These include intimate distance, personal distance, social distance, and public distance.

Intimate distance is that distance at which it is appropriate for highly personal communication encounters to occur. This area ranges from actual touching to a distance of approximately eighteen inches. These encounters are usually private and are reserved for communicating very special feelings. When we put an arm around the shoulder of a friend whose sister has just died, we are within the area known as intimate distance. The nature of this relationship dictates the appropriateness of our behavior. When a stranger stands within a few inches of us on a crowded bus during rush hour, however, we are likely to feel that our personal space has been invaded. To us it seems inappropriate for a stranger to be within this intimate distance.

According to Hall, **personal distance** is that area most appropriate for interpersonal interactions dealing with personal matters, that is, approximately eighteen inches to four feet. In interpersonal relationships, the closer the parties remain, the more private is the discussion. As people move farther apart physically, the likelihood is greater that the dialogue is becoming less personal. During an interview, for example, two parties usually sit across a table or desk from each other while having their discussion. If a person from another department enters the room, it is quite likely that the interview would temporarily cease while another type of interaction takes place. Perhaps the interviewer would stand up, introduce the other two individuals to each other, and establish a less personal conversation. Having a third party in the picture changes the dynamics of the interaction; personal distance is no longer appropriate or feasible for this new dialogue.

Social distance is that distance most appropriate for communication of a nonpersonal nature. A boardroom business meeting, a family picnic, a literature study group meeting in a member's home, or four couples enjoying an evening together playing bridge are all examples of situations where communication occurs at a social distance, that is, from approximately four to twelve feet. Social distance is the one category that cuts across both interpersonal and public communication. Of the examples just listed, the communication at a family picnic is purely interpersonal, yet it is entirely possible for a public presentation to be made by someone at a meeting of company executives.

Public distance, a distance exceeding twelve feet, is most appropriate for public communication. Situations involving public distance are usually more formal or defined by an audience and a speaker. For instance, when we purchase tickets for the performance of a popular comedian, we expect to watch his or her act as part of the audience. If, however, the comedian were to come down off the stage and mingle with the audience and even single out individual members to use in a few jokes, we might feel that the comedian has taken advantage of the personal space we perceive to be appropriate for this situation. We feel uncomfortable because the comedian has acted differently than we expected (*Note:* It is not necessarily inappropriate, however, for a public speaker to interact with an audience.)

Application Activity

PERSONAL DISTANCE

1. Visit your favorite restaurant or bar where people meet after work.

2. Observe two people who are having a conversation while sitting next to each other or across a table from each other.

3. What happens when a third individual approaches them and enters into their conversation? Are there any perceptible changes in their communication? List these changes.

4. At the school cafeteria, approach two people you know who are immersed in conversation. How does their communication change? Be specific.

5. In what ways do individuals alter their communication when others intrude on their personal space?

Territory

Territory is the space we stake out as our own. At home, we may have a special chair in the den or family room that we think of as our own; at work, our desk and the area immediately surrounding it are part of our territory. Because we often attach a special significance to territory, it is not uncommon for us to become protective of it. Whether it is a teenager communicating that her bedroom is off-limits to other family members, an employee who defines his territory by specially arranging his desk, posters, pictures, and plants, or a vice president who furnishes her office in order to convey a particular level of status or power, territory is an expression of our feelings and attitudes.

Application Activity

TERRITORY

1. Does any member of your family have a particular chair, room of the house, and so on that he or she considers special?

2. How does he or she communicate to others that the territory is special?

3. What happens when you invade his or her space? Be specific.

4. What does this say about the importance of territory in our communication with others?

TOUCH

Touch is a form of nonverbal communication that conveys a wide range of emotions. Usually, spontaneous touching behavior communicates such emotions as tenderness (a caress), concern (a hand on someone's shoulder, joy (a hug), anger (a slap or punch), or passion (a kiss). Sometimes it is easier to convey our feelings by touching someone than by finding the appropriate words to express our feelings. In such instances, touching is just as effective as a verbal message.

People react differently to touch. Many people respond positively to physical affection because it communicates concern and offers security. Others feel uncomfortable or nervous when touched—to them it is a question of having their personal space violated. As communicators, we need to be sensitive to these differences in people and to respect the feelings of others.

Several variables play a role in the way touching is interpreted: our socialization, our culture, and the context of the situation. Our *socialization* affects the way we respond to touch in that we tend to react more positively to touch if we have been exposed to touching behavior during our upbringing. On the other hand, if our childhood included minimal touching, we are likely to be more uncertain or uncomfortable with touching as adults.

Culture is another variable that affects the way we use touch. Some cultures have unwritten rules that dictate when touching behavior is appropriate. In European societies, for example, it is commonplace for men to embrace in public as a way of greeting each other, whereas in the United States greetings are usually done with a handshake. Public embraces are less common.

The *context* of the communication situation also can affect the way we use touch. For instance, a person may outwardly display affectionate touching behavior to an individual in private, yet the same behavior would be an intrusion of that person's privacy if done in public. Consider, too, that in a work environment intimate touching rarely occurs between colleagues. Under different circumstances, however, these same employees might embrace each other—a wedding or an announcement of a child's birth are two such occasions.

Sometimes touching is just as effective as a verbal message, as this photo of a basketball coach consoling one of his players shows.

. . . .

CLOTHING

The way we dress becomes part of the message we send to others, whether we intend it to or not. Our clothes and style of dress contribute to the way we see ourselves and the way others perceive us. Our style of clothing also reflects our ability or willingness to adjust to a variety of social situations. In other words, what we choose to wear can reflect our desire to gain acceptance within a given social situation. For instance, if we want to "fit in" among the other guests at a formal dinner party, we would wear a tuxedo or an appropriate evening dress. Moreover, our choice of dress reveals information about ourselves and affects our impact in both interpersonal and public-communication settings.

What specifically does our clothing communicate? One thing it can indicate is our age or an age we wish to project. If, for example, we want to appear youthful, we would dress according to the latest styles or trends. Beware, however, that we can inadvertently give away our age by wearing clothes considered to be out-of-date. Bell-bottom pants, polyester leisure suits, and go-go boots were popular in their day, but are definitely out of style today.

Certain types of dress identify individuals as members of particular groups or professions. When we see someone dressed in a blue uniform, we presume (usually correctly) that he or she is a member of a police department. Other examples include black collars worn by priests, military uniforms worn by men and women in the armed forces, uniforms representing different sports, leather jackets worn by members of motorcycle gangs, and native dress representing foreign nations (sarongs worn by Indian women, for example).

Sometimes we wear clothing specially selected to project an image that is different from the one we have ourselves. Consider these examples: (1) Mike, a college student, copies the style of popular TV star Don Johnson in order to appear sexy; (2) John, a recent graduate, wears a three-piece suit to his interview with a prestigious law firm in order to project an air of maturity and professionalism; and (3) Jill, a career woman, dresses in a business suit and carries a leather briefcase to her training seminar for local bank managers.

In selecting our clothing, we should keep the following in mind: Our clothes should not draw negative attention to ourselves. Whether we are speaking before an audience or interacting with only one or two other people, we should dress appropriately for the occasion. If we wear something outlandish, no one will pay attention to our message; they will be too busy studying our attire.

Application Activity

CLOTHING

1. Describe how you would dress for the following social situations:

    a. A football game with good friends

    b. A football game with a first date

    c. A New Year's Eve party at the Hyatt Regency

    d. Your first job interview

2. What motivates you to dress as you do?

3. What role does clothing play in our nonverbal communication?

PARALANGUAGE

Paralanguage is the vocal aspect of delivery that accompanies speech and other nonverbal utterances. It can include pitch (tone), volume (loudness), rate (speed), and quality (richness of one's voice), all of which work in conjunction with the spoken word. Chapter 13 presents a more detailed discussion of these factors.

What can we learn about someone from this special form of nonverbal communication? *Pitch* can bring with it certain associations. We sometimes associate youth or immaturity with a high-pitched voice. Of course, this is not necessarily the case; certain people maintain a high-pitched voice throughout their lives. A deep, resonant voice often communicates just the opposite—the image of someone who has a mature, steady, or dramatic nature.

The *volume* of a message communicates something extra. For example, when we desire to speak to someone on an intimate level, we often use a soft voice. Conversely, we use a loud voice to say "I want your undivided attention" or simply to ensure that our voice is heard in a noisy, crowded room.

The *rate* of our speech can convey our emotional state. When we feel nervous, for example, we tend to speak more rapidly. This happens in both interpersonal and public-speaking situations. Have you ever phoned someone you do not know very well and blurted out the purpose of your call in the first ten seconds? The interaction goes this way because you are nervous. Contrast this behavior with the normal speed at which we talk. A normal pace communicates that we are more comfortable with our surroundings.

The *quality* of one's voice is highly subjective. Generally speaking, someone with a nasal or grating voice is more annoying to listen to than someone who has a resonant voice.

One aspect of paralanguage that people universally find annoying is the use of **fillers,** sounds used to fill in the gaps between the words that comprise our messages. Words such as *you know, like, uh, uh,* or *um* are examples of commonly used fillers. It is more effective to pause between ideas than to repeatedly use fillers.

Application Activity

PARALANGUAGE

Ron has been working at the local paint store for eighteen months. His boss, Mr. Washington, owns the store. For the past two months Ron has thought about asking Mr. Washington for a raise. He thinks he deserves one; he is punctual, pleasant to the customers, and good at mixing paints. He is nervous about approaching Mr. Washington with his request, however. How might his voice reflect his nervousness? Specifically:

1. Does Ron talk fast or slowly?

2. Is the pitch of his voice different than usual?

3. Do you notice any change in the volume of Ron's voice?

4. Does he use any fillers during his interaction with Mr. Washington?

5. What does paralanguage communicate to others?

IMPROVING NONVERBAL COMMUNICATION SKILLS

As you have discovered throughout this chapter, the chief difficulty associated with nonverbal communication is its interpretation by others. It is easy to misunderstand the nonverbal cues you receive, yet it is more difficult to question these behaviors than it is to ask questions about particular verbal statements. As a result, you need to proceed cautiously when drawing conclusions about nonverbal communication. By using the following suggestions, you can increase your ability to accurately interpret nonverbal messages.

Explore All Possible Meanings of Nonverbal Messages

Because nonverbal messages can have a variety of meanings, it is easy to misinterpret them. This is one of the difficulties of nonverbal communication. To combat that problem, we should strive for greater accuracy in our interpretation of messages.

How do we achieve this? One way is to try to remain open-minded about the different meanings nonverbal behavior can suggest. For instance, if someone fails to establish direct eye contact with us, this might mean (1) that the person is extremely shy, (2) that the person is distracted because he or she has something else on his or her mind, (3) that the person is not interested in the conversation, or (4) that the person is showing respect as taught in his or her culture. (*Note:* A more detailed discussion of eye contact appears in Chapter 13.) Before an accurate conclusion can be reached, all the possibilities should be explored.

Look for Nonverbal Messages That Are Consistent with Verbal Statements

Nonverbal communication that supports verbal statements helps confirm the validity of the verbal message. Since nonverbal messages are more spontaneous than verbal messages, they *more accurately reflect* our feelings. Thus, if the verbal message is supported by the nonverbal behavior, we are probably interpreting the sender's message correctly. However, when the verbal and nonverbal messages are inconsistent, it is generally wiser to believe the nonverbal message. Consider the example of John and Kathy used in the beginning of this chapter. John's verbal statement of support for Kathy did not agree with his nonverbal behavior, which was an accurate indication of the envy and frustration he felt.

Use Questions and Descriptive Feedback to Achieve Accuracy

We will be able to communicate more effectively if we learn to focus on the behaviors of others and accurately describe what is observable *without* making unwarranted inferences. Asking questions about observable behavior may help us to avoid the trap of prematurely evaluating others. This process is known as perception checking. **Perception checking** is a verbal statement that reflects our understanding of a nonverbal message. If we can confront nonverbal behavior by asking specific questions about that behavior, we may find it easier to clear up misinterpretations and avoid unnecessary conflict. Look at the following example of Bob and Nancy on their first date:

Bob: I've noticed that you keep looking at your watch. You must be really bored!

Nancy: No, I'm not, It's just a habit of mine. I'm having a good time, but I'm just a little nervous.

Bob: Me too, I want to get to know you better, but it's always so hard in the beginning. That's probably why I'm rambling so much!

In this example we can see how perception checking helped clarify the communication between Bob and Nancy. Bob's comments focused on the behavior he observed without being critical. Table 5.2 provides a checklist for improving nonverbal communication skills.

TABLE 5.2   Checklist for Improving Nonverbal Communication Skills

✓ Explore all possible meanings of a nonverbal message.

✓ Look for nonverbal messages that are consistent with verbal statements.

✓ Use questions and descriptive feedback to achieve accuracy.

Application Activity

IMPROVING NONVERBAL COMMUNICATION

When Tony does not arrive home from work at his usual time, his wife, Brenda, begins to wonder what's keeping him. Forty-five minutes later he storms through the front door. His wife responds by saying, "Where have you been? When you didn't call to tell me how late to expect you, I began to think something awful happened. Is everything OK?"

"Everything's fine," Tony replies, but he avoids direct eye contact. He leaves the room a moment later, slamming the door behind him. When Brenda approaches him again, he backs away from her touch.

1. Come up with three explanations for Tony's nonverbal behavior.

2. Share your reasons with a classmate.

3. Does your partner have the same explanations as you? Note any other interpretations.

4. How do these multiple meanings create confusion for the receiver?

5. Reexamine the preceding dialogue, and develop a list of questions a receiver might ask Tony in order to better understand his behavior. These questions should focus on Tony's nonverbal communication.

6. How does the use of questions and descriptive feedback improve our interpretations of nonverbal communication?

SUMMARY

Nonverbal communication is that area of communication in which messages are sent without the use of words. This area includes kinesics, space, touch, clothing, and paralanguage.

Ekman and Friesen developed a classification system that divides bodily movements into five categories: (1) emblems—motions that take the place of words; (2) illustrators—nonverbal symbols that reinforce a verbal message; (3) affect displays—nonverbal signs of our emotional state; (4) regulators—nonverbal behaviors used to control or regulate communication between people; and (5) adaptors—nonverbal behaviors used to adjust to or cope with uncomfortable communication situations.

Proxemics is the study of physical space as it relates to human interaction. We need varying degrees of personal space, the area that exists between ourselves and others, for different communication encounters. Edward Hall identifies four distances that correspond to the levels of space people require: intimate distance, personal distance, social distance, and public distance. In addition to personal space, territory, the space we stake out as our own, is a factor in our nonverbal communication.

Through touch we communicate a wide range of emotions, including such feelings as tenderness, concern, and anger. How we use touch to communicate nonverbally and how we respond to touch depends on several variables: our socialization, our culture, and the context of the communication situation.

How we dress becomes part of the message we send to others. Our clothing can reveal such things as our age, our profession or membership in a particular group, or an image we wish to project.

Paralanguage, another component of nonverbal communication, is the vocal aspect of delivery that accompanies speech. It can include pitch, volume, rate, and quality, all of which work together with the spoken word.

Most problems with nonverbal communication center around misinterpretation. There are a number of techniques, however, that can increase our ability to accurately interpret nonverbal messages: explore all possible meanings of nonverbal messages, look for nonverbal messages that are consistent with verbal statements, and use questions and descriptive feedback to achieve accuracy.

REVIEW QUESTIONS

1. Describe the five components of the Ekman and Friesen classification system.
2. How do affect displays reveal our feelings?
3. List and describe the four categories of personal space discussed by Hall.
4. Describe two instances in which you have touched a person and gotten different responses. What might account for the differences?

5. How does clothing contribute to an individual's efforts to create a public image?
6. How does paralanguage reveal our feelings about a given situation?
7. List and describe three skills that help us improve our interpretation of nonverbal communication.

NOTES

1. Paul Ekman and Wallace V. Friesen, "The Repertoire of Nonverbal Behavior: Categories, Origins, Usage, and Coding," *Semiotica* 1:49–98, 1969.

2. E. T. Hall, *The Hidden Dimension* (Garden City, N.Y.: Anchor Books, 1969).

ADDITIONAL READINGS
An asterisk indicates an advanced reading.

*Ekman, P., and Friesen, W. V. *Unmasking the Face.* Englewood Cliffs, N.J.: Prentice-Hall, 1975.
This book presents a thorough study of the importance of facial expressions to nonverbal communication.

Hall, E. T. *The Hidden Dimension.* Garden City, N.Y.: Anchor Books, 1969.
This is a classic study of the importance of space in our communication with others.

Knapp, M. L. *Essentials of Nonverbal Communication.* New York: Holt, Rinehart & Winston, 1980.
This book offers an excellent overview on the subject of nonverbal communication.

Mehrabian, A. *Silent Messages,* 2d Ed. Belmont, Calif.: Wadsworth, 1981.
This is a highly readable introduction to nonverbal communication.

Morris, D. *Manwatching: A Field Guide to Human Behavior.* New York: Harry N. Abrams, 1977.
This is a visually fascinating account of nonverbal communication.

Part Two

Interpersonal Communication

6

Understanding Ourselves and Others

Learning Objectives

At the conclusion of this chapter you should be able to

1. Describe the four quadrants of the Johari window.

2. Explain three interpersonal needs.

3. Apply cost-benefit theory to one of your own interpersonal relationships.

4. Explain the benefits of self-disclosure.

5. Name the cautions associated with self-disclosure.

6. Explain four problems associated with interpersonal conflicts.

7. Apply four techniques to improve your ability to resolve conflicts.

If given the option of living in complete isolation or living in the company of others, the majority of us would choose a life that is shared with others. This selection does not imply that such a life would be easy; on the contrary, communicating with others demands considerable time, energy, and understanding.

In the preceding chapters we explored several fundamental components of the communication process. Each of these plays a significant role in our communication behavior with others. Chapter 2 focused, in part, on our self-concept—how it affects our perception of others and how it affects the way we send and receive messages. In Chapter 3 we discovered skills to help us become effective listeners, including such techniques as listening with empathy, questioning, and being supportive. After focusing our attention on the meaning of words and some of the problems we encounter with language, Chapter 4 went on to offer skills for improving our verbal communication. Finally, in Chapter 5 we explored the complex nature of nonverbal communication, including such topics as nonverbal behaviors; how such factors as space, touch, clothing, and paralanguage affect our nonverbal messages; and what we can do to become more skillful at interpreting nonverbal messages.

Taken as a whole, we have amassed a strong foundation of principles and skills that can now be used to assess our relationships with others. In this chapter we shall explore ways to improve our relationships by increasing our understanding of ourselves and the way we interact with others, by becoming aware of the benefits

and risks of sharing with others, and by exploring ways to confront conflict within our relationships.

OUR BEHAVIOR WITHIN RELATIONSHIPS

Several communication theories help to explain the dynamics of our interpersonal relationships. In this part of the chapter we shall discuss three of them. First, the Johari window illustrates the ways we communicate with others; second, Schutz's theory of interpersonal needs outlines our needs and explains the varying degrees of fulfillment; and finally, cost-benefit theory assesses why we choose either to remain in a relationship or to exit from it.

Johari Window

As we assess our relationships with others, we might ask ourselves, "Where is this relationship headed?" Are we involved in a growth relationship, or is the relationship going to remain at a superficial level? If we think we are in a blossoming relationship, we are likely to share increased information about ourselves. At the same time, we are interested in the other person's feedback. One way to gauge the stage of a particular relationship is to use the Johari window.

Joseph Luft and Harry Ingham developed the **Johari window,** which is designed to be a visual presentation of the self.[1] It can be used to explain our communication behaviors with others. Specifically, our interactions are classified as being either (1) open, (2) blind, (3) hidden, or (4) unknown (see Figure 6.1). Each of these behaviors represents part of the self, yet in any given interaction one of these behaviors outweighs the others. For example, Andrea *openly* discloses her career plans with her parents, yet she chooses

FIGURE 6.1 Johari Window

	Known to self	Not known to self
Known to others	1 **Open**	2 **Blind**
Not known to others	3 **Hidden**	4 **Unknown**

to *hide* the seriousness of her relationship with Mike when her parents raise the question. In the first situation, Andrea willingly shares her feelings; in the second, the opposite is true. The way we communicate, then, depends on our relationship with the other party. By assessing our Johari window, we can gain a better understanding of the way we present ourselves to others.

Of the four quadrants that comprise the Johari window, the **open** window represents that aspect of our self that we knowingly share with others and that others can readily determine about us. Information we are willing to divulge to others, such as our feelings about a political candidate, a piece of artwork, our job, or a movie we saw last week, comprises this open side of our self.

The **blind** quadrant of the Johari window represents that part of our self that we either unconsciously reveal to others or are actually unaware of, yet others have knowledge about. In social interactions, for example, our unconscious behavior can sometimes be annoying or distracting. Mary drums her fingers and sways from side to side when she delivers a speech. These unconscious gestures reveal her nervousness to members of the audience. Luther does not know that he is adopted, yet everyone else assembled for the family reunion is aware of the fact. If either Mary or Luther were made aware of the "unknown factors," the information would move from the blind to the open part of the self.

The third quadrant of the Johari window represents the hidden self. The **hidden** quadrant represents that part of us that we are

Application Activity

THE JOHARI WINDOW

Bob and Rick have been best friends since junior high school. As college roommates, they shared their dreams for the future, their feelings about the women they dated, and their feelings about their relationships with their parents. Both responded well to the feedback they gave each other. From this description it would be reasonable to expect either of them to construct a Johari window depicting their relationship this way:

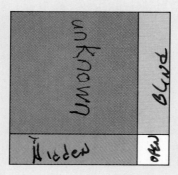

1. Describe the qualities of a relationship represented by this Johari window:

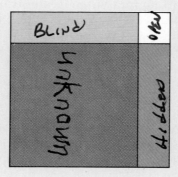

2. How would you describe a relationship characterized by this Johari window?

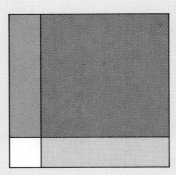

3. What does the Johari window teach us about the way we communicate with others?

aware of, but do not want to share or have not yet shared with others. This may include our dislike of Mexican food, our discomfort over participating in any athletic activity, our fear of being asked a question during class, or our fear of confronting a loved one about wanting to dissolve a relationship.

The last quadrant of the Johari window is that part of us that is **unknown** to both ourselves and to everyone else. We can think of this area as including our untapped potential or hidden talents, or simply that part of our self that remains unexplored. For example, we may not realize that we have an aptitude for speaking foreign languages, a special talent for gardening, or the agility to be a good tennis player because we have never pursued these areas.

Interpersonal Needs

William Schutz developed a theory based on the nature of our interpersonal needs.[2] His theory argues that people have certain needs that affect their communication in interpersonal relationships: the need for inclusion, the need for control, and the need for affection.

Inclusion   **Inclusion needs,** according to Schutz, deal with our desire to be part of a group and lead to a division of people into three

Building meaningful interpersonal relationships.

categories: undersocial individuals, oversocial individuals, and ideal individuals.

Undersocial individuals find it difficult to participate in groups, usually because they believe they are not capable of effective social interaction. Among the members of this group are those individuals who consider themselves to be shy, those who fear they will appear to be inarticulate or boring, and those who see themselves as significantly different from other members of the group. In order to cope with their lack of confidence, such individuals communicate by avoiding or retreating from group interactions.

Surprisingly, **oversocial individuals** also feel extremely uncomfortable in social interactions. Rather than shy away from social interaction, however, these individuals push full-speed ahead as a means of compensating for their anxiety. Many of us, for example, know a person like Kate, whose social calendar rivals that of a corporate executive. She is a member of several political organizations, three church committees, and she volunteers each Saturday morning at the hospital gift shop. Typically, such excessive group participation indicates an attempt to prove that we are capable of functioning comfortably in these situations.

Ideal individuals, according to Schutz, feel comfortable enough to participate in social groups, but do not feel a need to participate in *all* groups. More important, these individuals are comfortable *with themselves* in social interactions. They are likely to be skilled at presenting ideas to others and at the same time eager to listen to the ideas of others.

Control   **Control needs** refer to our desire to have power, influence, or responsibility for our social environment. The need for control is characterized by one of the following: abdicrats, autocrats, or democrats. **Abdicrats** find it extremely difficult to participate in the decision-making process because they are afraid of the possible consequences that accompany some decisions. They lack confidence, so they try to refrain from making either definitive or controversial decisions. For example, Edward is a classic "fence sitter"; he waits until others communicate their positions before he will share his. His reluctance encompasses a variety of decision-making situations. Internally, he may question his ability to make appropriate or wise decisions, so he avoids all kinds of decisions. Edward exhibits the communication pattern associated with the abdicrat.

At the other end of the scale is the **autocrat,** an individual who also may feel uncomfortable with decision making, but whose anxiety manifests itself in the opposite way. Instead of retreating from decision making, autocrats attempt to dominate the process. In an effort to camouflage their true feelings, autocrats believe that by making numerous decisions they will prove that they can be influential. Unfortunately, this type of behavior has an extremely negative effect on others. Autocrats do not listen to the ideas of others because they are too absorbed in their role of trying to be influential in the discussion. Many of us have encountered autocrats, perhaps at work or in our own families. These individuals seem obsessed with "having the final say" when making decisions, which, according to Schutz, stems from their efforts to prove that they are really capable of making decisions.

The ideal manifestation of control needs is displayed by the democrat. **Democrats** can cope with the responsibilities of decision making, yet they do not feel the need to have the final say in every decision-making session. They can assume a leadership role when necessary, but they also can function in a less active role without difficulty. These individuals are generally open to a variety of alternatives; they are receptive to ideas that differ from their own and are comfortable with having others participate in the process.

Affection   The third interpersonal need identified by Schutz is the desire for intimacy. **Intimacy** refers to the establishment of close personal relationships away from the group setting. An **underpersonal individual,** according to Schutz, will shy away from developing close, intimate relationships with others. Underpersonal individuals may avoid personal discussions or steer conversations to "safe" topics. They frequently have poor self-concepts and believe that they are not capable of sustaining intimate relationships. Consider the following:

> Many consider Kim to be someone who is difficult to get to know. When individuals attempt to get close to her, an invisible wall is erected that communicates "stay away." This pattern of communication surfaces in a variety of situations. At work, she spends very little time socializing with people. When she does socialize with others, she keeps the conversation at a safe level, being cautious not to reveal much about herself.

Kim's desire to protect herself suggests a fear of intimacy. She engages in little sharing with others because she may not feel that she is capable of participating in close relationships.

The fear of intimacy also can cause another type of behavior, exemplified by the **overpersonal individual.** Overpersonal individuals try to compensate for their anxiety by establishing many relationships. In an effort to feel better about themselves, they try to be closely involved with several people. In addition, these individuals are typically possessive of their relationships, which is often stifling and aggravating for all parties involved. A phone call to ask "Why haven't you called lately?" represents the sort of behavior caused by such anxiety. These individuals have an excessive need for support that is both draining and seemingly unending.

Personal individuals feel comfortable with their ability to handle close personal relationships. They realize that relationships are constantly changing and can adjust to this fact. As relationships grow more distant, well-adjusted individuals can, in time, let go without guilt. That is, they will not blame the other person, and more important, they will not feel guilty when the nature of a particular relationship changes. Such individuals realize that sometimes people grow closer together, but at other times people grow apart, that change is a function of the dynamics of the relationship, not the result of a guilty party's actions. Individuals whose needs

Application Activity

INTERPERSONAL NEEDS

1. Identify a person with whom you find it difficult to communicate.

2. As you observe this person's interactions, do you notice any of the deficient or excessive types of behavior identified by Schutz?

3. Can you detect any repeatable patterns?

4. How does Schutz's theory contribute to your understanding of this person's communication behavior? Be specific as you assess his or her interpersonal communication.

for affection are neither deficient nor excessive are better equipped to cope with intimacy.

Schutz's theory of interpersonal needs can contribute to our understanding of the ways people's needs dictate their behavior within different communication situations. Our ability to recognize both deficient communication (*deficient* meaning either undersocial, abdicratic, or underpersonal) and excessive communication (*excessive* meaning oversocial, autocratic, or overpersonal) enables us to better understand the dynamics of a particular relationship. Furthermore, such understanding allows us to step back and analyze the communication of others. Being able to explain another person's communication behavior helps us to avoid personalizing the unmet needs of that person. Accordingly, our responses to interpersonal communication situations are likely to be more sensitive.

Cost-Benefit Theory

A theory developed by John Thibaut and Harold Kelley attempts to explain how people assess their relationships.[3] **Cost-benefit theory** (also called **cost-reward theory**) suggests that people choose to maintain or exit relationships based on the rewards they receive within those relationships. If the rewards, which may be either emotional, psychological, financial, or physical, are perceived to outweigh the costs, which can include emotional stress, financial expense, amount of time spent in the relationship, or physical abuse, then an individual will likely remain in the relationship. If the costs are perceived to outweigh the rewards, he or she will probably leave the relationship. Consider the following:

> In his relationship with his father-in-law, Judd examines the rewards versus the costs in working for his father-in-law. He acknowledges that the salary he receives constitutes the chief reward in the relationship, yet he is bothered by the costs/drawbacks: lack of independence, the social stigma associated with working for a relative, and the tension that it sometimes creates in his marriage to Elaine.

According to Thibaut and Kelley's theory, if Judd believes the costs outweigh the benefits, he will sever the relationship. Conversely, if Judd determines that the benefits (in this case, financial security) outweigh the costs, he will probably decide to remain in his father-in-law's employ. Furthermore, he may work to increase his involvement in the business, perhaps by assuming a greater role in the decision making or by striving to become a partner.

Relationships are seldom as simple as the one just outlined. There are times, for example, when we choose to remain in uncomfortable relationships because the alternative is even less desirable. Judd's decision to remain in his father-in-law's firm, despite his frustrations over feeling financially dependent, may be colored by the fact that the employment outlook for architects is bleak in the city where he lives. In this case, the alternative is less appealing than remaining in the relationship.

Cost-benefit theory can be a valuable tool in understanding how we assess relationships. When we feel frustrated in a relationship, we may choose to leave the relationship, or we may try to discuss the problem in an effort to improve the relationship. For example, Judd might attempt to change the dynamics of his working relationship with his father-in-law if his goal is to reap additional rewards. After discussing the situation with his father-in-law, he might be able to identify an area of the business that needs developing and then concentrate his efforts in that direction. If he is successful, he will have achieved a measure of independence that he desired all along. By doing so, Judd has improved his relationship with his father-in-law. Applying cost-benefit theory to relationships may help us understand some of our relationships more fully, why they are satisfying or dissatisfying to us, and whether or not they are worth trying to improve.

Application Activity

COST-BENEFIT THEORY

For the past three years, Eduardo, a full-time college student, has worked part time as a shoe salesman. The salary from this job provides Eduardo with additional money to meet his expenses. A constant irritant at work, however, is Eduardo's boss, who is rude and who occasionally embarrasses him in front of the customers. On the other hand, his boss does allow Eduardo to work around his class schedule.

1. Given both the positive and negative factors surrounding this relationship, why might Eduardo decide to keep the job?

2. How might Eduardo try to improve his relationship with his boss?

3. Describe both the positive and negative aspects of one of your own relationships.

4. How does cost-benefit theory explain why we choose to remain in or quit a relationship? *p. 115*

SELF-DISCLOSURE WITHIN RELATIONSHIPS

One way to improve the quality of relationships is through self-disclosure. **Self-disclosure** is the conscious decision to share personal information about ourselves. Its purpose is to help others get to know and understand us better. What we disclose about ourselves can be of little or high risk, or somewhere in between. For example, voicing an opinion about Oliver North's testimony at the Iran-*contra* hearings would probably be nonthreatening for us, whereas telling a colleague that the pressure of the job is becoming a problem for us would involve some degree of risk. Likewise, revealing to a spouse that our emotional needs are not being met is certainly a more difficult task. The degree to which we self-disclose depends on how we feel both about ourselves and our relationship with the other person.

Benefits of Self-Disclosure

The process of self-disclosure has a number of benefits, namely, an increased understanding of ourselves, the ability to express our feelings, and an increased likelihood that others will be more open with us. The end result is that our understanding of our interpersonal relationships grows.

One benefit of self-disclosure is an increased understanding of ourselves. By communicating our feelings to someone else, we are forced to acknowledge these feelings and even analyze why we feel a particular way. Simply stated, in the process of sharing with others, we end up taking a better look at ourselves. Our strengths, weaknesses, beliefs, and ambivalences are not only shared with others, they are reaffirmed for us as well.

Another potential benefit of self-disclosure is the relief we experience from letting our feelings out. In general, we are more inclined to self-disclose with someone whom we trust or know well. After doing so, we generally feel better about ourselves and the possible strengthening of our relationship. In this dialogue from Judith Guest's *Ordinary People*, Conrad bares his feelings to Berger, his psychiatrist:

"Out of the box!" He shakes his fists at the ceiling, in a parody of rage.

"That box," he says. "I feel like I've been in it forever. Everybody looking in, to see how you're doing. Even when they're on your side, they're still looking in. Like, nobody can get in there with you."

"Yeah, not much fun, is it?"

"No. But sometimes I can get out of it, now. And then, there's you." He clears his throat nervously. "I never saw you out there, you know? You, I always saw inside the box. With me." He laughs, suddenly embarrassed. His face is hot. He brings his gaze to the opposite wall, glaring at the books, daring them to move from the shelves, daring the windows to shatter. "What I'm saying . . . I guess I think of you as a friend."

There is movement at the edge of his eye. Berger, nodding.

"Well, I think of you as mine, too, kiddo."

"You don't have to say that."

"Right. I don't. So, I wouldn't."

They look at each other, and, abruptly, he relaxes, grinning.

"You understand, there weren't a helluva lot of people standing in line."

"Good," Berger says. "I hate competition."[4]

Conrad feels better for having taken the risk with Berger. His openness allowed him to release pent-up emotions with someone he trusted, which also helped lay the groundwork for a stronger relationship.

A third benefit of self-disclosure is the increased likelihood that the other party will begin to share his or her feelings and concerns with us. When both parties feel comfortable enough to do this, understanding between individuals is strengthened. An example will clarify this point:

> Stephanie and her neighbor Linda are discussing their three-year-old sons, Chad and Larry. During the course of their conversation, Linda reveals that she sometimes has tremendous feelings of guilt because she works full time and therefore has less time to spend with Larry. She worries that he is being denied a "full-time" mother.
>
> Linda is surprised by Stephanie's response— Stephanie, too, doubts how good a job she is doing as a mother. Although she does not have a job outside her home, Stephanie wonders if her influence is too controlling or smothering. She also admits that she often feels that she would have a better attitude about motherhood if she had some outside activity, such as a job.

By sharing with each other, each woman sees that she is not alone in her concerns; both have similar feelings of guilt over not being the "perfect" mother. Their understanding of each other is increased because of this shared information.

Cautions of Self-Disclosure

Trust is a prerequisite for self-disclosure in relationships. We would not consider an open discussion of our feelings with someone we barely know, nor would we expect an acquaintance to disclose something highly personal or sensitive to us.

It is conceivable to trust someone, yet not feel comfortable enough with this person to reveal private feelings. Basically, we look for someone whom we believe will be both a good listener and responsive to our needs. Empathy is often a key ingredient in these interactions. We want the other party to be an uncritical listener who shows support and understanding for our position and ultimately feels comfortable enough to share some of his or her own feelings with us. This give and take between two individuals pro-

Application Activity

SELF-DISCLOSURE

1. Reread the dialogue from *Ordinary People* on page 118.

2. What part of the dialogue represents the greatest risk for Conrad? Why?

3. Examine one of your own relationships in which trust is an established fact.

4. Are there any similarities between the dynamics of your relationship and the one between Conrad and Berger? Explain.

5. How do trust and selectivity affect self-disclosure?

motes better understanding of each other and improves communication.

Finally, in order for self-disclosure to be a meaningful process, it should occur in an environment or setting that is natural. For example, if we want to discuss our anger over the way our daughter's teacher handled a situation at school, we would make an appointment with the teacher. We would not bring up the subject if we saw the teacher waiting in line with her husband at a crowded restaurant; the time and place are all wrong. Instead of resolving the problem, we would likely put the teacher on the defensive and create a potentially more uncomfortable situation. Consider the individual and the communication climate before making a decision to self-disclosure.

CONFLICT WITHIN RELATIONSHIPS

Conflict is a natural and common occurrence within relationships, but by its very nature it produces discomfort for the parties involved. An area that builds on several of the communication skills discussed in this and previous chapters in *conflict resolution*. According to Joyce H. Frost and William W. Wilmot, **interpersonal conflict** is "an expressed struggle between at least two interdependent parties who perceive incompatible goals, scarce rewards, and interference from the other parties in achieving their goals. . . ."[5] In this definition, *expressed struggle* refers to the fact that both parties acknowledge that a problem exists; by contrast, there is no conflict if only one party perceives that there is a problem. Consider the following: Simon is angry with Althea because she did not phone him; however, because Althea is unaware of his frustration, she does not perceive that there is a conflict.

In expressing feelings, people send either verbal or nonverbal messages. Linda, for example, raises her voice when she is upset about something, whereas Jayne shows her discontent by "glaring" at others. When Linda and Jayne express their feelings to each other, the conflict is brought out into the open.

What is meant by *incompatible goals?* Basically, in order for one party to gain, there is a perceived loss to the other party. In other words, one party gains at the other party's expense. If your neighbor announces, for example, that he plans to erect a five-foot fence along your adjoining properties, you might tell him that you are against such a proposal. However, if the neighbor succeeds in getting the necessary papers to allow this action, you might perceive yourself to be the loser, while your neighbor perceives himself to be the winner.

Frequently, conflicts arise over scarce rewards which take up considerable time. We have all been in a position where we feel we do not have adequate time to deal with a situation. In these instances we are likely to ask ourselves the question, "Is it really worth spending two to three hours trying to justify to an aunt why her grandson is not invited to our daughter's wedding?" The aggravation is bound to outweigh any measure of understanding we achieve with our aunt.

Problems

Several factors contribute to the difficulties people experience when involved in conflicts, such as denial, suppression, aggression, and status. These factors inhibit our attempts to resolve conflicts because they stifle open communication between parties (see Table 6.1).

First, we shall look at denial. **Denial** is our refusal to acknowledge that a problem exists. When we refuse to see a problem, it

TABLE 6.1   Conflict at a Glance

Denial	Our refusal to acknowledge that a problem exists.
Suppression	We acknowledge a problem, but we minimize its importance.
Aggression	We are hostile toward the other party and try to intimidate him or her into a resolution.
Status	Either we or the other party use status to intimidate.

generally creates tremendous frustration on the part of the second party who may wish to resolve the problem. For example,

> Martina usually resorts to yelling when she and her husband, Eric, disagree over an issue. Eric has a serious problem accepting Martina's communication style (that is, her yelling), yet he cannot convince Martina that she has a problem; she contends that venting emotions by yelling is a perfectly natural and acceptable behavior. By denying the problem, Martina makes it very difficult for Eric to take any further steps to resolve their differences.

Suppression is a second problem in conflicts. With **suppression,** we acknowledge that a problem exists, but we attempt to minimize its importance. Our fear is that confronting the problem may result in consequences that are too difficult or painful for us to deal with. Like denial, the amount of frustration experienced by the other person can be substantial. For example, Gloria's anger increases each time Joel's mother interferes in their personal affairs and Joel fails to talk to his mother about it. Instead, Joel tries to make light of the problem with Gloria.

Aggression is a problem in conflicts because we are hostile toward the other party and try to intimidate him or her into a resolution that is clearly more advantageous to us. Consider the following:

> Alec and his wife Audrey discuss on a daily basis Alec's desire to move from their current neighborhood to a suburb populated predominantly by successful young professionals. Despite Audrey's pleas that she will not feel comfortable living in the more affluent suburb, Alec insists that the move is right for them. After four months of these persuasive talks, Audrey finally consents to give it a try. The resolution of Alec and Audrey's conflict is only temporary, because from Audrey's point of view, Alec pressured her into something she genuinely opposed. Furthermore, if her discontent about the move persists, she will continue to harbor angry sentiments toward her husband, and the underlying conflict will go unresolved.

A final problem that interferes with conflict resolution is status. **Status** is the relative standing of one party in relation to the other. An individual's status can be either achieved or dictated by society.

Reprinted with special permission of NAS, Inc.

In interpersonal conflicts, status can act as an inhibitor in two ways: (1) we can use our perceived status to intimidate others, or (2) we can feel intimidated by others who use their status to control interactions. For example,

> Eileen is extremely upset over her principal's decision to cut funds for the remedial reading program she supervises at the middle school, yet feels too intimidated by the principal's superior status to strongly voice her objections. The principal, on the other hand, sensing that he will have a difficult battle over the issue, firmly announces that "he has given the matter considerable thought and will not reverse his decision to cut the program." He uses his status to prevent an open discussion of the conflict with Eileen.

As with denial, suppression, and aggression, the problem with status is that conflicts are left unsatisfactorily resolved.

Improving Our Efforts to Resolve Conflicts

After learning about the problems that impede conflict resolution, it is natural to wonder how we can best approach the area of conflict resolution. While no simple formula exists, primarily because each relationship has unique characteristics, several skills can help us deal with conflict in our relationships. These skills include dealing with feelings, keeping the discussion focused on the problem, being a sensitive listener, and being flexible.

Deal with Feelings When we suspect we are having a conflict with someone, the first step is to examine our own feelings concerning the problem. This self-examination helps us better understand exactly what it is that is making us angry, hurt, or frustrated. Once we have acknowledged our feelings, we can more effectively express what is bothering us to the other person. Let us examine the following situation:

Mary is furious with her son Adam for staying out past midnight. Initially, she decides to "let him have it" when he comes walking through the front door; then she reconsiders this tactic. She decides that her chief feeling is not anger, but concern for his safety. When Mary realizes this, she pledges that she will calmly express her feelings to Adam rather than yell at him for being late.

Adam arrives home ten minutes later and finds his mother waiting for him just inside the front door. He begins to apologize for being so late, but he allows his mother to speak instead. In getting her feel-

The most beneficial strategy in family discussions is to try to remain focused on the problem.

ings out, Mary is surprised and pleased with herself for not turning the situation into a shouting match. By remaining calm, she succeeds in having an open discussion with Adam. Furthermore, they are able to resolve this conflict together.

Keep the Discussion Focused on the Problem When we discuss our conflict with another person, the most beneficial strategy is to remain focused on the problem. How? The easiest way is to try to **describe** our feelings about the issue, about the other person's behavior and how it offends or angers us. We should avoid attacking the other person; rather, we should focus on observable behavior that contributes to the problem. By doing so we avoid the pitfall of getting too personal.

Keith decides to discuss his work relationship with Gus, his manager. He resolves that he will remain calm and keep the discussion problem-centered. After work, he lets Gus know that he needs to talk. The following is a summary of their interaction:

Keith: I need to talk with you about a problem I'm having here at work.

Gus: What's on your mind, Keith?

Keith: I'd like you to show more respect for me. I find it extremely embarrassing when you yell at me in front of the customers.

Gus: O.K. What would you like me to do?

Keith: It would make me happier if you would just stop barking from across the store, "Wait on this customer, Keith."

Gus: Well, I see your point. I'll try to stop doing that to you.

Keith: Thanks. I appreciate it.

In this example, Keith's effort to keep the discussion focused on the problem helped both parties have a productive interaction. In addition, because Keith avoided making statements that personally attacked Gus, his manager did not get *defensive* (a concept that will be discussed extensively in the next chapter).

Be a Sensitive Listener Looking at a conflict from the other person's perspective can lead to greater understanding of the problem.

As indicated in Chapter 3, *empathy* means being able to look at something from someone else's viewpoint. In our attempt to understand the other person's position, we can use the skills associated with effective listening, such as paraphrasing, listening without being judgmental, and being supportive.

Empathy also can help diffuse a conflict. When we take the time to reconstruct the other person's position, we gain insight into why that person communicates the way he or she does. A by-product is that we take a better look at our own reactions to this person's communication. The overall effect is to have a more positive understanding of each other.

Finally, by being a sensitive, supportive listener, we encourage the other party to more freely express his or her feelings. This is a desirable way to get at the core of a conflict. If anger, resentment, doubts, or pain remain unspoken, the conflict cannot be resolved and the communication between the individuals will continue to be strained.

Be Flexible   Interpersonal conflicts are more easily resolved when the individuals involved are flexible. Being **flexible** means having the ability to adapt to a variety of situations. Flexibility suggests that there is more than one way to work through a conflict. Consider the following:

> Claire and her son John disagree over the type of punishment John should receive for denting the family car. Claire would like to bar him from driving for one month, particularly because he took the car without her knowledge and permission, whereas John contends that no punishment is warranted because the accident was the other driver's fault. Realizing that their individual stands are narrow-minded, they decide to openly discuss the matter in order to arrive at a more equitable solution. In this case, Claire and John reach a compromise—Claire agrees to let John continue to drive the car, and John agrees to get his mother's okay before taking the car in the future.

This is an ideal situation, because both parties walk away from the conflict having "won" something. Their willingness to talk about the problem and cooperate with each other by collaborating on the solution demonstrates their flexibility. Table 6.2 provides a checklist for conflict resolution.

TABLE 6.2   Checklist for Improving Our Efforts to Resolve Conflicts

√ Deal with feelings.

√ Keep the discussion focused on the problem.

√ Be a sensitive listener.

√ Be flexible.

Application Activity

CONFLICT RESOLUTION

1. With a partner create a hypothetical situation in which a conflict needs to be resolved.

2. Together use the following skills to work through a solution:

    a. Deal with feelings.

    b. Keep the discussion focused on the problem.

    c. Be a sensitive listener.

    d. Be flexible.

3. Apply these same skills to a conflict you are having in one of your personal relationships.

4. How can these skills improve your effectiveness in resolving conflicts?

SUMMARY

People need people—for sharing feelings, for support, for confirmation of their beliefs. Our interpersonal relationships teach us much about ourselves and the way others communicate. There are a number of ways to assess the dynamics of these relationships, including the Johari window, Schutz's theory of interpersonal needs, and cost-benefit theory.

    The Johari window, developed by Joseph Luft and Harry Ingham, classifies our interactions as either open, blind, hidden, or unknown. This theory represents a visual presentation of self. William

Schutz's theory of interpersonal needs argues that our needs for inclusion, control, and affection have an impact on our communication in interpersonal relationships. Finally, John Thibaut and Harold Kelley's cost-benefit theory explains how we assess our satisfaction within a given relationship.

Self-disclosure, the conscious decision to share personal information, is one way to improve the quality of our relationships. Its benefits include an increased understanding of ourselves, the ability to express our feelings, and an increased likelihood that others will be more open with us. Despite these benefits, a few cautions exist; namely, (1) we need to be selective with whom we share, and (2) self-disclosure should occur under natural conditions.

Conflict is an integral part of interpersonal relationships. A number of factors inhibit our attempts to resolve conflicts, including denial, suppression, aggression, and status. In order to improve our efforts in this area, the following skills are recommended: deal with feelings, keep the discussion focused on the problem, be a sensitive listener, and be flexible.

REVIEW QUESTIONS

1. Distinguish among the four quadrants of the Johari window: open, blind, hidden, and unknown.
2. What are the similarities between undersocial and oversocial behavior?
3. Apply cost-benefit theory to one of your current relationships.
4. Describe the benefits of self-disclosure.
5. Why is it important to be selective when engaging in self-disclosure?
6. Differentiate between denial and suppression.
7. How does being a sensitive listener help resolve an interpersonal conflict?

NOTES

1. Joseph Luft, *Group Processes: An Introduction to Group Dynamics,* 3rd Ed. (Palo Alto, Calif.: Mayfield, 1984).
2. William Schutz, *The Interpersonal World* (Palo Alto, Calif.: Science and Behavior Books, 1966).
3. John W. Thibaut and Harold H. Kelley, *The Social Psychology of Groups* (New York: John Wiley & Sons, 1959).

4. Judith Guest, *Ordinary People* (New York: Ballantine Books, 1975), pp. 127–28.

5. Joyce H. Frost and William W. Wilmot, *Interpersonal Conflict* (Dubuque, Iowa: William C. Brown, 1978), pp. 9–14.

ADDITIONAL READINGS

An asterisk indicates an advanced reading.

*Berger, C. R., and Bradac, J. J. *Language and Social Knowledge: Uncertainty in Interpersonal Relations*. London: Edward Arnold, 1982.
> Chapter 4 includes an interesting discussion of the relationship between language and self-disclosure.

*Littlejohn, S. W. *Theories of Human Communication*, 2d Ed. Belmont, Calif.: Wadsworth, 1983.
> Chapter 10 provides a valuable discussion of self-disclosure and conflict.

Rogers, C. R. *On Becoming a Person*. Boston: Houghton Mifflin, 1961.
> This is a highly readable classic by a well-respected humanistic psychologist.

7

Creating a Positive Communication Climate

Learning Objectives

At the conclusion of this chapter you should be able to

1. Explain why people communicate defensively.
2. Identify eight types of defensive communication.
3. Explain how altering a defensive climate can improve our communication with others.
4. Identify the six pairs of communication behaviors in the Gibb study.
5. Compare and contrast the six pairs of communication behaviors in the Gibb study.
6. Explain two benefits of stepping back from defensiveness.

Neil, Jim's supervisor, steps into Jim's office and proceeds to fire a series of questions: (1) "George wants to know how you can afford to add twenty-five new titles to the periodicals collection next year." (2) "George asked me why you haven't arranged for the microfilming of the local newspapers yet. How much is it going to cost?" (3) "Why is only one person scheduled Tuesday mornings?" (4) "Branches have complained to George about not receiving their new subscriptions. Has the subscription agency been notified about the problem?" (5) "When will the new periodicals list be ready?"

Jim fires back a few sarcastic responses, feeling his anger (and his blood pressure) rising by the minute. He views this barage of questions as an attack on his performance as head of the library's periodicals department, and he resents the way that Neil conducted the interaction.

Have you ever been in a similar position? It is difficult to know how to react in a communication setting where you feel threatened. When feelings of self-doubt or insecurity surface, people attempt to protect themselves. This self-protection often manifests itself in the form of defensive communication. **Defensive communication** is a person's reaction, either verbal or nonverbal, to a communication

situation in which he or she feels personally threatened or uncomfortable.

Neil's probing questions, for example, triggered a defensive response from Jim, who began to feel uncomfortable within this interpersonal setting. Likewise, a public speaker who exhibits "forced"
humor in front of an audience is also reacting defensively to the fact
that he or she is uncomfortable in the situation. The communication
we use to protect our "public" self places a shield between ourselves and others. This protective shield, however, creates a number of problems that affect our communication, including an inability to effectively confront problems. Consider, too, that it requires a
tremendous amount of energy to simply maintain these protective
walls.

Although defensiveness is an understandable reaction to an uncomfortable situation, learning how to cope with defensive communication, both our own and that of others, can lead to greater confidence as a communicator. Becoming aware of the different defense
mechanisms is a major step toward self-improvement. One important lesson is learning not to take personally the defensiveness of
others. Equally important is learning how to implement a positive
communication climate, which may lead to a reduction of defensiveness and an improvement of our communication with others. These
objectives are the subject of this chapter.

DEFENSE MECHANISMS

When we feel threatened by a situation or by another person, we
often engage in defensive communication, which is simply our effort to protect ourselves. We can exhibit a variety of defensive communication behaviors, and these are called **defense mechanisms.**[1]
Developing an understanding of the different defense mechanisms
people use should help us to recognize the types of feedback we
receive from others. Several defense mechanisms are explained in
this section: avoidance, psychological withdrawal, distancing, reaction formation, sarcasm, outdoing others, overly critical communication, and formula communication.

Avoidance

Avoidance occurs when we retreat from a problem in a relationship.
We are troubled about something, but we decide not to confront the
problem or the person associated with the problem. Instead, we
convince ourselves that the problem will go away. Avoidance is evident in the following example:

This couple seems to be practicing avoidance, psychological withdrawal, and distancing all at the same time.

. . . .

Ann and Dolores are co-owners of a small bookstore. For several weeks Dolores has arrived late to open the shop, has missed appointments with sales representatives, has had several personal phone calls, and so on. Ann is angered by Dolores's numerous excuses and by the additional responsibility she has had to shoulder; however, rather than discuss her feelings with Dolores, she avoids a direct confrontation.

A satisfactory resolution to the problem is not achieved because the two women do not discuss the resentment Ann feels toward Dolores.

In significant relationships, avoidance also can pose a problem. In some families, for example, problems are never worked through because the individual members are unwilling to discuss their feelings. Minor incidents are seen as insignificant events and are dismissed or repressed. The frustration associated with these minor episodes may build over the years, resulting in bad feelings between family members. When these feelings finally surface, the interaction is often a heated shouting match, the result of buried frustrations.

Psychological Withdrawal

Closely related to avoidance is the defense mechanism known as psychological withdrawal. **Psychological withdrawal** occurs when we feel terribly uncomfortable in a particular situation but at the same time feel forced to be physically present. Because we are unable to leave the social setting, we mentally attempt to escape from it. This type of behavior is different from daydreaming during a lecture. Daydreaming can be attributed to boredom or preoccupation with other thoughts; psychological withdrawal can be attributed to uncomfortable feelings. For example,

> Donald feels obligated to attend his cousin's wedding even though he realizes his ex-wife will be in attendance as well. When he arrives, he feels extremely uncomfortable seeing ex-relatives. Although he cannot leave the church, he withdraws psychologically.

People also use this defense mechanism in professional settings. Mike experiences extreme discomfort each time he attends staff meetings. Because he is usually shy and quiet, he believes that others will not listen to his ideas. Rather than risk rejection, he withholds his comments and avoids direct eye contact with others.

Distancing

Distancing is a defensive response which communicates "Do not get close to me." It is our way of shielding or hiding our perceived weaknesses from others. Adjectives sometimes used to describe such people include *conceited, cold,* and *aloof.* In reality, people who use distancing are shy and afraid of opening themselves up to criticism. Distancing communicates that we do not wish to be approached. George is a good example:

> George has just been promoted to a managerial position. Because he feels unsure of himself in his new role, he decides to make himself inaccessible to those employees he now supervises. He explains in a written memo that his new responsibilities will keep him busy for the next several weeks and that all requests to see him should be cleared with his secretary.

George's actions communicate to his employees that he wishes to distance himself from them. At the same time, his behavior reveals his lack of confidence in his new position.

Reaction Formation

In **reaction formation,** we behave contrary to the way we really feel. This behavior grows out of our need to present an image that is completely different from the one we believe is true. For example, an individual who exhibits reaction formation may feel uncomfortable in certain situations but will put on an act to appear confident. Consider the case of the class clown. This person actually feels uncomfortable in a group setting; however, in order to compensate for that feeling, he or she strives to "prove" to everyone else that he or she enjoys being the center of attention:

> Richard is our class clown. His daily efforts at humor are contrived and predictable. It does not take very long for Richard's classmates to realize that his communication behavior is extreme; they sense that it is unnatural for someone to always crave the attention he seems to demand.

Richard's communication is not intended to be annoying; rather, it represents an effort to be accepted by others.

Application Activity

REACTION FORMATION

Joe always seeks center stage at social gatherings, yet he behaves awkwardly in interpersonal encounters. On several occasions you have observed Joe's lack of direct eye contact when he talks to others.

1. Explain the difference between Joe's communication at social gatherings and his communication in interpersonal encounters.

2. Can you identify someone from your own circle of friends or family who communicates as Joe does? If so, how does recognizing this defensive behavior help you communicate more effectively with this person?

Sarcasm is generally more biting than humorous and is designed to keep people at a distance or put them down.

. . . .

Sarcasm

Sarcasm is the use of a biting sense of humor designed to keep people at a distance and to maintain control in a situation. Humor is meant to be spontaneous and nonmalicious. The sarcastic person, however, often plans his next retort, intent on making others uncomfortable or simply putting them down. Initially, we may find the sarcastic person to be humorous or witty; after repeated contact with this person, however, we may feel on guard or tentative. Consider the following:

Deneen: Can you clarify the role of the CIA in the sale of arms to the *contras?*

Professor Casey: Where were you vacationing? What do you think I have been lecturing about for the past five days?

Professor Casey's remarks in this example demonstrate how sarcasm can play a detrimental role in communication. Because the professor is in a position of authority, Deneen may take his remarks personally and begin to question her own intelligence. Moreover, the professor's sarcastic remarks can adversely affect other class members.

In general, the sarcastic person appears unapproachable. As a result, other people tend to avoid interactions with that person. Let us take another look at the effects of Professor Casey's defensive communication. Danielle, an extremely quiet student, may decide never to speak up in class after the preceding incident, reasoning that she, too, will be put down. If other class members develop a similar attitude and stop asking questions, what has Professor Casey been able to accomplish? The use of sarcasm allows the professor to place a shield around himself and at the same time makes it difficult for students to question and challenge him. This technique enables the professor to maintain distance between himself and his students; he stays in control by remaining unapproachable.

Outdoing Others

Outdoing others happens when we feel the need to constantly top the achievements of others. We tend to define our self-worth in relation to others. When we exhibit "one-upmanship," we rarely listen to the communication we receive, because we are too busy worrying about our role in the interaction. Despite an inability to take the focus off ourself, we are not self-centered; rather, our discomfort in interactions causes us to see only how things personally affect us. The following dialogue illustrates this point:

Mary: I studied the entire weekend for my math test, and I think it was worth it because I received 82 percent on the exam. I finally think I understand what we've been learning this past semester.

Amanda: I got 91 percent on the test. I'm really pleased because I didn't have to stay home over the weekend to study. I'm glad math comes so easily to me.

While Mary was attempting to *share* her good news, Amanda felt the need to overshadow her friend's achievement. The dialogue started out by focusing on Mary, but it transferred to Amanda in the end.

Overly Critical Communication

Overly critical individuals judge the behavior of others; they compare the accomplishments of others to their own feelings of inadequacy and believe that by criticizing others, their own self-esteem

The traffic argument is a classic example of defensive communication.

. . . .

will be enhanced. Their critical style of communication reflects their own critical nature. Consider the following:

Paul: I'm going to apply for the position in management that just opened up. I see it as a significant advancement for my career.

Steve: Do you really think you are talented enough to be promoted? I think you would be better off keeping your present position. You haven't been terribly successful as a supervisee, so how do you expect to be a capable manager?

Steve is critical because his self-esteem is weak. If Steve is repeatedly critical in his communication with others, it is probably the result of a negative self-concept. His critical communication in this example would explain his attempt to boost his self-esteem.

Formula Communication

Formula communication is safe, nonthreatening communication that involves little or no risk on the part of the communicator. It is often evident in the superficial dialogue that people exchange. There is the potential for greater depth in these relationships, but the people involved are hesitant to share their feelings. Consequently, the barriers remain and the communication stays at a superficial level. For example,

> Bob and Emily have been married for six years. During their third year of marriage Bob changed jobs, so the two of them relocated. They still, however, make regular trips back home to see everyone. The beginning of each visit is devoted to small talk and bringing everyone up to date. Afterwards, the conversation wanes; dialogue seems stuck at this superficial level. Emily and her mother are grateful for the television that fills the long moments of silence; this "third party" gives them a welcome excuse to keep their conversation to a minimum.

Although the parties believe there is more to their relationship, no one is willing to take the risk to change the communication pattern. Thus the parties continue to rely on superficial communication to survive the weekend. Table 7.1 presents a summary of defense mechanisms.

TABLE 7.1　Defense Mechanisms at a Glance

Avoidance	We retreat from a problem in a relationship.
Psychological withdrawal	We feel uncomfortable in a particular situation, yet feel forced to be physically present.
Distancing	We prevent others from getting close to us.
Reaction formation	We behave contrary to the way we really feel.
Sarcasm	We use a biting sense of humor to keep people at a distance and to maintain control in a situation.
Outdoing others	We feel the need to top the achievements of others.
Overly critical communication	We judge or criticize the behavior of others.
Formula communication	We engage in superficial dialogue as a means of self-protection.

Application Activity

DEFENSE MECHANISMS

1. Review the summary chart on defense mechanisms (Table 7.1).

2. Identify one defense mechanism you recognize in your own communication.

3. During the next two days record those instances when you exhibit this defensive behavior. Include the following information in your log:

   a. The circumstances that triggered your defensiveness.

   b. The names of those individuals also involved.

4. Is there a noticeable pattern to your defensive communication? Explain.

COPING WITH DEFENSIVENESS

As discussed in the preceding section, people communicate defensively in an attempt to protect themselves. Although their frustration is often with themselves, they defend themselves by directing their frustration, anger, or anxiety toward others.

As a result of our discussion about defense mechanisms, we should be able to at least recognize defensive communication. The next logical step is to learn how to communicate more effectively when we encounter defensive behavior. Realistically, there is no escaping defensive communication; therefore, it helps to know how to combat defensiveness when we encounter it. Our increased understanding of defensiveness will help us break through the walls others erect in order to shield themselves. Our reward for having accomplished this significant task is a level of communication that is more meaningful.

Altering the Communication Climate

We bring a particular state of mind with us when we engage in the act of communicating. This emotional atmosphere is known as the **communication climate.** It includes such factors as our feelings toward the person or persons with whom we are interacting, our attitude about the subject under discussion, and how we feel about ourselves in the particular interaction. The climate, therefore, often

The supportive climate is obvious as this family enjoys looking at family photos.

determines the degree of comfort we experience while interacting with others.

Jack Gibb differentiates between supportive and defensive communication climates.[2] **A supportive climate** is one that encourages a free and open interaction between individuals. For instance, a family gathering in which members pore over photo albums and talk nostalgically of bygone days represents a supportive climate. Inhibitions lessen as the individuals get caught up in their reminiscences.

A defensive climate, on the other hand, inhibits the interaction between individuals. Consider the following situation:

The assistant director has been invited to the reference department's meeting in order to answer questions concerning the administration's unpopular proposal to have one of the reference librarians "volunteer" to work six months at a branch library. All seven librarians are upset at the outset of this

meeting, and the assistant director knows he will be
met with antagonism.

Both parties contribute to a defensive climate in this example.

The Gibb study identifies six "pairings" of behaviors that contribute to a defensive/supportive climate. In other words, for each of the six behaviors Gibb associates with a defensive climate, there is a counteractive behavior that contributes to a supportive climate. The follow subsections will focus on the Gibb pairings: evaluation versus description, control versus problem orientation, strategy versus spontaneity, neutrality versus empathy, superiority versus equality, and certainty versus provisionalism.

Evaluation versus Description   Highly evaluative communication contributes to a defensive climate. **Evaluative behavior** is judgmental; it attacks the individual rather than that person's actions. In the following example, both parties resort to this type of communication:

Application Activity

EVALUATIVE VERSUS DESCRIPTIVE COMMUNICATION

1. For this activity, consider an interpersonal relationship that is important to you.

2. Identify an aspect of the other person's behavior that you find irritating.

3. Write down your observations. Try to avoid using evaluative language. For example:

   Wrong: Bob always cuts me off because he's rude.
   Better: Last night Bob cut me off three times while I was talking with Paul.

4. Share your observations with a classmate. Practice making descriptive statements about the observable behavior of others with your partner.

5. What are the advantages of using descriptive language?

6. How can you use descriptiveness to improve your relationship with the person identified at the beginning of this activity?

Susan: Why don't you ever pick your stuff up around here? You're so lazy! I'm always the one who cleans up this place. You never care about anyone but yourself.

Jill: I'm not lazy! You're the one with the problem. You're always criticizing! Everything has to be "just so" all the time. You know what? You're impossible to please!

Susan: I can't believe how nasty you are!

Jill: How about you?!

In this exchange, both Susan and Jill become defensive, which is reflected by their communication with each other. In order to ensure a more supportive climate, Susan needs to use a technique known as **descriptiveness,** the ability to focus on observable behavior. If Susan were to explain to Jill why she has a problem with their messy apartment, the interaction would probably go more smoothly—perhaps something like this:

Susan: Jill, it bothers me that this place is so messy. Since we're having company this weekend, I was wondering if you could do some cleaning. How long will it take you to finish?

Jill: Well, I don't know. I'm really busy today, but I'll try to get everything straightened up by tomorrow evening.

Susan: I'd really appreciate that.

In this dialogue, Susan attempts to focus on the problem *she* has with her roommate's sloppiness rather than attacking Jill personally. When we have difficulty with others, it usually deals with their *behavior;* therefore, it makes sense to have our feedback focus on those actions.

Control versus Problem Orientation   Sometimes we try to resolve a conflict with a one-sided solution. When this approach is taken, one party decides it is the other party who needs to change. **Control** is a means of making the other party conform to our way of thinking. Furthermore, it suggests that there is only one way to see a problem. Consider the following:

Melanie was rebellious as a teenager. She repeatedly challenged the authority of her parents, which contributed to tense family communication. When dialogue did occur, shouting and screaming were typical. Melanie's parents felt that she was the one with the problem, that she was the one who needed to change. They encouraged her to seek therapy, yet they refused to participate in family counseling.

With a **problem orientation,** the parties involved realize that several people contribute to the problem and that adjustment of behavior is necessary on all fronts. The focus of the discussion rests with the assumption, "We have a problem. Let's try to resolve it"— as in the following case:

Debbie is Melanie's age. Like Melanie, she went through a rebellious stage during her teens. There was considerable tension in her household, yet Debbie's family did not assume that the problem was entirely hers. Instead, the whole family participated in counseling sessions. Over a period of several months the problems between Debbie and her parents improved. This meant, however, that all the parties involved eventually altered their communication.

Strategy versus Spontaneity   Efforts to manipulate interactions between people indicate that some **strategy** is in motion. This frequently creates a defensive climate between parties. Sometimes when we have a conflict with another person, we try to preplan the dialogue, often with disastrous results. When we discuss our differences with the other party, our comments can lack spontaneity and sincerity. Consider the following situation:

A conflict is brewing between Paula and Ruth. They have been friends for over twenty years. Lately, however, Paula has been troubled over the tension that has developed between them. She invites Ruth out for lunch. Paula is nervous about the meeting and stays up until 2:00 A.M. planning what she wants to say. When they meet, Ruth surprises Paula by bringing up some unexpected points. Paula's preplanned comments are inappropriate for their current conversation. The outing is a failure for both women.

Spontaneity is the opposite of strategy. **Spontaneity** refers to an open discussion of feelings. You know the major points you wish to bring up in a discussion, but you do not have an exact script for the interaction that is about to take place. "I feel bad about the present strain in our relationship and I hope we can repair the damage" will go much further than a preplanned script.

Neutrality versus Empathy   **Neutrality** implies indifference toward another individual. This apparent disinterest can be interpreted as a lack of caring and can therefore have a negative effect on the communication climate. For example,

> Allan is excited about his decision to go to graduate school. He wants to share his news with Barbara, a fellow student. Barbara shows little interest, prompting Allan to wonder why he spoke to her in the first place.

Empathy, the ability to look at something from someone else's perspective, is the antithesis of neutrality. Empathy communicates an understanding of the other person's viewpoint. In essence, it means taking the focus off yourself so that someone else's position can be readily seen. Consider the following circumstances:

Application Activity

NEUTRALITY VERSUS EMPATHY

1. Using the preceding example of Jan and Linda, answer the following questions:

   a. What evidence is there that Jan is able to take the focus off herself?

   b. How does Jan's behavior make it easier for Linda to disclose her feelings?

2. Consider the individual you named in the preceding Application Activity. Analyze his or her irritating observable behavior by placing yourself in his or her position.

   a. List the possible explanations for this person's communication.

   b. How can the use of empathy create a more positive communication climate?

Jan's two children have been home from school for the past two and a half weeks because of a teachers' strike. Jan is angered by the disruption the strike has caused her boys' education, their family's daily schedule, and so on.

Linda, one of Jan's closest friends, teaches in the school district. Linda visits Jan one afternoon following another unproductive negotiating session. She is frustrated by the long ordeal, but she firmly believes the strike is justified. Despite her differing views, Jan allows Linda to discuss her feelings and explain her reasons.

The empathy displayed by Jan in this example creates a communication climate in which Linda feels free to express her views.

Superiority versus Equality Superiority communicates an attitude that an individual is better, more important, or more valuable than someone else. Designed to intimidate others, superiority discourages people from expressing themselves freely and therefore can contribute to a defensive communication climate. Consider the following:

Carol, a member of the Blue Ridge school board, is presiding over a meeting of parents concerned about the recent firing of a popular teacher. When questioned about the board's reasons for the firing, Carol prefaces her response by citing the collective credentials of those who serve on the board. This tactic is chosen intentionally to intimidate the parents and make them feel less qualified to speak up.

This reply sets the tone for the remainder of the meeting—a tense, defensive climate in which ill feelings dominate.

Equality, treating others on a par with ourselves, represents a supportive climate. The dialogue between individuals tends to be much freer and more supportive because the status of the individuals does not interfere with the interaction. For example, if Carol had responded to the parent's question by first acknowledging her importance as an *involved* parent, the meeting would likely have proceeded more productively.

Certainty versus Provisionalism We have all encountered individuals who believe that their way is the only way to proceed. Gibb refers to this type of person as one who has a high degree of **cer-**

tainty, one who believes that others cannot possibly contribute new knowledge to the situation. This individual frequently promotes defensiveness in others by inhibiting others from describing their ideas.

Provisionalism, on the other hand, is a willingness to explore new ideas. Individuals in this category realize that theirs is not the only way to look at a situation; they welcome input from others. For example,

> Karen and Angie are both receptionists for Dr. Johnson. After eight weeks on the job, Angie suggests a different method for handling insurance claims to Karen, who has worked in this position for three and a half years. Rather than being threatened by Angie's suggestion, Karen recognizes the merit of the proposed change and decides to approach Dr. Johnson about implementing it.

Provisionalism, as illustrated in this example, creates a supportive communication climate that encourages an open exchange of ideas. Table 7.2 presents a checklist for creating a supportive communication climate.

Stepping Back from Defensive Communication

If we find ourselves responding to someone else's defensive communication by behaving defensively in turn, it is time to step back and take stock of our actions or risk developing a habit of defensive communication. By analyzing the interaction, we can gain insight into the communication behavior of both parties and choose a more productive course of action than that provided by a defensive re-

TABLE 7.2   Checklist for Creating a Supportive Communication Climate

√ Be descriptive.

√ Try to resolve the problem together.

√ Openly discuss feelings.

√ Try to see the other person's point of view.

√ Treat others on a par with yourself.

√ Show a willingness to explore new solutions.

sponse. In the example at the beginning of this chapter, Jim responded defensively to what he perceived to be an attack on his job performance by his supervisor. His defensive response to Neil's defensive communication was unproductive; the only result was shared ill feelings between the two men. Certainly this situation could have produced different results. For example, had Jim recognized that Neil was acting defensively, he could have responded by saying, "I realize that George caught you off guard by asking you all those questions, and I don't want to get defensive about the whole thing. Please tell me what precipitated this incident and I'll do my best to answer your questions."

It is also time to step back if we find ourselves internalizing another person's defensiveness. This occurs when we perceive ourselves as the cause of someone else's defensiveness. For example,

> Lisa feels she is the cause of her colleague's coolness toward her. If, however, she were to analyze both Kim's behavior and her own attempts to establish a good working relationship with Kim, Lisa would soon realize that it is Kim who has difficulty communicating with others.

Application Activity

STEPPING BACK FROM DEFENSIVENESS

At parties, Tom always feels the need to be the center of attention. Because he believes he has to entertain everyone, he imposes tremendous pressure on himself. Sometimes he uses a biting sense of humor to accomplish this goal. It is his own need to protect himself that motivates this behavior.

Henry is at the same party. Experience has made him edgy around Tom; he has been the brunt of Tom's sarcastic humor more than once. To avoid further incidents, Henry watches what he says during the evening.

1. What's happening to Henry?

2. What advice would you give Henry in order to change his communication?

3. Examine one of your own relationships in which you react as Henry does. How would you change your own communication behavior?

Kim's way to deal with this problem is to exhibit the defense mechanism known as *distancing* (see earlier discussion). Lisa is *not* responsible for Kim's behavior.

Finally, there are times when others are theatened by *who we are,* so they lash out at us. A number of emotions may account for this behavior—anger, jealousy, and resentment are common reactions to such circumstances as our position at work, our perceived wealth, our attractiveness, or our popularity among our peers. If we realize that insecurities often motivate these individuals to communicate defensively, then it will be easier for us to detach ourselves from their defensiveness. By stepping back and analyzing their behavior, we reduce our chances of becoming defensive in return.

SUMMARY

Defensiveness is our response to a threatening situation, one that makes us feel anxious, uncomfortable, or fearful. Defensive communication acts as a shield that protects us from others, yet it creates barriers to effective communication.

We use a variety of defense mechanisms when we feel threatened by a situation or by another person. These include avoidance, psychological withdrawal, distancing, reaction formation, sarcasm, outdoing others, overly critical communication, and formula communication.

Since all of us use defensive communication and encounter its use by others, it is only natural that we should be interested in learning how to cope with defensiveness. Jack Gibb suggests that creating a supportive communication climate helps alleviate much of the tension and inhibitions that exist between people. In his work he identifies six pairings of behaviors that contribute to either a defensive or supportive climate: evaluation versus description, control versus problem orientation, strategy versus spontaneity, neutrality versus empathy, superiority versus equality, and certainty versus provisionalism.

In addition to adopting Gibb's techniques for establishing a supportive communication climate, another way to cope with defensiveness is to step back from the other person's defensive communication. In order to do this, we must first realize that it is the other person's insecurities that trigger the undesirable communication. Our ability to avoid internalizing the defensiveness of others allows us to analyze their communication and minimizes our chances of becoming defensive in return.

REVIEW QUESTIONS

1. Why do people behave defensively?
2. List eight defense mechanisms that emerge in social situations. Write a short example of each one.
3. Why is reaction formation a difficult behavior to change?
4. Differentiate between avoidance and psychological withdrawal.
5. What are the benefits of alleviating a defensive climate?
6. Briefly explain six ways to create a supportive climate.
7. Create or describe a situation in which empathy is used to establish a supportive climate.
8. How does internalizing another person's defensiveness stifle effective communication?

NOTES

1. For a sensitive discussion of defensive communication which helped shape this author's approach to teaching defensiveness, see Ronald B. Adler and Neil Towne, *Looking Out/Looking In: Interpersonal Communication,* 3d Ed. (New York: Holt, Rinehart & Winston, 1981), pp. 122–63.

2. Jack R. Gibb, "Defensive Communication," *The Journal of Communication* 11: 141–48, 1961.

ADDITIONAL READINGS

An asterisk indicates an advanced reading.

Adler, R. B., and Towne, N.   *Looking Out/Looking In: Interpersonal Communication,* 3d Ed. New York: Holt, Rinehart & Winston, 1981.
     Chapter 4 provides an insightful discussion of defensive behavior.

*Fitts, W. H.   "Issues Regarding Self-Concept Change." In M. D. Lynch, A. A. Norem-Hebeisen, and K. J. Gersen (Eds.), *Self-Concept: Advances in Theory and Research.* Cambridge, Mass.: Ballinger, 1981.
     This article examines the relationship between self-concept and defensiveness.

Gibb, J. R.   "Defensive Communication." *The Journal of Communication* 11: 141–48, 1961.
     The six categories of defensive and supportive behaviors first appeared in this article.

Howell, W. S. *The Empathic Communicator,* rev. ed. Prospect Heights, Ill.: Waveland Press, 1986.

This book focuses on the important theme of empathy.

Powell, J. *Why Am I Afraid to Tell You Who I Am?* Niles, Ill.: Argus Communications, 1969.

This book includes a valuable discussion of defense mechanisms.

8

Interviewing

Learning Objectives

At the conclusion of this chapter you should be able to

1. Define and differentiate between *open* and *closed, primary* and *secondary,* and *neutral* and *leading questions.*

2. Explain the function of each of the following interview parts: the introduction, the body, and the conclusion.

3. Construct an informational interview.

4. Prepare a résumé and cover letter for an employment interview.

5. Apply four techniques to improve your communication in an employment interview.

> You have been sitting in the small waiting room for ten minutes, trying to talk yourself into being calm. ("Take a deep breath. . . . There, that's better. You know you're qualified for this job. Just relax and you'll do fine.")
>
> You look up as your name is called. Your heart begins to beat more rapidly. As you walk into the adjoining room, you spot the man you are about to meet for the first time. Is he going to hire you? You certainly would like to get this job! ("Remember, offer a firm handshake. I hope my hands aren't clammy!")
>
> "Hello, my name is Michael Lapeer. I'm pleased to meet you."

Does this scenario sound familiar? When we think about being interviewed, one word comes to mind—*fear*. What are some factors that contribute to our anxiety? First, there is the risk of participating in an interview. We are not certain about whether or not we will get the job, and if we do not, can we handle the rejection? Second, it is difficult to interact with someone we have just met, especially when we realize this person will be judging our responses. And third, many of us are unsure about how to conduct ourselves during an interview. This chapter attempts to alleviate some of our anxieties about interviewing by explaining what an interview is and how we can improve our part within the interaction.

An **interview** is a planned interaction between two parties in which questions are asked and answers are given. The party who asks the questions is the **interviewer;** the responding party is the **interviewee.** The "interviewer" can be more than one person, such as a group of board members, department personnel, or panel members. When we think of interviews, the first kind that comes to mind is the employment interview. There are, however, several other types of interviews: physicians gather information from their patients; mortgage loan officers gather information from prospective homeowners; contractors ask customers about the special features to be included in their kitchen, bathroom, or sunroom; reference librarians ask patrons about the kind of information they need to answer their questions, and so on.

The interview builds on several of the concepts discussed earlier in this book. For instance, *listening* plays a crucial role in the interviewing process, since both participants must listen carefully to each other's responses. Questions need to be worded with precision and clarity so that they communicate the intent of the sender. *Nonverbal communication* is also crucial to the process. Participants need to observe both deliberate and accidental responses. Both parties need to be sensitive to their own interactions in order to respond appropriately to the other party's communication.

INTERVIEW QUESTIONS

Interviews contain a wide range of questions. While interviewers must formulate appropriate questions, interviewees should try to anticipate the types of questions that will be asked. On a job interview, for example, we expect to be asked about former positions we have held or why we think we are qualified for the job. Anticipating such questions can help us feel more comfortable with the interviewing process and, in turn, increase our ability to respond to questions. Several kinds of questions emerge during an interview, including the following pairings: open and closed, primary and secondary, and neutral and leading.

Open and Closed Questions

Open questions are nonrestrictive questions designed to give the respondent maximum latitude in formulating an answer. They provide an opportunity for interviewees to reveal more information about themselves—their feelings, philosophies, and biases. A question such as "What was your reaction to Senator Gary Hart's reentry into the 1988 presidential campaign?" allows us to voice our opinion about the issue. At the same time, open questions are often successful in establishing an atmosphere of give and take between the interviewer and interviewee.

Open questions can be problematic, however. Consider the fact that our response to an open question, both in terms of the subject matter covered and the amount of time utilized, is beyond the interviewer's control. In fact, much of the information we yield in response to an open question can be far removed from the interviewer's purpose. For example, if our response to the question about Hart's reentry digressed into a discussion of previous presidents' indiscretions, the interviewer would be getting more than he or she bargained for (in this case, the interviewer was simply looking for some indication of the degree of public support Hart might anticipate receiving). Consider, too, that inexperienced interviewees or those with a low self-esteem might feel particularly anxious about responding to open questions because they are afraid to disclose personal information or they are afraid that their responses might be too off-base.

Closed questions are designed to elicit specific feedback from the respondent. They are especially useful in conducting surveys or polls in which the interviewer plans to statistically compare the responses. The interviewee's responses to closed questions should be brief.

The following series of closed questions could be used in a political poll:

1. Did Senator Hart exercise good judgment in reentering the presidential race?
2. Does Gary Hart's alleged infidelity disqualify him for the Presidency?
3. Does Hart's judgment in the Donna Rice affair disqualify him for the presidency?
4. Does Gary Hart's campaign rhetoric include "new ideas"?
5. Do you agree with Senator Hart's ideas concerning military reform?
6. Would you vote for Gary Hart if the election were held tomorrow?

These questions, and several more like them, are necessary in order to gauge the public's attitude toward Gary Hart. It might take dozens of closed questions to determine the attitudes expressed in response to just one open question. Closed questions, however, are not meant to probe or explore another person's feelings or values; rather, their intent is to simply gather facts or confirm what is already suspected by the interviewer.

Primary and Secondary Questions

Primary questions are those questions which introduce a major area of discussion to be guided by the interviewer. Whenever the interviewer summarizes one area of discussion and then moves in a new direction, the initial question he or she asks is known as a *primary question*. For example, a sportscaster might kick off each new area of an interview by asking the following questions of a baseball manager whose team just clinched the American League Pennant: "What did you say to your players before the start of today's game?" "What was the turning point in this deciding game?" "Did you ever lose confidence in your team?" "Who do you plan to start in game one of the World Series?" The sportscaster is able to introduce several key issues, each with a separate primary question. Interviewers generally prepare primary questions ahead of time. By the same token, interviewees can usually anticipate that some of these questions will be asked during the interview.

Secondary questions are designed to gain additional information from the interviewee. The interviewer is asking that we clarify or expand our response to the primary question. General questions such as "What do you mean?" "I don't think I fully understand your point," or "Why do you say that?" can be used, or the secondary questions can be more specific. For instance, as a follow-up to the primary question, "Who do you plan to start in game one of the World Series?" the sportscaster might ask: "Will his arm have enough rest with only three days off?" "Are you worried about the number of walks he gave up during the two games he pitched in the Championship Series?" Certain nonverbal behaviors also can function as secondary questions. A raised eyebrow or a searching look might indicate that the interviewee needs to clarify or expand on his or her response to the last question.

Secondary questions also provide an opportunity for both parties to clear up any misunderstandings about statements made earlier in the interview. In addition, they allow the interviewee to give more detailed answers. Ultimately, this may affect how the interviewer interprets information, or reaches a decision, in the case of job interviews.

Neutral and Leading Questions

Neutral questions are those questions which reveal nothing of the interviewer's biases, preferences, or expectations. There is no "right" or "wrong" response to such questions as "Are accounting courses better at night or in the day?" "How do you like to spend your leisure time?" Here the interviewee would not feel the pres-

Application Activity

RECOGNIZING TYPES OF QUESTIONS

After reading each of the following questions, determine whether it is (a) open or closed, (b) primary or secondary, and (c) neutral or leading.

Example: What is your favorite sport? (*Answer:* This question is closed, primary, and neutral.)

1. When you talk about baseball, you mean hardball, don't you?

2. In your opinion, what is the best major for a career in public relations?

3. Your composition courses helped prepare you for a career in public relations, didn't they?

4. Is the IBM personal computer the best buy for the money?

5. What in your background persuaded you to become a fireman?

6. Are there any additional factors that led you to choose this career?

sure of "I have to get this one right!" Frank, honest replies are the only requirement.

Leading questions are designed to move the interview in a specific direction. "Don't you agree that part-time students who work are more serious about their courses?" "Television coverage can make or break a politican's career, wouldn't you agree?" In the preceding questions, the interviewee is being led to a specific response. Leading questions can create problems, however. People can become extremely defensive when they feel forced to give responses that do not truly represent their views. This can increase the level of tension within the interview.

ORGANIZING THE INTERVIEW

How do we incorporate the different types of questions discussed in the preceding section into the interview itself? To answer this question, we need to explore the issue of organizing the interview. This section attempts to do just that. While the discussion is presented from the perspective of the interviewer, it should be of equal value to the interviewee. An awareness of the interview's structure can help the interviewee anticipate the types of questions he or she will be asked.

In many ways, the structure of an interview follows the pattern of a speech. Consequently, there are three parts to the interview: the introduction, the body, and the conclusion.

The Introduction

The **introduction** opens the interview. Its general function is to establish rapport between the two parties and to clarify the interview's purpose and scope. What the interviewer says during the introduction generally sets the tone for the rest of the interview. His or her ability to create a positive communication climate depends, in part, on how interpersonally skilled he or she is.

The introduction is an appropriate place to ask some general

The introduction generally sets the tone for the rest of the interview.

questions in order to relax the interviewee. These warm-up questions, often open in nature, give the interviewee an opportunity to express himself or herself in general terms: "Did you have any trouble finding the office?" "Have you been enjoying this unseasonably warm weather?" This process often reduces the tension for both interviewer and interviewee alike. The sequence should remain brief, however, lest the interviewee become nervous about supplying "correct" answers to these questions.

The Body

The next segment of the interview is the **body.** This is where the major part of the interview occurs. In developing the body, we must first determine the degree of flexibility we feel is appropriate for the interview. We might characterize the body in one of three ways: highly structured, moderately structured, or loosely structured.[1]

Highly Structured Body   A **highly structured body** includes all the questions that the interviewer plans to ask. Most of these questions are closed, leaving little opportunity for secondary questions to arise. Marketing surveys and public opinion polls follow a highly structured body. In employment interviews, the highly structured body generally works best for the inexperienced or untrained interviewer. The security of having a prepared list of questions *in advance* simplifies the process, especially for the novice. For instance, a newly promoted store manager may have little or no experience interviewing others for a position in sales. For her first interviewing experience, an already prepared list of questions might be a wise choice. She can move from one question to the next, taking time to listen to the response given after each question. What a highly structured body does not invite, however, is a spontaneous exchange between interviewer and interviewee. This is generally achieved during a moderately or loosely structured interview, where the interviewer is more experienced.

Moderately Structured Body   In a **moderately structured body,** the interviewer determines the primary questions ahead of time. These serve only as a foundation for the rest of the interview, however. The interviewer proceeds on the premise that the interviewee's responses will trigger secondary, related questions. In other words, the interview is open to give and take between the two parties. The moderately structured interview offers flexibility and a sense of naturalness. It is an excellent format for someone who has experience as an interviewer.

For example, the interviews conducted by Ted Koppel on

Johnny Carson uses a moderately structured interview style. Some of the questions are scripted ahead of time, but there is plenty of room for give and take between Johnny and his guests.

ABC's *Nightline* follow a moderately structured format regardless of the evening's topic or invited guests. Mr. Koppel determines the ground he wants to cover prior to airtime. Once the initial questions are asked, however, he allows the interviewees' responses to dictate some of his follow-up questions. Of course, as a highly skilled interviewer, Mr. Koppel is always able to bring the topic back into sharp focus if the conversation goes too far afield.

Loosely Structured Body   The loosely structured body provides maximum flexibility for both interviewer and interviewee. The interviewer works from a list of possible questions or a list of possible topics and subtopics. These questions tend to be open ended, which allows the interviewer to observe the interviewee more closely. The loosely structured interview works best when the interviewer has no time constraints and has considerable experience. For example,

> Harvey owns four children's clothing stores. Over the years, he has interviewed and hired dozens of people; at present, he is seeking a new manager for one of his stores. In order to find the right person for the

Application Activity

ORGANIZING THE INTERVIEW

1. Observe how a seasoned television interviewer (Ted Koppel, Barbara Walters, William F. Buckley, Morley Safer) or talk show host (Phil Donahue, Oprah Winfrey, Johnny Carson) conducts an interview.

2. What type of body does this interviewer use?

3. Evaluate the interview's effectiveness.

4. What variables should one consider when constructing the body of an interview?

job, he decides to ask the applicants a few open-ended questions and then pay close attention to their responses. Harvey's experience as a businessman allows him to conduct a loosely structured interview. If the candidate's responses are too unfocused, Harvey can easily redirect his or her attention.

The Conclusion

In some respects, an interview's conclusion is similar to the introduction. One of its purposes is to end on a positive note, reinforcing the positive climate created in the introduction. To end an interview abruptly could destroy an otherwise positive climate. In "winding down" the interview, the interviewer might say, "I would be pleased to answer any questions you might have." This invitation provides the interviewee with an opportunity to ask a few final questions in order to clarify any uncertain factors: "Do the four store managers meet on a regular basis to discuss sales and advertising strategies?" "Do you encourage your managers to submit their suggestions for the company's advertising campaign?" After the interviewee's questions are addressed, the interviewer thanks him or her for participating in the session: "I'm glad you and I had this opportunity to talk. Thanks for coming in today."

TYPES OF INTERVIEWS

As adults, we have many opportunities to participate in interviews, including those related to job hiring, parent-teacher conferences, and questioning salespeople about particular consumer products, among others. Of the numerous interviews conducted daily, two are especially significant—the informational interview and the employment interview. The informational interview is presented from the interviewer's perspective; in it we discuss how to conduct this type of interview. In the section on the employment interview, the focus shifts from interviewer to interviewee. Preinterview preparations are explained, followed by a discussion of communication skills designed to improve our performance during an employment interview.

The Informational Interview

The purpose of an informational interview is to acquire facts about a specific topic. Perhaps our purpose is to gain an understanding of a company procedure or policy, to elicit an octogenarian's oral history, to determine the strategies employed by the local high school football coach, or to learn about the successful techniques of a prominent business executive. In all these cases, we must interview someone knowledgeable in a specific area. There are several steps to consider when conducting an informational interview. These include (1) developing the objective, (2) adequately researching the subject, and (3) carefully planning the interview questions.

Developing the Objective A clearly defined interview objective serves several purposes; namely, (1) it communicates the intent of the interview, (2) it helps the interviewer develop appropriate questions, and (3) it establishes a time frame for the interview. By having a clear picture of the interview's intent, both parties better understand the purpose of the interaction and the importance of each of their roles. Having a good idea of where the interview is headed allows the interviewer to outline meaningful questions that remain focused on the stated purpose. Finally, a clearly established objective helps determine a reasonable time frame for the interview. This forces the interviewer to take into consideration the interviewee's time. For example,

Ineffective objective: To learn about your business.

Effective objective: To learn the procedure that your company uses for hiring accountants.

Ineffective objective: To learn about the newspaper business.

Effective objective: To learn about the typesetting and printing stages in publishing the late edition of the paper.

The first statements in the preceding list are vague, while the second statements clearly establish the parameters of each interview. The interviewer can then proceed to develop concrete questions, while the interviewee has a strong sense of the direction of the interview.

Researching the Topic If the purpose of the interview is to gain information, it is advisable to research the topic ahead of time. Researching the topic helps the interviewer determine what he or she needs to find out during the interview, it prepares the interviewer to ask pertinent questions, and it enhances the interviewer's credibility with the interviewee. Furthermore, researching the topic avoids wasting interview time asking questions that could already have been answered by doing some groundwork. A basic understanding of the interview topic allows the interviewer to respond to the interviewee's comments by asking spontaneous follow-up questions. This task becomes difficult if the interviewer is generally unprepared for the interaction.

Planning the Interview Questions Once the interview objective is determined, the interviewer is ready to develop interview questions. In part, the purpose of the interview dictates the types of questions used; an oral history, for example, lends itself to open questions because its purpose is to learn about the individual's experiences. As discussed earlier in this chapter, open questions encourage the interviewee to reveal personal thoughts or attitudes concerning a particular topic. Open-ended primary questions should be formulated prior to the interview; so, too, can some anticipated follow-up questions. Other secondary questions are interjected *during* the interview, since they grow out of the interviewee's responses. Whatever questions are used in the interview, they should conform to the structure (high, moderate, or loose) deemed most suitable by the interviewer.

Example: Informational Interview

The purpose of this interview is to gather information about the college football team from the coach. It might cover the following three points:

I. Objective: To discover the decision-making structure of the football team.
   A. How are the practice sessions planned?
   B. Who develops the game plan for the quarterback?
   C. Who calls the plays for the quarterback?

Application Activity

INFORMATIONAL INTERVIEW

In order to gather first-hand information about a particular event in history (that is, the Great Depression, the assassination of John F. Kennedy, the Vietnam war), you decide to interview a family member.

1. Develop a set of questions for each of the following categories:

　a. The event's effect on the family.

　b. The event's impact on the neighborhood.

　c. The event's impact on the person's choice of career and/or future goals.

2. How does this information affect your perception of the event?

　　D. How many times a week do you meet to discuss the offensive and defensive strategies with your assistants?
　　E. Do the offensive and defensive teams scrimmage every other day?
　II. Objective: To find out about the team's players.
　　A. Has the quarterback recovered from his injury?
　　B. Do you think he will be ready to play this week?
　　C. If he does start, do you think he will play the entire game?
　　D. Since Rob Jackson came off the bench and scored the winning touchdown this week, will he be the starting quarterback next Saturday?
　III. Objective: To discuss the strategy for this week's game against Central State University.
　　A. What type of offense are you going to implement?
　　B. Are you going to primarily rely on the run?
　　C. How will you stop their strong passing game?
　　D. Will you use the blitz to capitalize on the strength of your linebackers?
　　E. How will you improve the performance of your special teams?

The Employment Interview

For an employer, the purpose of an employment interview is to uncover information about potential employees and to use that information to hire a new employee; for an applicant, the purpose is to find out more information about a position and to persuade the employer to hire him or her. Such factors as experience, educational background, interpersonal skills, and appearance enter into the employer's decision-making process. In the past, some employers selected applicants on factors *not* related to job performance, such as gender, race, or religion; today, guidelines prohibit this practice. The Equal Employment Opportunity Commission (EEOC) has developed strict guidelines for interviewing and testing potential employees. Both employers and employees should be aware of these guidelines, in addition to state laws that govern hiring. In this section we will focus on two aspects of the employment interview: (1) preinterview preparations, and (2) communication skills during the interview.

Preparing for an Interview   There are several ways for an applicant to prepare for an employment interview. Take the time to assess your employment potential, to compile a clearly structured résumé, to write a solid cover letter, to research the company or organization, and to evaluate the interviewer's perspective in the interviewing process. Each of the steps described in this section has the potential to make you a better prepared, more confident employment candidate.

Self-Assessment   In assessing your employment potential, you want to evaluate your suitability for a particular career. To do this, you must appraise your capabilities and talents in order to determine how well you might fit a particular position. Self-assessment involves asking yourself such questions as (1) Why am I interested in this position? (2) How important is my work to me? (3) Do I have the necessary background for this job? (4) Could I grow into the position?

Many people look to their job to fulfill personal interests. For instance, a person who enjoyed doing research as a history major in college also might enjoy being a research assistant for an advertising firm. It is equally important to take stock of such personal qualities as motivation, intelligence, and sensitivity, since these directly affect your work behavior. For example, Nancy's desire (motivation) to save money for medical school may account for her aggressive sales techniques at the car dealership where she works part-time.

Do any of your personal accomplishments make you a viable candidate for a particular position? For instance, during your term as president of a college fraternity, you probably demonstrated supervisory abilities that are applicable to a management position. Likewise, if you were responsible for financing your college education, you certainly demonstrated your ability to manage a budget.

Self-assessment forces you to realistically examine and evaluate your strengths and weaknesses. This internal review helps you to get a better sense of yourself and at the same time helps you to decide whether or not you are a good candidate for a particular job.

The Résumé   A **résumé** is a short account of one's qualifications for a particular position. The purpose of a résumé is to present one's educational and experiential backgrounds, emphasizing their relations to the job under consideration. The résumé requires thoughtful preparation and organization, since it is often a key factor in determining which applicants get interviews.

A carefully prepared résumé should include the following information: (1) the applicant's name and current address, (2) current place of employment, (3) prior employment and related experience, (4) education/training, and (5) awards, honors, and professional recognition. In addition, the résumé may include (1) activities and experiences which highlight leadership potential, (2) career goals, and (3) references.[2] Figure 8.1 presents a sample résumé.

The Cover Letter   The **cover letter** is a short letter that introduces you to a prospective employer. Its overall intent is to express your interest in the job and to create a positive first impression. To achieve this goal, the letter must be free of grammatical errors. Additionally, the cover letter should be tailored to the particular job vacancy. You want the organization or company to believe your letter is written expressly for them.

The first paragraph states your reasons for writing to the company. This is the place to indicate the specific position you are applying for and *why* you are applying for that position.

In the second and third paragraphs, explain your interest in the position and, more important, what you can do for the employer. Refer to specific professional and/or academic experiences, as well as job experiences, that contribute to your qualifications for the position. For instance, college courses in public relations and an internship at the county welfare department are details worth mentioning in a cover letter for a public relations position at the community hospital. This information gets the attention of those individuals who screen applications.

Next, refer to the enclosed résumé, which summarizes your training and experience. Also mention where the employer can check your credentials.

In the final paragraph indicate your desire for a personal interview. You can suggest possible dates or simply indicate your flexibility. Remember, do what you can to encourage further communication. You may wish to call on a certain date to arrange an

FIGURE 8.1 Sample Résumé

ERIN C. OKAMOTO
9207 Highland Street
Highland, Indiana 46322
(219) 924-4617

OBJECTIVE: To obtain a position in public relations/advertising, where I can apply my communication experience and education.

EDUCATION: Purdue University Calumet (PUC), Hammond, Indiana. Communication, Emphasis in Public Relations. May, 1988 5.35/6.0 Major Grade Point Average

WORK EXPERIENCE: Highland Public School System, Highland, Indiana
Assistant Speech and Debate Coach (8/85–present).
Teach/train high school students the fundamentals of oral interpretation for state wide competition.

Substitute Teacher (1/88–present)
Teach high school Communication, English, Speech.

Purdue University Calumet, Department of Communication and Creative Arts
Editor, Communicator
Create department newsletter from beginning to completion, write articles, conduct interviews, edit articles written by faculty, do layouts.

Assistant Editor of Communicator (9/86–5/87)
Assist editor in layouts, proofreading.

Arby's Restaurant, Highland, Indiana
Counter clerk/sandwich maker (4/87–12/87)

Jewel Food Store, Highland, Indiana
Service Clerk (9/84–9/85)

Highland Nursing Home, Highland, Indiana
Cook's Assistant (4/81–12/83)

HONORS: Presented paper at the Depauw University Undergraduate Honors Conference (3/88)

ACTIVITIES/ INTERESTS: PUC Theatre Company, *Public Relations Coordinator*.
Publicize upcoming events, promote theatre company to increase student/faculty/community support and attendance. (1/88–present)

Public Relations Project, *Grant Proposal Contributor*.
Participated in writing the successful $15,000 matching funds grant proposal for Hammond Tourism, "Wander Indiana" campaign. (1986)

Advertising Project, *Calumet Area Humane Society*.
Researched, wrote and assisted in the production of two Humane Society commercials, which are currently running on four cable television stations. (8/87–12/88)

PUC Student Leadership Program, *Student Leader*.
Introduced Freshmen students to campus facilities and programs, as part of orientation week. (8/87)

REFERENCES: Available upon request.

interview or to find out when a company representative plans to be in the area (such as on your college campus) so you can set up an interview then. Figures 8.2 and 8.3 present the cover letter format and an example.

Company Research   Finding out all you can about a particular company or organization will help you be better informed at the time of the interview. What kinds of things should you research? If the po-

FIGURE 8.2 Cover Letter Format

```
                                              your street address
                                              city, state zip
      _____

      Today's Date

      Employer Name, Title
      Department
      Company Name
      Address
      City, State Zip

      Dear Mr./Ms. Last Name:

      First paragraph—Why you're writing; use reference, source of
      information, exact position title you're applying for (if
      you have it).

      Second (and possibly third) paragraph—Tell employer why he
      or she should hire you. Cite your qualifications (skills,
      strengths) in terms of experience, education; and document
      these skills/strengths.

      Final paragraph—Tell employer you would like an opportunity
      to discuss your qualifications and interest in the
      organization in further detail. Thank employer for
      consideration.

      Sincerely,

      (sign here)

      John Doe


      enc
      (which indicates you have enclosed a résumé)
```

sition is with a manufacturing company, learn about its products, the location of its plants, and the company's history, financial status, and growth potential. For service organizations, such as hospitals, libraries, and social service agencies, comparable information is important: the type of service provided to the public, the number of employees, and its reputation in the community, annual budget, organizational structure.

FIGURE 8.3 Sample Cover Letter

```
                                              316 Kent Street
                                              Gary, IN 46406


March 9, 1988

Mr. Robert Gray, Staffing Specialist
Northern Electronics, Inc.
1605 Revere Street
Morton Grove, IL 60053

Dear Mr. Gray:
I am seeking a cooperative education or internship position
in electrical engineering technology (EET). The University's
Placement Office has informed me that Northern Electronics
hires EET co-ops.

I am a hard worker and eager learner. I believe that my high
school and college achievements reflect that. Another reason
for high achievement in my current academic studies is my
enthusiasm for the curriculum that I have chosen. I would
like to bring that enthusiasm and hard work to Northern
Electronics.

I enjoy interacting with my co-workers as well as with the
public. This quality makes it easy for me to assume a team
position as an employee. The production-line atmosphere in
my work at Burger King has certainly taught me the value of
each employee to the overall operation.

I am available for employment immediately and would be
interested in starting work this summer or fall. I can be
contacted at (219) 989-2241.

Sincerely,


Douglas Evans

enc
```

Another sound practice is to conduct research in your field or discipline. Find out about such things as average starting salaries, trends, current and future problems, and what the work is like on a day-to-day basis. For instance, if your field is accounting, you might want to investigate current practices regarding the use of computers, required continuing-education classes, and special training for the Tax Reform Act of 1986, among others.

The Interviewer Ideally, a prospective employer comes to an interview prepared to ask pertinent questions of the applicant and to supply information about the company. In many instances, the interviewer alone determines whether or not the interviewee will be considered for the position. In a well-structured interview, the interviewer has a clear set of primary questions which constitute the body of the interview. Typical questions might include "What prompted you to apply for a job with our company?" "On your application you state that you have work-related experience. Would

"Interesting résumé, but what have you done lately?"

Application Activity

PREPARING FOR AN EMPLOYMENT INTERVIEW

Visit the placement office at your college or university. From the list of job openings, select a position of interest to you.

1. Prepare a résumé and cover letter for this position.

2. Share your work with a classmate. Ask that classmate to evaluate the effectiveness of both the cover letter and the résumé.

3. Use the feedback to revise both documents.

you please elaborate?" "What are your career goals?" "What qualities do you possess that would convince me to hire you over applicants with similar training for this position?" The interviewee's responses to these questions can be revealing; from them the employer assesses the applicant's general knowledge, ability to communicate, prior achievements, ambitions for the future, and suitability for the job.

Improving Your Interviewing Skills Anxiety and nervousness are common reactions to an impending employment interview. To a degree, relief is possible by immersing ourselves in the process, that is, by concentrating on the questions generated by the interviewer and by applying specific communication skills to our responses. These skills include effective listening, honesty, direct language, and effective nonverbal communication. While these topics are treated in previous chapters, their specific application to the employment interview is discussed in the following subsections.

Listening Without question, listening is an important aspect of the interview. Effective listening requires that we do two things: (1) listen closely to detect the exact nature of the interview questions, and (2) listen to the interviewer's responses to our answers in order to gauge how well we are doing in the session, to learn more about what is important to the interviewer, and to be able to keep conversing intelligently.

One of our chief concerns in an interview is to be able to provide intelligent answers to interview questions. In order to do so, we must first understand the question. Listening closely to the interviewer is essential; however, a second step is sometimes warranted—asking for clarification when we do not fully understand what the interviewer wants. For example, to make sure that we are on target, we might paraphrase an interviewer's question this way: "Am I interpreting your question correctly? You want me to explain what steps I would take to correct an employee's chronic tardiness?" When the interviewer confirms that we have understood the question correctly, we feel comfortable offering our response.

Following our answer, the interviewer may make some comments before moving on to the next question. Listening to this feedback is just as important as listening to the questions themselves, because it provides us with clues concerning our performance. For instance, if the interviewer clearly misunderstands our reply, we need to clarify our position in order to eliminate the misunderstanding. This problem can be rectified only if we are listening closely to the feedback being given.

Finally, by listening carefully to the interviewer's questions and feedback, we can avoid asking questions or making comments about something that has already been mentioned in the interview. When we are nervous, this happens more frequently. The key here is to shift the focus away from ourselves (that is, our preoccupation about how stressful this interview is) to the other party, to pay close attention to the interviewer's message.

Honesty   One of our objectives during an interview is to present an honest picture of ourselves. This requires that we represent our skills accurately and that we take responsibility for any difficulties that we may have had in previous jobs. Misrepresentation of skills and/or experiences threatens both the likelihood that we will be selected for the position and, if we are selected, the chances of maintaining our employment. Consider the following:

> Leonard tells a prospective employer that he has auditing experience in order to appear better qualified for the job; despite his misrepresentation of the facts, Leonard lands the position. Two months later he is asked to work on an audit with his boss. It becomes immediately apparent to Leonard's boss that Leonard misrepresented his abilities during the job interview. Leonard may even have jeopardized his employment with the firm.

During the interview, questions may be raised about our reasons for leaving a previous job. It is best to offer straightforward responses to such questions: "I saw no place to advance within the company's structure." "After four years I grew tired of doing the same job day after day. I needed a change to feel self-motivated again." "I found myself increasingly frustrated by the unresolved problems and tension between my supervisor and myself. Because I saw no sign of improvement for the future, I decided to find another job." Avoid placing the blame on other parties; it suggests a weakness on our part, an inability to adequately work through difficulties with others.

Direct Language   Answering interview questions with direct, precise language communicates both a knowledge of the subject and a confidence in our own abilities. Precise language, especially terminology related to a specific occupation or profession, demonstrates our familiarity with the field: "I've worked with children at two preschools during the past seven years. In my opinion, a preschool curriculum should stress the development of gross motor skills, socialization skills, and reading readiness skills." Furthermore, being able to provide direct, concrete explanations communicates our self-assurance: "Reading readiness includes teaching such concepts as letter recognition and sounds, numbers, left and right, and sequencing [first, second, third]." Conversely, vague or general responses indicate a lack of knowledge or expertise and an apparently weaker job candidate. The lesson here is to know the subject and to show the interviewer that we know the subject by expressing ourselves with appropriate language.

Nonverbal Communication   Nonverbal communication can indicate our level of confidence within the interviewing situation. When we are nervous, for example, we communicate our discomfort not only through our verbal responses, but also through our nonverbal behavior. Signs of discomfort include averting our eyes each time the interviewer looks directly at us, repeated shifting in our seat, wringing our hands, and forced smiles.

In an employment interview, we want our nonverbal communication to support our other efforts to appear confident in the interaction. In other words, our effort to listen carefully to the interviewer's questions and comments can be accompanied by our effort to maintain direct eye contact. If we look away when the interviewer speaks to us, we will seem nervous and uninvolved. Likewise, our verbal replies to interview questions can benefit from appropriate gestures and paralanguage. For example, when we talk enthusiastically about our career goals, we can add to that positive image by using hand gestures, by increasing the rate of our speech, and by raising the pitch of our voice. (Chapter 5 has an indepth discussion of these and other nonverbal communication behaviors.) Table 8.1 provides a checklist for improving interviewing skills in an employment interview.

TABLE 8.1   Checklist for Improving Your Interviewing Skills in an Employment Interview

✓ Listening	Listen closely to detect the exact nature of the interview questions. Listen to the interviewer's feedback to gauge your performance.
✓ Honesty	Present an accurate picture of yourself.
✓ Direct language	Answer interview questions with precise language and concrete explanations.
✓ Nonverbal communication	Maintain direct eye contact with the interviewer. Have appropriate gestures accompany your verbal responses.

Application Activity

THE EMPLOYMENT INTERVIEW

The advertising firm of Barnes and Roberts is interviewing applicants for an entry level advertising position. After introductions are made, the interviewer spends a few minutes providing information about the firm and describing the current job opening to the interviewee. Following this introduction, the interview moves into high gear. These primary questions are asked of the applicant:

Why do you want to work for Barnes and Roberts?

What is it about this particular job that appeals to you?

What special qualifications do you bring to this job?

Which of your college courses best prepared you for this position?

What experiences outside the classroom helped prepare you for this job?

Describe an ideal supervisor.

What are your strengths?

What are your weaknesses?

What type of experience do you expect to gain from this job?

What do you hope to be doing five years from now?

1. Choose a classmate, and assume the role of the interviewer, asking the questions listed above. Add your own secondary questions based on your partner's responses.

2. Choose a different classmate, and this time assume the role of the interviewee. Practice using effective listening, honesty, direct language, and effective nonverbal communication as you formulate your responses to the interview questions. Elicit feedback about your performance from your partner.

SUMMARY

An interview is a planned interaction between two parties in which questions are asked by an interviewer and answers are provided by an interviewee. The interview consists of a variety of questions. Generally, each question can be classified as open or closed, primary or secondary, and neutral or leading. Open questions are designed to give the interviewee maximum latitude in formulating an answer, whereas the purpose of closed questions is to elicit specific feedback. Primary questions focus on the major concerns of the interviewer; secondary questions serve as a follow-up and are designed to gain additional information from the interviewee. Neutral questions reveal nothing of the interviewer's biases, preferences, or expectations; leading questions are designed to move the interview in a specific direction.

The basic structure of an interview is similar to that of a speech—both have an introduction, a body, and a conclusion. The introduction opens the interview and sets the tone for the interaction. The body is the heart of the interview; it is where the questions are asked and the responses are given. In the conclusion the interviewer draws the session to an end, hopefully on a positive note.

Two types of interviews are especially significant: the informational interview and the employment interview. The purpose of an informational interview is to acquire facts about a specific subject. Generally, the most effective way to prepare for this type of interview is to develop an objective, research the topic, and plan the interview questions.

In an employment interview the interviewer's goal is to uncover pertinent information about potential employees in order to select a qualified candidate; the interviewee's goal is to find out more about the position and to persuade the employer to hire him or her. The employer should be ready to supply information about the vacancy and the company offering the position. Before the interview, applicants should take the time to assess their employment potential, compile a well-structured résumé, write a solid cover letter, research the company, and evaluate the interviewer's perspective on the process. There are specific ways to reduce anxiety and at the same time improve our communication in employment interviews. These skills include active listening, honesty, using direct language, and using effective nonverbal communication.

REVIEW QUESTIONS

1. What is the difference between open and closed questions, primary and secondary questions, and neutral and leading questions?
2. Explain three ways to structure the body of an interview.
3. What steps are involved in preparing for an informational interview?
4. What is the primary purpose of a cover letter?
5. Why should you go through a self-assessment in preparing your résumé?
6. Discuss the importance of listening, honesty, direct language, and nonverbal communication when participating in an employment interview.

NOTES

1. For a discussion of a similar interviewing structure, see Charles J. Stewart and William B. Cash, Jr., *Interviewing: Principles and Practices*, 4th Ed. (Dubuque, Iowa: William C. Brown, 1985), pp. 68–70.
2. *Ibid.*, pp. 201–2.

ADDITIONAL READINGS
An asterisk indicates an advanced reading.

Bostwick, B. E.   *Résumé Writing: A Comprehensive How-To-Do-It Guide*, 2d Ed. New York: John Wiley & Sons, 1980.
     This book provides several tips on how to prepare a résumé.

*Gorden, R. L.   *Interviewing: Strategy, Techniques, and Tactics*, 3d Ed. Homewood, Ill.: The Dorsey Press, 1980.

This book provides a thorough discussion of the process of interviewing.

Stewart, C. J., and Cash, W. B., Jr.   *Interviewing: Principles and Practices,* 4th Ed. Dubuque, Iowa: William C. Brown, 1985.

This is an important book on interviewing by respected leaders in the field.

9

Small-Group Communication

Learning Objectives

At the conclusion of this chapter you should be able to

1. Define *small-group communication.*

2. Explain the importance of norms, cohesiveness, consensus, commitment, and arrangement to small-group communication.

3. Identify small-group discussion questions of fact, questions of value, and questions of policy.

4. List the steps involved in formulating a discussion question.

5. Identify and describe three perspectives of leadership.

6. Compare and contrast democratic, autocratic, and laissez-faire styles of leadership.

7. Describe task-related and process-related leadership behaviors.

8. Explain the four phases a small group goes through to reach a decision.

9. Apply three communication techniques to improve your participation within a small group.

Five faculty members are meeting to discuss their choices for filling the vacant position in the department. Their task is to rank order the three candidates under consideration and to make a recommendation to the dean about which of the three to hire.

The group agrees to focus the discussion on each candidate's merits and liabilities. During the discussion, Theo and Jack voice markedly different opinions about one of the candidates; they even get into a heated argument over which candidate is best for the department. Their behavior does not surprise the other members of the committee; these men have clashed over issues in the past. The three members do, however, feel uncomfortable about what is happening, yet they are not sure how to bring the group back to a more civil discussion. Finally, Donna suggests that they call another meeting for the following afternoon.

This example illustrates some of the problems associated with small-group communication; namely, additional players make the interaction more complex, difficulties between two individuals can affect the entire group process, and prior interrelationships affect the present interaction.

The complexities of small-group communication make it a fascinating area to study. Because so much of our time is spent in small groups, acquiring skills in this area will help increase our confidence and self-esteem. By participating in small groups, we have an opportunity to learn a great deal about ourselves, especially from the feedback other group members provide. At the same time, our participation increases both our understanding of how others communicate and our general knowledge of various issues and topics.

AN OVERVIEW OF SMALL-GROUP COMMUNICATION

Our lives are filled with group activities: business meetings, dinners with friends, bowling teams, study groups that review for midterms and finals, bridge games, and planning committee meetings. Does our communication in small groups require special understanding and skill? The answer to this question is an emphatic *yes.*

The dynamics of small-group communication are vastly different from those of either *dyadic* communication (two parties) or *public* communication (speaker and audience). Specifically, while small-group communication retains some of the spontaneity of interpersonal communication, it has the added pressure associated with interacting in public. In order to successfully communicate in small groups, we must be tuned in to the various interpersonal relationships within any given group.

Small-group communication—exactly what is it? Steven A. Beebe and John T. Masterson offer this definition: "face-to-face communication among a small group of people who share a common purpose or goal, feel a sense of belonging to the group, and exert influence upon one another."[1] Most small groups are composed of three to eight members. *Face-to-face communication* means that people interact with each other on a personal level, either verbally or nonverbally; it is not enough to simply be designated a "member" of a group. A common goal or purpose binds the group together. Consider the shared purpose of individuals charged with raising money for the library foundation. This shared goal contributes to an overall feeling of belonging to the group. Finally, efforts to meet a goal or reach a decision demand that members work cooperatively. At various times during a group's interactions, individuals voice their suggestions or ideas; their comments or actions end up influencing the group as a whole.

In this chapter we shall discuss several aspects of small-group communication, ranging from types of small groups, to variables of the group process, to preparing for small-group discussions, to leadership, to our participation in small groups. The concepts covered in preceding chapters—perception, listening, verbal communication, nonverbal communication, understanding relationships, and building a positive communication climate—determine to a large degree how successfully we communicate in small groups. The relationship between these factors and small-group communication will become more apparent as you read this chapter.

TYPES OF SMALL GROUPS

Small-group communication occurs in a variety of situations, ranging from loosely structured social gatherings to highly structured public presentations. The purpose of social groups is not to solve problems or accomplish specific tasks, but to interact with others on an informal basis and to maintain interpersonal relationships. Members may meet once a week to play softball, watch and discuss a film, or meet for a drink after work.

Somewhat more structured than a social group is a **committee,** a "small group of people given an assigned task or responsibility by a larger group (parent organization) or person with authority."[2] Although the group has a specific function, "business" tends to be conducted rather informally. For example, a campus club committee charged with planning programs for the year is likely to conduct its business in a member's home, with the discussion taking place while refreshments are served. A faculty textbook-selection committee meeting is slightly more structured—minutes are taken and votes are held over competing texts.

A number of small-group discussions take place publicly. These group presentations range from the less structured forum, to the panel discussion, to the highly structured symposium. Generally speaking, in a **forum,** a group presents its ideas to an audience, which is then invited to join the discussion. A town meeting is typical of a forum. A second type of public small-group discussion occurs when a **panel** of individuals attempts to solve problems or inform an audience about a topic. In many cases, a chairperson is selected to act as a moderator. (Although the audience may ask panel members questions, the role of the audience is diminished.) The more structured **symposium** includes a small group of speakers who share a topic, but who discuss it individually, often focusing on a specific aspect of the topic. A symposium on the 1988 presidential election, for example, might include separate presentations on the primary races, the candidates' campaign strategies, and the vice presidential hopefuls. The presenters listen, along with the audience, to the comments of their fellow participants. Interaction among the speakers and between the audience and speakers is minimal.

VARIABLES OF THE GROUP PROCESS

What factors contribute to the communication that takes place in a small group? This section explores a number of variables affecting group communication, namely, norms, cohesiveness, consensus, commitment, and arrangement.

Norms

In part, the communication behavior of small groups centers around **norms,** rules that dictate how group members ought to behave. Whether these norms are implied or openly expressed, they often provide a basis for predicting the behavior of group members. Consider the following:

> In the first two staff meetings Chris noted that the other accountants never questioned or challenged the instructions of the senior partner. Their behavior implied that this was the accepted practice or norm for staff meetings. When Brad joined the firm, Chris told him about the expected behavior at the staff meetings (an openly expressed norm).

Appropriate dress is another type of norm often dictated by the group. For instance, we dress differently when we spend time with business associates than we do when we are with family members or close personal friends. An office holiday party at a local restaurant would dictate a certain type of dress; we might feel comfortable wearing something more casual to a comparable holiday party with close friends.

Cohesiveness

Cohesiveness is a demonstrated sense of purpose within a group. A cohesive group works together as a unit to solve problems, reach goals, or accomplish a specified task. Cohesiveness develops as in-

It is obvious that certain norms dictate behavior as these investment company executives meet around a mirror-finish conference table.

. . . .

dividuals in the group become more committed to a project, as they get to know one another better, and as trust between them grows. For example, individuals serving together on a committee for the first time are likely to be reserved with one another. If, however, during their subsequent interactions they recognize the shared purpose among themselves, they will likely proceed with renewed enthusiasm. Decisions can be reached more easily this way. The importance of cohesiveness is evident in a group's accomplishments— generally speaking, the achievements are greater in a group that demonstrates this quality.

Consensus

Consensus is the genuine agreement among members that an appropriate decision has been made; it is not the result of pressure applied by others in the group. If, for instance, members of a group, as a result of peer pressure, feel they must agree with a decision, then a true consensus has not been achieved. A consensus allows the group to reach closure on an issue or to complete the group's task. A group should be careful to avoid at least the following two things when engaged in the decision-making process: (1) making premature decisions, and (2) succumbing to pressures to conform. A premature decision often indicates a lack of analysis by the group. Many sides of an issue or decision need to be explored before a consensus is reached. Sometimes individuals feel pressured to comply with a stand taken by other members who are in positions of power. We have all experienced instances when we have felt it is wiser to agree with a supervisor, parent, teacher, or some other person in authority than to subject ourselves to their displeasure. Our agreement does not constitute a true consensus.

Commitment

Commitment, the motivation of members to meet the goals of the group, also plays a significant role in the outcome of small-group interactions. Are the members genuinely committed to the stated goals of the group? Do they identify with the values expounded by the group? If the answer to these questions is yes, then the members are likely to be more productive and work as a cohesive unit. For example,

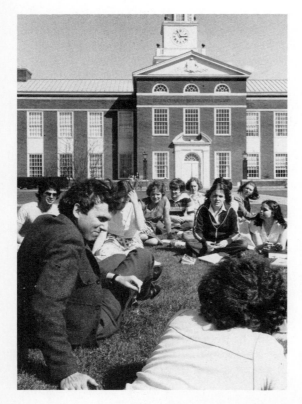

Altogether different norms dictate behavior in this outdoor class.

> Seven elementary school teachers are charged with studying a plan to implement a computer curriculum in grades one through three. Five of the seven teachers are enthusiastic about the idea; as a result, they devote considerable energy to writing their recommendations to the school administration. The remaining two members have little interest in the project, which is apparent by their minimal participation during meetings.

Commitment, then, can energize or renew a group's interest in achieving a goal.

There are some potential drawbacks to commitment. First, we are often blind to others' viewpoints because we are convinced that ours is the best (and only) way. Second, when we are committed to a project, there is a tendency to try to persuade others to see things as we do. At times the pressure we apply is overbearing.

Arrangement

Another variable that affects group participation is the communication **arrangement,** the physical placement of the individuals within the group. Is everyone sitting in rows, around a conference table, or on the floors and couches in someone's living room?

Often the placement of individuals in the group determines the amount of interaction that takes place. For example, if a group is arranged in a row, as panel members often are, direct eye contact is limited, especially for those who are seated at either end of the row. Dialogue is generally limited to those sitting next to one another. Interaction is increased when members are able to see each other better. When we have a better view of those we are talking to, it is easier for us to detect the feedback others send and alter our message, if necessary. Having group members seated in a half-wheel or circle facilitates direct eye contact and greater participation among everyone.

PREPARING FOR A SMALL-GROUP DISCUSSION

Frequently, the task of a small group is to discuss a question or resolve a problem. As participants, we feel more comfortable if we adequately prepare for the discussion in advance. Just as we feel ready to take an exam when we have read the assigned texts and studied our class notes, the same applies to our participation in a group discussion. Necessary preparation includes assessing the question, gathering material, and developing an agenda.

A jury is a common example of a small group that must discuss the facts in a case and determine guilt or innocence.

. . . .

Assessing the Question

One of the preliminary steps of small-group discussions is to assess the question before the group. To help focus the discussion, the group might first determine whether the question is one of fact, value, or policy. A second step involves formulating the question. Both these steps help shape the discussion that follows later on.

Types of Questions   When dealing with a **question of fact,** the group argues whether or not a statement is true or false. Its purpose is to explore a "fact" and draw some conclusions based on its accuracy. A group of jurors, for example, must weigh the statements of various witnesses in order to judge whether these statements are true or false.

A second type of question centers around **value.** The group in such a situation must determine the *morality* of an issue, that is, whether something is good or bad, right or wrong. For instance, our jury must decide whether a defendant's actions are unlawful and, therefore, punishable by law, or whether the actions do not violate present laws.

Application Activity

ASSESSING DISCUSSION QUESTIONS

Identify the following as questions of fact, value, or policy:

1. Does lowering your blood cholesterol level reduce your risk of developing heart disease?

2. How can the laws be changed to reduce the number of drunk drivers?

3. Is it important to have an ideologically balanced Supreme Court?

4. Should parents receive a tax credit if their children attend private schools?

5. Many psychologists agree that viewing violence on television can lead to acts of violence by individuals. Is their stand on this issue useful?

6. Should surrogate mothers be granted visitation rights?

7. Should cigarette smoking be banned on all commercial airplane flights?

Finally, with a **question of policy,** the group must decide if any specific action is in order. Such a decision often rests on taking another look at questions of fact and value that help shape policy. For example, if our jury decides in favor of the defendant (based on weighing earlier questions of fact and value), it might have to tackle the sticky issue of how much to award the defendant in damages—should the defendant be entitled to damages, and if so, how much?

Formulating the Question   Once the group determines whether the question is one of fact, value, or policy, the next stage is to formulate the question. Is the question stated clearly? Is the question neutral? Does it promote discussion? These three factors should be considered when constructing the question.

Is the Question Clear?   "Do you feel that music videos are eroding traditional values?" Each member of the group may have a different interpretation of "traditional values" in the preceding question. To ensure that each member understands the topic, it is best to use concrete language, as discussed in Chapter 4. Additionally, it is useful to construct a question that contains only one idea; the more complicated the question, the greater is the confusion among group members.

Now consider this question: "Are the sexual themes portrayed in rock videos harmful to the lasting impressions formed by adolescents regarding sexual relationships?" In this second question the language is concrete, providing the group with a greater sense of direction than the first question allowed.

Is the Question Neutral?   In constructing the question, care should be taken to avoid alienating group members. "Should the racist practice of the school board be stopped?" This question would undoubtedly provoke some individuals and might lead to an unproductive conflict within the group. A question can be **neutral,** that is, one that does not "take sides," yet still promote natural conflict and discussion among group members. For example, "What steps should the school board take to desegregate the schools?" Because the second question neither condones nor attacks the present policies of the school board, it is unlikely to alienate group members before the discussion starts. Its neutrality can lead to a more fruitful discussion.

Does the Question Promote Discussion?   The question should be one that generates a meaningful, engaging discussion. Controversy frequently stimulates members to participate in a discussion. A question that is controversial, then, should successfully accomplish this task. "Are the welfare agencies and juvenile courts justified in returning abused children to their homes?" This question does not suggest that there is a simple answer. The issue is obviously a complex one and can certainly lead to a lengthy debate. Table 9.1 provides a checklist for formulating the question.

Gathering Material

Once the discussion question is decided, the next step is to gather research material. This process is discussed at length in Chapter 11;

TABLE 9.1   Checklist for Formulating the Question

✓ Is the question clear?	Use concrete language. Construct a question that contains only one idea.
✓ Is the question neutral?	The question should avoid "taking sides."
✓ Does the question promote discussion?	Controversy stimulates discussion.

however, a basic explanation is included here as well. To support our position or contentions, we need to gather reliable information that is culled from either **primary sources,** documents such as letters, manuscripts, and taped interviews, or **secondary sources,** interpretations of primary material. For example, to prepare for a discussion on President Reagan's reaction to the October 1987 stock market crash, we would want to examine his personal copy of his address to the nation. This primary source, however, is unavailable to the general public. What is available in its place is a wide range of secondary sources: newspaper accounts, reports by television journalists, and analyses in magazines and journals. Of course, sources that include a transcript of the President's message, such as the *New York Times* or *Vital Speeches of the Day,* are considered to be more accurate than interpretations of his message that appear in other periodicals. Further, assessments of the meaning and impact of Reagan's message are offered by many, but those of noted authorities are better secondary sources than those of lesser known individuals.

The Agenda

Our preparation for a discussion should include an **agenda,** an outline of the points to be discussed. One member of the group may be asked to prepare the agenda (this individual may assume a position of leadership within the group), an agenda subcommittee may be assigned this task, or all members can suggest points to be discussed. Although the group is likely to shift back and forth as the

Application Activity

PREPARING FOR A DISCUSSION

1. Given the topic "surrogate mothers," formulate a discussion question.

2. What kinds of resources would you use to gather information about the subject?

3. Develop an agenda for the discussion. Take into account the various arguments, both pro and con, surrounding this subject. Consider how much time to allow for each point discussed.

4. Share your agenda with a small group to elicit feedback.

5. Use this feedback to improve your agenda.

members discuss the topic, an agenda will help them stay focused. The agenda should allow for adequate time both to discuss the problem and to explore several solutions.

It is important to let all group members have an opportunity to share their ideas. This process guarantees that several different approaches to the problem will be explored and adequately discussed before moving on to a solution. Even after a tentative solution is reached, the group is likely to debate the positive and negative aspects. The agenda should take this fact into account.

LEADERSHIP

Regardless of a group's purpose, whether it is planning a class reunion or deciding which computer to purchase for the office, the group's success depends, in part, on its leadership. **Leadership** is the ability to exert influence on a group by providing a sense of direction or vision. This influence can come from an individual designated as the leader or be shared by several members of the group. In this section we shall discuss a variety of leadership perspectives, ranging from the trait perspective with its "born leaders," to the situational perspective with its democratic, autocratic, and laissez-faire styles, to the functional perspective with its shared leadership by means of task-related and process-related behaviors. Knowing about these perspectives can help us to recognize the leadership roles played by others and assist us in developing our own leadership capabilities.

Trait Perspective

The **trait perspective** of leadership suggests that certain individuals are "born leaders" because they possess such qualities as a forceful personality, marked intelligence, and dynamic communication skills. While we can think of individuals who have these characteristics, they are not necessarily effective leaders when placed in small groups. Why? This perspective has some serious flaws. The chief flaw with the trait perspective is that its outlook is too narrow: it does not take into account the other individuals in the group. The leadership qualities just described do not guarantee that an individual will be a successful leader. So what if Mary is aggressive, intelligent, and a skillful communicator? If she has no interest in a group's intended purpose or function, she may prove to be an ineffective leader. A second flaw of this perspective is its failure to recognize the motivational drive and commitment of those who want to lead groups, nor does it take into account the fact that individuals often have potential leadership qualities that need only be tapped.

Situational Perspective

In most groups the type of leadership required depends on two chief ingredients: (1) the reason for the group's existence (that is, to set a preliminary budget or to plan a surprise birthday party), and (2) the composition of the group, including how these individuals interact. In other words, each group creates a new situation, and this situation dictates which style of leadership is most appropriate. This is called the **situational perspective.** We frequently label a leader's style as either democratic, autocratic, or laissez-faire. Let us take a look at what each of these means. A **democratic leader** demonstrates his or her confidence in the group by involving group members in decision-making matters. Rather than dominate the group, the democratic leader allows the group to decide who will tackle specific tasks or jobs. Such involvement generally increases both the group's cohesiveness and the overall satisfaction with the group process. We take pleasure in knowing that we have contributed to the group's efforts, that we have been personally involved.

The role of the **autocratic leader** is one characterized by a more domineering presence. This individual usually decides what direction the group will take; he or she assigns tasks to members, dictates the nature of all activities, and makes policy statements. The separation between "leader" and "group member" inhibits input from the group; the lack of involvement often leads to dissatisfaction on the part of group members. Because the process is more expedient under an autocratic leader, group members are frequently more productive. However, the satisfaction of participating in the decision-making process is absent.

A **laissez-faire leader** gives minimal direction or instruction to group members; rather, members have complete freedom to make decisions. The laissez-faire leader offers advice only when directly asked by the group or one of its members. Practically speaking, this style of leadership is the least effective of the three. The group often fails to make progress because it is unsure about where it is headed.

From the descriptions just given, we might easily conclude that the democratic style of leadership is the best approach. While this is true in many cases, there are instances when either an autocratic leader or a laissez-faire leader is warranted. Consider, for example, two groups who are given the same assignment in their public administration class: to write a job description for a town manager serving a population of 18,000. Group A has three members with no work experience and a fourth member who served for five years as a clerk in a mayor's office. Because of her experience, Julia "takes charge" of the group, especially after fifteen minutes of floundering and indecision by the other members. Her role as an autocratic leader succeeds in mobilizing the group.

The four members of Group B, however, all have work experience. Suggestions for the town manager's job description seem to come easily, and there is agreement among the group members about the necessary qualifications. For this group, a laissez-faire style of leadership is appropriate. There is no need to have a controlling presence when the individual members already function as a cohesive group.

Functional Perspective

A **functional perspective** of leadership focuses on the kinds of leadership behaviors that *any* member of the group can exhibit which collectively result in the group's making progress. This perspective differs from the other leadership perspectives discussed so far because it does not promote the role of a single leader. Two primary types of behavior associated with functional leadership are task-related leadership behavior and process-related leadership behavior.

Task-related leadership behaviors include those actions whose purpose is to keep the group focused on the problem or question. Groups frequently get sidetracked from their intended function; to rescue them there are such task-related behaviors as initiating ideas, elaborating on the ideas of others, raising questions, and summarizing thoughts.

An individual who offers new or fresh ideas helps the group move closer to solving a problem. This is especially true if the group seems stuck on a particular point. When an idea generates enthusiasm, someone can take that idea a step further by elaborating on the subject. For example,

> Monica's idea is to make the theme of their fifteen-year high school reunion "The Way We Were," the top single in 1974. The planning committee likes her idea, and Jim responds by suggesting that this theme be carried out in the invitations and music. He thinks the invitations should request that all guests dress as they did during their senior year and that the band play songs popular during 1973–74.

Another behavior that moves the group forward is asking questions. Even a simple question such as, "Where do we go from here?" refocuses the group's attention to the task at hand. Finally, summarizing a discussion accomplishes two things: (1) it clarifies the various points by restating them, and (2) it brings into sharp focus what has already transpired and, by doing so, points out what remains to be done. This gives the group an opportunity to hear the ideas or arguments once again and to ask for clarification if necessary.

The task-related behaviors just described go hand in hand with **process-related leadership behaviors**—those behaviors concerned with maintaining a positive climate within the group. These include such things as relieving tension, gatekeeping, and offering encouragement to other group members.

When the interaction within a group becomes tense, it is a relief to have someone say, "Let's take a break for a few minutes," or to interject a little humor to ease the tension. An equally important function is carried out by a **gatekeeper,** one who attempts to regulate the flow of communication within the group. This role requires that the individual draw quiet members into the discussion (perhaps by asking a direct question) and, at times, take the center stage away from a group member who is dominating the discussion. The person who acts as a gatekeeper believes that each member has something to contribute to the group. This is also the belief of one who en-

Application Activity

LEADERSHIP

The Chief of Medicine at Parkline General appoints a five-member committee to recommend changes in the hospital's present emergency room procedures. The committee consists of the two senior ranking emergency room nurses, two emergency room physicians, and the physician in charge of the emergency room.

1. The emergency room chief is the appointed leader of this committee. Describe how he or she would operate:

   a. As a democratic leader

   b. As an autocratic leader

   c. As a laissez-faire leader

2. Describe two task-related and two process-related behaviors that members of this committee might demonstrate in a functional approach to the assignment.

courages other group members to participate in the group discussion. Praising an individual's ideas, for example, can lead to increased self-esteem and satisfaction as a group member. When members feel better about themselves, the overall quality of the group process is enhanced.

PARTICIPATING IN SMALL-GROUP DISCUSSIONS

Thousands of committees meet each day to discuss issues and make decisions. Asking a small group of individuals to solve a problem suggests a belief that collectively a better decision can be reached than by asking an individual to do the same thing. Of course, this is not true for all types of decisions. Some decisions are highly personal, such as the brand of toothpaste we choose or the kind of car seat we purchase for our child. However, participating in small-group decision making can be more effective if we understand two basic facts: (1) that every group decision is reached as a result of going through specific phases, and (2) that the use of special communication skills can bring out the best in people.

Phases of a Discussion

Every small-group decision is a process that goes through several phases. In order to become better participants in the process, it is helpful to recognize that decision making is frequently a slow, frustrating exercise that requires considerable patience and tolerance. In the subsections that follow we shall explore four phases of the decision-making process of a small group: orientation, conflict, emergence, and reinforcement (see Table 9.2).[3] Further, a basic understanding of these phases provides a framework for the skills discussed in the final section of this chapter.

TABLE 9.2   Phases of a Discussion

Orientation phase	A time for establishing a comfortable communication climate and becoming familiar with the topic.
Conflict phase	Disagreements surface; tension is a natural by-product.
Emergence phase	There is a gradual shift toward an apparent decision.
Reinforcement phase	Consensus is achieved; dissent all but vanishes.

Asking a small group of individuals to solve a problem suggests a belief that a better decision can be reached by a collective than by an individual.

· ·

Orientation Phase   During the **orientation phase,** or the beginning of a group discussion, members are chiefly concerned about establishing a comfortable social climate. Dialogue is apt to be guarded and superficial as members pay particular attention to "getting along" with everyone. This is also a time for individuals to become acquainted with the subject about to be discussed. For example,

> The library administration appoints a five-person committee to decide how to spend an additional $68,000 on library materials during the remaining two months of the fiscal year. At the initial meeting the committee members discuss the circumstances surrounding the acquired funds and voice their pleasure at being involved in this assignment. Everyone is in agreement that they can work out an equitable way to spend the allotted money. "I feel like we've hit the jackpot on *Wheel of Fortune!* I can't wait to spend this money."

Conflict Phase   As ideas begin to surface regarding the decision making, it is natural for disagreement and tension to surface as well. This stage is known as the **conflict phase.** It would be unrealistic to expect a group to reach a decision without first experiencing conflict. The degree of conflict, however, varies from one group to the next and influences how much time is spent in this particular phase of the process. Our tolerance during this phase is particularly important (more on this in the final section of this chapter).

As individuals become passionate about their ideas and coalitions (subgroups) start to develop, the interaction becomes less inhibited. When individuals align themselves for or against a particular proposal, tension frequently results from any differences of opinion.

> The library committee (mentioned earlier) is now splintered into two coalitions, each having a vastly different idea about what kinds of materials and equipment to purchase. One group proposes that the majority of the money be used to purchase print materials: "The library should maintain its image as an institution that provides books on all subjects." The other group favors audiovisual materials: "We disagree. The patrons who use the library today want to check out compact discs, computer software, and videos!" Will they be able to resolve this problem?

Emergence Phase   As discussion continues, most groups grow anxious to reach a decision. This stage is called the **emergence phase.** In an effort to reach a consensus, there is a tendency among those members who expressed dissent during the conflict phase to now take a more ambiguous stand. These individuals attempt to disengage themselves from the passionate stands taken just a short time ago, but at the same time they avoid embracing the opposing position wholeheartedly. Ambiguity replaces passion as a modified form of dissent. As coalitions break up and dissent weakens, there is a gradual shift toward an apparent decision. Let us look once again at our library committee:

> A decision to purchase more audiovisual material is gaining favor. Those who voice strong opposition during the conflict phase now make ambiguous comments about the same proposal. These comments reflect a shift in attitude from dissent to resigned acceptance. "The public would probably react enthusiastically to a larger collection of feature-film videocassettes."

Reinforcement Phase In the final phase of the decision-making process, consensus is achieved; this is called the **reinforcement phase.** Members typically reinforce their positive feelings concerning the decision and also show their support of one another. Dissent all but vanishes.

> The members of the library committee applaud their efforts and state that they acted on behalf of the public which they serve. "Our patrons will be thrilled with all the new materials we've agreed to purchase. Everyone on the committee did a terrific job."

The example of the library committee used throughout this discussion of orientation, conflict, emergence, and reinforcement phases is idealistic; few group discussions go so smoothly. Even the most heated, emotionally tense discussions, however, proceed through these phases. In the final section of this chapter we will learn skills to help us cope with the frustrations of small-group discussions and to help us successfully participate in the process.

Communication Skills within Small Groups

Small-group communication challenges our ability to communicate effectively with others. It requires that we make constant adjustments to the various personalities within the group, that we exert a special effort to make our message understood by others, and that we, in turn, strive to understand the views held by other individuals in the group. Furthermore, the potential for conflict and communication breakdowns is substantially higher in small groups than it is in one-to-one encounters. This is particularly true for task-oriented or problem-solving groups, where ideas are apt to clash. Fortunately, we can overcome these obstacles by applying specific skills in the areas of verbal and nonverbal participation and by maintaining a positive communication climate.

Verbal Participation As a member of a small group, each of us has an obligation to let others know our ideas or positions regarding a specific topic. While the degree of participation varies with each member, it is important to remember that a lack of participation fails to serve the best interests of the group. Sometimes groups are dominated by one person who tries to monopolize the conversation. What can be done to remedy this situation? To steer the attention away from this person, one can ask someone else in the group a pointed question, such as "What course of action would you suggest?" or "How will the proposed schedule affect people who work in your department?"

Application Activity

COMMUNICATION SKILLS WITHIN SMALL GROUPS

1. Begin by forming two small groups, each with five members. Have each group select one of the following topics to discuss:

   a. Should a city's public funds be used to purchase and display a Nativity scene?

   b. Should smoking be prohibited in hospitals?

   c. Should sterilized needles be given to intravenous drug users to stem the spread of AIDS?

   d. Do television commercials that advocate the use of condoms for "safe sex" erode the morality of our nation?

2. Group A discusses its selected topic for twenty minutes. Members should concentrate on practicing the communication skills discussed in the previous section: verbal participation, nonverbal participation, and maintaining a positive communication climate. During this discussion, each member of group B observes one member of group A. (*Note:* These pairings should be decided prior to the discussion.)

3. At the end of twenty minutes, members of group B begin discussing their topic. Group A observes their communication skills.

4. At the conclusion of the second discussion, each set of partners from group A and group B meets to give each other feedback on their participation within the group. Use empathy and descriptive language when communicating with your partner.

Questions serve many purposes: (1) they maintain your involvement in the group discussion, (2) they can refocus the group's attention or provide direction for a discussion that has strayed from the main points, and (3) they can be used to draw other members of the group into the discussion, especially quiet members. Any group member can use the technique of asking questions to improve the quality of the interaction.

Nonverbal Participation   Another way to communicate our feelings is through nonverbal participation. Perhaps the most effective nonverbal behavior is that which communicates our agreement with or support of an idea. The simple act of nodding our head or smiling when someone makes a humorous comment offers encouragement to the person who is speaking. When we perceive another group member's nonverbal signals as negative (that is, a head shaking "no," a glaring look, or eyes directed away from the person talking), there are specific actions we can take. One method is to ask the person why he or she disagrees with what is being said or proposed to the group. Another similar method is to confront the person about his or her negative nonverbal communication by saying something along these lines: "I noticed you shaking your head a moment ago. Are you having a difficult time understanding or accepting my proposal? I'll try to clarify my position if you want." The person's response to our comments and questions will indicate whether we have perceived this person accurately; then we can proceed accordingly.

Maintain a Positive Communication Climate   A positive communication climate, discussed at length in Chapter 7, encourages discussion among group members. During the orientation phase of a group discussion the climate is likely to remain positive; however, this is not always the case during the conflict phase. As individuals begin to take sides on an issue or proposal, the climate can quickly change. Our efforts to reduce defensiveness can restore a positive climate and at the same time improve the overall interaction.

   The group process is disrupted when one or two people dominate the discussion and others begin to withdraw from it. How do we combat this? When a group discussion deteriorates to the point where individuals resort to name-calling or threaten to walk out, we can remind everyone involved to avoid personal attacks on others. Instead, the discussion should be brought back to the issue at hand. We also can remind group members to allow others to voice their opinions without being interrupted. This forces us to listen atten-

TABLE 9.3   Checklist for Communication Skills within Small Groups

✓ Verbal participation	Let others know our ideas or positions; ask questions to maintain involvement of ourselves and others.
✓ Nonverbal participation	Communicate our support; respond to nonverbal feedback of others.
✓ Maintain a positive communication climate	Reduce defensiveness by avoiding personal attacks and interruptions; provide descriptive feedback to others.

tively. If we have any questions, we can ask them after the person stops speaking. Finally, our comments, including the feedback we give to others, should be descriptive (not judgmental) and reflect our empathy for the positions taken by these individuals. Group discussion will progress more smoothly when these steps for maintaining a positive climate are taken. Table 9.3 provides a checklist for communication skills within small groups.

SUMMARY

Small-group communication is communication involving three to eight individuals who share a common purpose, feel a sense of belonging, and influence each other. Small-group discussion occurs in social groups, in committees, and in public presentations ranging from forums to panels to symposiums.

Several variables affect small-group communication, including norms, rules that dictate how group members ought to behave; cohesiveness, the demonstrated sense of purpose within a group; consensus, the genuine agreement that an appropriate decision has been reached; commitment, the motivation of members to meet the goals of the group; and arrangement, the physical placement of the individuals within the group.

Three steps help us prepare for a group discussion: (1) assessing the question, which includes determining whether the question is one of fact, value, or policy, and formulating the question, which means deciding whether the question is clear, whether it is neutral, and whether it promotes discussion; (2) gathering material, either from primary or secondary sources; and (3) having an agenda or outline of the points to be discussed.

Leadership is the ability to exert influence on a group by providing a sense of direction or vision. It is defined by a variety of perspectives, ranging from the trait perspective, with its notion that certain individuals are "born leaders," to the situational perspective, in which the group situation dictates the most appropriate leadership style (either democratic, autocratic, or laissez-faire), to the functional perspective, which focuses on the kinds of leadership behaviors any group member can exhibit which result in the group's making progress.

Effective small-group participation is based on two facts: (1) that every group decision is reached as a result of moving through specific phases, and (2) that the use of special communication skills improves our communication. The four phases of the decision-making process include the orientation phase, where the climate is established and the members acquaint themselves with the topic; the conflict phase, in which disagreements surface; the emergence phase, in which the desire for the group to reach a decision takes hold; and the reinforcement phase, where members voice their support for the decision which has been reached and for one another.

Finally, our effectiveness within groups depends on how skillfully we communicate in the following areas: verbal participation, nonverbal participation, and maintaining a positive communication climate.

REVIEW QUESTIONS

1. Briefly describe the following variables that affect small-group communication:
   a. Norms
   b. Cohesiveness
   c. Consensus
   d. Commitment
   e. Arrangement
2. Differentiate between a question of fact, a question of value, and a question of policy. Give an example of each.
3. List three factors a group should consider when formulating its discussion questions.
4. Compare and contrast the situational and functional perspectives of leadership.
5. Under what circumstances is the laissez-faire style of leadership effective?
6. Briefly describe the four interpersonal phases of small-group decision making.
7. List and describe three communication skills that can improve our participation in small-group discussions.

NOTES

1. Steven A. Beebe and John T. Masterson, *Communication in Small Groups: Principles and Practices* (Glenview, Ill.: Scott, Foresman, 1982), p. 12.

2. John K. Brilhart, *Effective Group Discussion*, 4th Ed. (Dubuque, Iowa: William C. Brown, 1982), p. 3.

3. For further discussion, see B. Aubrey Fisher, *Small Group Decision Making: Communication and the Group Process*, 2nd Ed. (New York: McGraw-Hill, 1980), pp. 144–49.

ADDITIONAL READINGS

An asterisk indicates an advanced reading.

Beebe, S. A., and Masterson, J. T.　*Communicating in Small Groups: Principles and Practices*. Glenview, Ill.: Scott, Foresman, 1982.

　　　This is an impressive overview of small-group communication.

*Cathcart, R. S., and Samovar, L. A. (Eds.).　*Small Group Communication: A Reader*, 4th Ed. Dubuque, Iowa: William C. Brown, 1984.

　　　This reader includes several important articles on small-group communication.

*Fisher, B. A.　*Small Group Decision Making: Communication and the Group Process*, 2d Ed. New York: McGraw-Hill, 1980.

　　　This book provides a systems approach to small-group communication.

*Janis, I. L.　*Groupthink: Psychological Studies of Policy Decisions and Fiascoes*, 2d Ed. Boston: Houghton Mifflin, 1982.

　　　This is a fascinating application of groupthink to foreign policy decisions.

Part Three

Public Communication

10

Selecting a Speech Topic and Analyzing the Audience

THE SPEECH PURPOSE

After choosing a topic, you must establish the purpose of your presentation. If your stated purpose is in line with the expectations of the audience, you will likely feel more comfortable about presenting your ideas. The development of your speech purpose usually follows three steps: (1) determining the general purpose, (2) determining the specific purpose, and (3) creating a thesis statement (see Figure 10.1).

General Purpose

Establishing the **general purpose** of your presentation means deciding whether your overriding goal is to inform, to persuade, or to entertain. In most instances, your purpose is to inform or to persuade, although these frequently overlap. When your purpose is to inform, your chief concern rests with presenting information as clearly and accurately as possible. For example, as personnel director, you set a time and date to explain each of the three medical plans now available to company employees. As you try to increase the audience's understanding of your topic and to broaden their knowledge, clear, descriptive language is essential.

FIGURE 10.1 Establishing Your Purpose

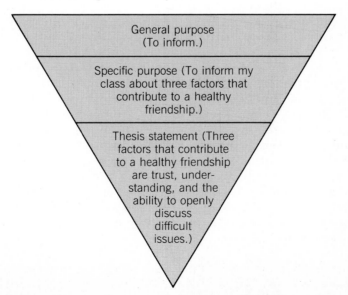

General purpose
(To inform.)

Specific purpose (To inform my class about three factors that contribute to a healthy friendship.)

Thesis statement (Three factors that contribute to a healthy friendship are trust, under-standing, and the ability to openly discuss difficult issues.)

When your purpose is to persuade, you want to go beyond simply presenting information. With this type of speech, your primary goal is to induce change in the audience; that is, you want to move them to action. Your goal as a speaker is to get the audience to empathize with your position, to feel the concern that you feel. If you are successful, the audience will be motivated to change. You are scheduled to speak to 110 employees about XYZ health maintenance organization, one of three health plans to be voted on by the group. As a representative of this health insurance company, your aim is to convince (persuade) the group that XYZ is the best plan on the market. While you are concerned about presenting the information clearly, your speech goes one step further—it asks the audience to respond in some way.

When your purpose is to entertain, you strive to make others happy. This is usually accomplished by interjecting humor into your speech. Johnny Carson and David Letterman make entertaining presentations on their nightly television shows. Although their monologues sometimes fail to draw laughter, their overriding purpose is to entertain.

Specific Purpose

In order to make your speech more manageable, both for you to develop and for your audience to understand, you must determine its specific purpose. Stated in a single sentence, your **specific purpose** takes into account the following factors: (1) what you hope to accomplish, (2) which aspect of the topic you will cover, and (3) your intended audience. This process moves you from your general purpose (to inform, to persuade, or to entertain) to a more focused speech topic. Consider the following:

> Amy, a freshman speech student, must give a four-minute informative speech. She was advised to describe something to her audience and to base her speech on a personal experience. This meant choosing a topic she was familiar with. Amy knew she would be more convincing if she discussed a topic she cared about. She wrestled with several topics before finally deciding on the topic of friendship. Because friendship is a broad topic, she knew she would have to narrow its focus. After some additional thought, she decided to focus on the different aspects of friendship.

When Amy began developing her speech, she started with the general purpose "to inform." Now she has to determine which as-

pect of friendship she wants to talk about. Her first attempt to narrow her topic produced the following results:

Specific purpose A: To talk about friendship.

Would an audience have a strong sense of the speech purpose
after hearing this statement? Probably not. Amy still needs to decide
exactly what she wishes to tell her audience. She tries it again, this
time with better results:

Specific purpose B: To inform the audience about
the way friendships work.

Amy is now offering more information, but she still is not telling us anything specific. Amy needs to determine the ingredients of
a successful friendship. She might try looking at a specific friendship in order to determine why that relationship works so well. By
doing so, she will have a better idea of what to share with her audience. Upon further reflection, Amy comes up with this statement:

Specific purpose C: To inform the audience about
three factors that contribute to an effective friendship.

This shows some improvement, but Amy still has not identified
the group to whom she wishes to deliver the speech. This seemingly minor point is important, because it helps her to keep her audience in mind as she delivers her speech. Here Amy's final effort:

Specific purpose D: To inform my class about the
three factors that contribute to a healthy friendship.

Do you see what Amy has accomplished? She has moved from
a very general treatment to a more specific treatment of the topic.
As a result, Amy should have an easier job constructing an effective
speech because she has created specific guidelines for herself.

What process can you use to develop your specific-purpose
statement? Let us analyze the preceding example. Amy's final statement, "To inform my class about the three factors that contribute to
a healthy friendship," clearly states her specific purpose. Note that
it is written in the form of a statement, not a question, that it contains only one idea, and that the language is concrete.[2] Also note
that Amy needed to revise her statement several times before constructing an effective one. The message is clear: You must refine
your statement until it includes all the components just mentioned.

Application Activity

DEVELOPING A SPECIFIC-PURPOSE STATEMENT

1. Develop a specific-purpose statement for each of the following topics:

   a. Dieting

   b. Soap operas

   c. Sports competitions

2. Keep the following in mind:

   a. What do you want to accomplish?

   b. What specific aspect do you wish to cover?

   c. Who is your intended audience?

3. Share your results with a classmate.

4. Use the feedback from your classmate to refine your specific-purpose statements.

Thesis Statement

Once you have constructed an effective specific-purpose statement, the next logical step is to develop your thesis statement. A **thesis statement** includes the major ideas of your speech; at the same time, it refines your specific purpose.

Whereas the specific-purpose statement lays the groundwork for constructing your speech, the thesis statement reflects the outcome of your research. In fact, your research may cause you to construct a thesis statement that is different from the one you initially envisioned. For example, prior to conducting any research on your topic (accidental deaths), you develop the following specific-purpose statement and thesis statement:

> *Specific purpose:* To inform my classmates about the two leading causes of accidental deaths.
> *Thesis statement:* The two leading causes of accidental deaths in the United States are automobile accidents and fires.

Your research, however, turns up different evidence; you must now change your thesis statement to reflect your findings:

Application Activity

DEVELOPING THE THESIS STATEMENT

1. Select one of the three specific-purpose statements you developed in the preceding Application Activity regarding dieting, soap operas, or sports competition.

2. Identify the major points in this speech.

3. Write a thesis statement incorporating the major points.

4. Write a full sentence for each separate idea in the thesis statement, which in turn will become the major ideas in the speech.

Amended thesis statement: The two leading causes of accidental deaths in the United States are automobile accidents and falls.[3]

In constructing your thesis statement, there are a few guidelines to follow: (1) put your thesis statement in a complete sentence, (2) avoid general or vague language, and (3) consider the amount of time allotted for your speech. By taking these factors into account, your thesis statement will provide a good basis for developing the major ideas in your speech.

The previous section included this example of a specific-purpose statement: "To inform my class about the three factors that contribute to a healthy friendship." Fine-tuning resulted in the following thesis statement: "Three factors that contribute to a healthy friendship are trust, understanding, and the ability to openly discuss difficult issues." While this thesis statement refines Amy's specific-purpose statement, it also reflects what she wants her audience to remember after her presentation.

ANALYZING THE AUDIENCE

Audience analysis goes hand in hand with selecting and developing the speech topic. For instance, preparing for a speech on "safe sex" depends, in part, on the audience. Consider the different approach you would take when talking to 150 ninth-grade students from the approach you would take when talking to 15 administrators of social service agencies. Such factors as audience size, attitudes, and knowledge must be taken into account.

Before developing any speech, consider the audience; your efforts to develop an effective speech will be wasted if you fail to consider who you are talking to. For example, your speech is headed for failure if your audience has no interest in your topic, if the information you are providing is beyond the audience's level of comprehension, or if your message runs counter to beliefs firmly held by the audience.

What criteria do you use to assess your audience? This section will explore the areas of demographics, traits and characteristics of an audience, appropriate methods for gathering audience information, and adapting to the audience.

Demographic Factors

Segments of the population are routinely analyzed according to **demographics,** that is, easily identifiable characteristics such as age, sex, and socioreligious background. Demographic analysis of an audience should be considered for the purpose of preparing a public speech because it can assist you in tailoring the topic to a specific audience.

Age   The composite age of the audience often plays a role in the selection of a speech topic, because some topics are better suited to one age group than another. These topics are based on the unique frame of reference of a particular audience. Topics based on World War II, for example, will have a different impact on those Americans who "lived the war" via the front line or who worked for the war effort "stateside" than on those Americans too young to have anything but secondhand experience.

The age of the audience also can affect how you develop the topic. It may even be a primary factor in determining how you will discuss a topic that you consider highly sensitive. In such cases, your choice of words might change with the audience's age in an effort not to alienate them. The age of the audience suggests a general frame of reference that may or may not be in tune with the topic. Consider the following:

> Bob is a member of the local public school board. In recent months the board has been discussing the issue of sex education in the classroom. Bob is the only board member under the age of forty-five. Many of the other board members have children who were teenagers during the rebellious '60s and early '70s. Since Bob is speaking in favor of sex education in the

classroom, he is cautious as he puts his words together. He knows his audience is sensitive to the issue, so he avoids language that might remind them of
rebellious times.

As you become more sensitive to the age of your audience, you
should find yourself feeling better able to communicate with them.

Sex   As our society changes, so do the attitudes we hold concerning
sex roles. Consequently, there are very few topics that are regarded
as strictly "male" or "female." More men are spending time participating in child-rearing responsibilities, while more women are
spending a significant amount of time expanding their careers. It
would be dangerous, then, to cling to outdated stereotypes that cat-
egorize people's interests according to sex roles. In fact, men and
women often have similar responses to a topic.

We cannot, however, avoid the fact that many people are raised
in an environment filled with sexual stereotypes, and it would be
impossible for those individuals not to be influenced by those stereotypes. An all-female audience, for example, may have a high
level of knowledge concerning child care; likewise, an all-male audience may be familiar with the standings of the hometown football
team. Still, it is important to remember that not *all* members of a
sexual group will possess knowledge about a particular subject. In
Chapter 2 I admitted to a personal lack of confidence in my mechanical abilities. A speaker who does not know me might incorrectly
assume that I have a special knowledge of auto mechanics simply
because I am a male. Can you see a problem here?

Socioreligious Background   The United States has been aptly la-
beled as a great "melting pot" of racial, ethnic, and cultural groups,
as well as of diverse religions. This is as true today as it was during
the great wave of immigration during the 1800s and early 1900s. It
is important to keep these differences in mind when you prepare
your speech so as not to alienate a particular segment of the audience. On the other hand, discovering that the audience's background is similar to your own, or that because of its cultural or ethnic background it is sympathetic to your topic, makes it easier for
you to prepare your speech.

During his 1984 bid for the the presidency, Jesse Jackson made
some denigrating remarks about Jews that created quite a stir. Hos-
tility developed between the Jewish and black communities because of these purported anti-Semitic remarks and the coverage this
incident received by the newspaper and television media. At the
Democratic National Convention, Jackson attempted to heal those
wounds:

If in my high moments, I have done some good, offered some service, shed some light, healed some wounds, rekindled some hope . . . or in any way . . . helped somebody, then this campaign has not been in vain. . . . If in my low moments, in word, deed or attitude, through some error of temper, taste or tone, I have caused anyone discomfort, created pain or revived someone's fears, that was not my truest self. . . . Please forgive me. Charge it to my head . . . so limited in its finitude; [not to] my heart, which is boundless in its love for the entire human family. I am not a perfect servant. I am a public servant . . . Be patient. God is not finished with me yet.[4]

Jackson, aware of the tension his remarks had caused, made an effort to unite the black and Jewish communities and to heal some wounds. Students can certainly learn from Jesse Jackson's experience. Table 10.1 provides a checklist for demographic factors.

Application Activity

ANALYZING THE DEMOGRAPHIC FACTORS OF AN AUDIENCE

The topic "Sex and Violence in Music Videos" is to be presented to two hypothetical classroom audiences. How would the demographics of each audience assist you in developing your speech?

AUDIENCE 1

AGE		SEX		COLLEGE MAJORS	
18–22	85%	Female	45%	Liberal arts	60%
22–30	10%	Male	55%	Education	30%
Over 30	5%			Business	10%

AUDIENCE 2

AGE		SEX		COLLEGE MAJORS	
18–22	30%	Female	55%	Liberal arts	20%
22–30	30%	Male	45%	Education	20%
Over 30	40%			Engineering	20%
				Business	40%

TABLE 10.1   Checklist for Demographic Factors

✓ Age	Is your audience all the same age or different ages? If the same age, are your choices of topic and references appropriate for that age group?
✓ Sex	Is your audience all male? All female? Mixed? How will this factor affect the way you develop your topic?
✓ Socioreligious background	Is your audience composed of individuals of various ethnic, religious, or cultural backgrounds? How does this composition affect the way you develop your topic?

Audience Traits and Characteristics

In addition to the demographic factors just discussed, it is possible to assess an audience based on such criteria as size, knowledge, attitude, and needs. Knowledge of these characteristics can help you adapt or adjust the speech to fit the audience. This applies to both the structure of the speech and the style of delivery you choose.

Size   Some obvious adjustments need to be made in developing your presentation based on the audience's size. For example, with a larger audience, you may find it necessary to be more formal in your presentation, right down to the way you deliver the speech. With a large audience you are less likely to interact directly with members of the audience. In addition, it is more difficult to respond to feedback because it is so difficult to establish direct eye contact with members of the audience. Conversely, you will probably find that with a smaller audience you can present a speech with abstract ideas, because it is easier for you to detect any nonverbal feedback the audience generates and act on it. Consider the following:

> Professor Gerard's lecture was on the subject of how the media create pseudo-events. As he was explaining the concept of a pseudo-event, he noticed a look of confusion on Andrea's face. Because of the relatively small size of the group, he was able to detect her nonverbal cue and respond to it. To further illustrate his point, he used Oral Roberts' $4.5 million "deal" with God, in which Roberts appealed to his

The size of your audience dictates the way you deliver your speech. A large audience frequently requires a relatively formal presentation.

flock of televiewers to come up with the money or God would "call him home." He emphasized how both the television and print media made an issue of this event by continuing to monitor the evangelist's efforts to reach his goal of $4.5 million. Andrea's nod communicated that she now understood the concept. In a larger group, a response to Andrea's cue would have been less likely.

Knowledge   The amount of information the audience possesses about your topic may give you some insight concerning the way you want to approach the speech. If your audience is unfamiliar with your topic, you may need to take an elementary approach; on the other hand, if your audience is familiar with the topic, you can take a more detailed approach. Suppose you select the subject of identical twins as your topic. For a group of expectant parents whose knowledge of the subject is limited, a successful speech would likely focus on raising twins, with perhaps a brief biological explanation of how twins are created. If, however, your speech is directed at a group of biology majors, the genetic factor would likely be the focal point of your talk. With this group, the level of detailed information would be much greater.

A speech on a subject about which you are especially knowledgeable, such as kayaking, needs to take into consideration the audience's level of understanding of the subject matter.

. . . .

Attitude   Generally speaking, at the outset of a speech the audience has formulated an attitude toward both the topic and the speaker. Knowledge of the audience's attitude toward the topic can help you adapt what you say to the group. Consider this example:

> Elizabeth plans to speak to a group of disgruntled parents about the school board's recommendation to close Taft Elementary School at the end of the year. Realizing that her audience strongly opposes this action, she begins by stating that the board gave serious attention to this issue and regretted having to make this difficult decision. Her opening remarks are meant to reduce some of the audience's hostility, so she can proceed to explain the reasons for the board's decision.

In the situation described here, it is reasonble to presume that the sentiment toward Elizabeth was probably negative prior to her speech. Her remarks were intended to diffuse some of the natural resentment both toward an unpopular board decision and toward herself as president of the school board. Had Elizabeth not taken the audience's resentment into account, her speech would not have been as sensitively prepared.

Needs   According to Abraham Maslow, people have the same basic needs, which are best understood when explained in terms of a hierarchy.[5] These needs are classified as physiological, safety, belonging, esteem, and self-actualization (see Figure 10.2).

As a speaker who is familiar with Maslow's hierarchy, you have the advantage of being able to develop your topic according to the appropriate audience need. What does this mean? First, it means examining the topic you have selected (this time from the audience's perspective) and asking yourself, "What is the connection between my topic and people's needs as identified by Maslow?" What, for example, is the relationship between the threat of nuclear disaster (your topic) and Maslow's hierarchy of needs? Answer: This topic appeals to the audience's need for safety. Second, once you have established the link between your topic and the audience, you can begin the process of adapting your speech to appeal to these needs. Need identification is simply one more way of analyzing the audience.

Physiological needs are the lowest-level needs on Maslow's hierarchy; food, water, and air are examples. A speech on the starvation of Indian children relates to physiological needs on Maslow's hierarchy; such a speech appeals to the physiological needs of the members of the audience and therefore most likely evokes their

FIGURE 10.2   Maslow's Hierarchy of Needs

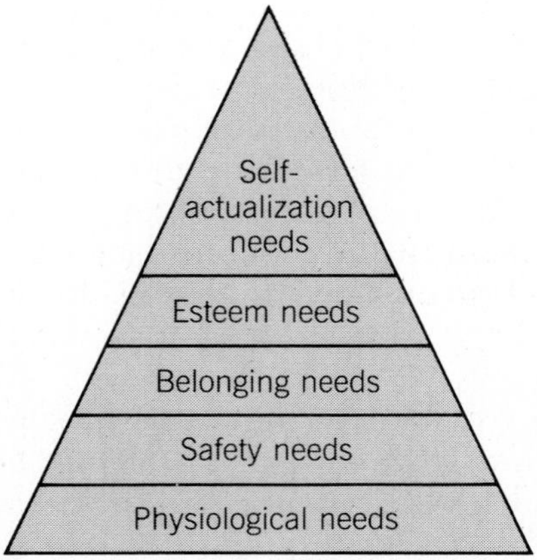

sympathy and interest. You might, for example, develop a speech with the specific purpose "To inform the assembled clergymen about two U.S. programs aimed at alleviating hunger in Third World countries."

Safety needs, the second level on Maslow's hierarchy, refer to our desire to feel secure. They function on two levels: (1) physical security and (2) personal security in social situations. The example given earlier about the threat of nuclear disaster deals with physical security. A speech that focuses on the difficulties of social interactions also may relate to an audience's need for safety. Your specific purpose could be "To inform my classmates about three techniques to increase their comfort at parties."

The need to belong refers to the desire to be part of a group. The group, of course, may vary in composition. Some individuals join a fraternity because of their desire to be part of a group that is popular on a college campus. Other individuals participate regularly in religious organizations because they enjoy being with people who hold convictions similar to their own. If your audience happens to be twenty-five students taking a course entitled "Introduction to News Writing and Editing," your specific purpose might be "To offer members of this class three ways in which joining the student newspaper staff can help them feel more involved in campus activities."

Esteem needs, the desire for influence or status within the social structure, are next on Maslow's hierarchy. Consider the following situation:

> Tom Laufer, Executive Director of Parents Without Partners, is asked to speak to the twenty charter members of a new chapter. He plans to speak about the importance of the organization, but he refines his topic to arrive at this specific purpose: to persuade these charter members that they can shape the future of this chapter by serving as officers during this important first year.

Self-actualization is perceiving that you are at the highest level of what you believe to be your potential. Maslow emphasizes the importance of reaching your full potential as you grow toward self-actualization. On the day before a final exam, you might try to inspire your students to put forth their best effort. The specific purpose of your "pep" talk becomes "To persuade my students that by studying and reviewing their notes, they can write their best possible exam tomorrow."

Application Activity

TARGETING THE NEEDS OF THE AUDIENCE

For each of the following topics, develop a specific-purpose statement that ties the topic to one of the needs on Maslow's hierarchy (physiological, safety, belonging, esteem, or self-actualization):

1. Health clubs

2. Wall Street

3. AIDS

4. 1987 U.S.–Soviet summit meeting

5. Stress

Example

> *Topic:* Yuppies
>
> *Specific-purpose statement:* To inform my classmates about the level of success one must achieve to be considered a Yuppie (need for esteem).

Gathering Information

How do you determine the audience characteristics described in the previous two sections? Basically, there are three methods for gathering information: observation, interviews, and questionnaires. Whether you have an opportunity to observe your audience ahead of time, whether you manage to interview some of the members individually, or whether you prepare a questionnaire for each member to complete, you will undoubtedly draw some inferences based on your observations and the responses you receive from members of the audience. In turn, these will be used to develop and adapt your speech to the audience.

Observation   A great deal can be learned about an audience by simple observation. It is not difficult to determine such demographic factors as sex, age, and race. You also can note how a group reacts to what others say; in particular, how they react to other speakers. For example, if you are scheduled to deliver a lecture during the fourth week of an eight-week management course, you may want to attend a couple of lectures prior to your speech. This gives you a chance to observe how the class reacts to the different speakers' styles, content, and so on. Use this information as you work on developing your speech. Are there any special appeals you can make because of the group's composition, attitudes, and needs? In a communication class you have a perfect opportunity to practice this method.

Interviews   A more time-consuming method of gathering information is the interview. In an interview, your purpose is to gain background information about the audience by asking another party specific questions. This approach is especially useful in situations in which you have been asked to speak to an audience about whom you know nothing. To avoid speaking to the group "blindly," you would want to ask one of the members (probably the person who invited you to speak) about the audience's interests, age, knowledge about the topic, and so on. His or her response to your questions will help you prepare a more appropriate speech. Further information on constructing interview questions and conducting an information interview can be found in Chapter 8.

Questionnaires   Questionnaires can pose a variety of general questions, such as number of years of education, marital status, age, and income bracket, and they can ask questions that relate to a specific topic, such as "Do you support U.S. aid to the *contras?*", "Was Judge Robert Bork treated fairly during the Senate confirmation hearings?", "What is your favorite type of exercise?". Such specific questions can help you to analyze an audience's knowledge, attitudes, and needs concerning your selected topic. You can choose from three types of questionnaires: closed, open, and graduated scale.

In a **closed questionnaire,** the respondent must select an answer from two or more choices:

> Do you believe regular exercise prolongs a person's life?
> Yes _____   No _____   Not sure _____

While a questionnaire composed of questions such as the preceding does not provide much detail, it does offer additional information in a limited way. Because responses are clear-cut, you can generally detect whether or not there is a consensus of opinion among the members of the audience. If there is, you will have a better idea of how to develop your presentation.

An **open questionnaire** gives respondents the opportunity to fully express their feelings:

> How well is the American public coping with the
> AIDS epidemic?

Application Activity

DEVELOPING A QUESTIONNAIRE

1. You have selected the following topic for a public speech: "Television Advertising Aimed at Children."

2. Consider the following sets of questions:

a. *Closed questions:*
Do you believe advertisers take advantage of children's programming to promote certain products?
Yes _____   No _____   Not sure _____

Do you think special regulations should be developed for this area of advertising?
Yes _____   No _____   Not sure _____

b. *Open questions:*

How would you respond to this claim: Advertisers take advantage of children's programming to promote certain products.

What types of special regulations, if any, should be developed in the area of television advertising directed at children?

c. *Graduated-scale questions:*

For the following statements, circle the number that most accurately represents your feelings:

Advertisers take advantage of children's programming to promote certain products.
    1   2   3   4   5
Strongly agree Agree Undecided Disagree Strongly disagree

Special regulations should be developed in the area of television advertising directed at children.
    1   2   3   4   5
Strongly agree Agree Undecided Disagree Strongly disagree

3. Based on the preceding example, how do the different types of questionnaires yield different types of results?

4. What are the implications for you as a public speaker?

Responses to such questions, which tend to be more detailed, often provide insight about people's reasons for feeling strongly about a topic. Despite the sense of "knowing" the audience better, there is the drawback of having to sift through a great deal of extraneous information in an open questionnaire.

The **graduated scale,** also known as the **Likert scale,** gives individuals the opportunity to rank their feelings on a continuum:

> For the following statement circle the number that most accurately represents your feelings:

The American public is responding effectively to the AIDS epidemic.

1	2	3	4	5
Strongly agree	Agree	Undecided	Disagree	Strongly disagree

The responses can indicate the intensity of audience feelings toward a particular topic. This information is valuable to a speaker.

Adapting to Your Audience

Analyzing an audience takes considerable time and effort; however, this generally translates into a better understanding of your audience. How do you use the information you have gathered (through observation, interviews, and questionnaires) about an audience's demographics and such related characteristics as size, knowledge, attitudes, and needs? Simply stated, you must use these data to adapt your topic to your audience.

In the process of analyzing your audience, you make inferences and draw conclusions. For example, perhaps you realize that your audience, 80 percent female between the ages of twenty and forty-five, has a very positive attitude about preschool education. Obviously, a speech that advocates additional state funds for preschool education should be well received. Your next step, then, is to develop both your topic and your style of delivery, keeping this information in mind.

You will be a better public speaker if you can take what you have learned about your audience and temporarily become one of its members as you begin to develop your speech. Your efforts to empathize with your audience, a skill so essential to successful interpersonal communication, will lead you to a successful public presentation. The next two chapters will take you through the process of preparing your speech; gathering information about your topic is treated in Chapter 11, while organizing your speech is the subject of Chapter 12.

SUMMARY

Selecting a topic is the first order of business in preparing a public speech. A key variable in the selection process is *you*—your concerns, experiences, knowledge, and curiosity often provide excellent speech topics. Brainstorming, either by yourself or with your peers, is an alternative method for exploring additional topics.

Once you have selected your topic, you must determine the purpose of your presentation. The development of your speech purpose usually follows three steps: (1) determining the general purpose—either to inform, persuade, or entertain—(2) determining the specific purpose, and (3) creating a thesis statement. The move from general purpose to specific purpose helps you focus your topic by taking into account such factors as (1) what you hope to accomplish, (2) which aspect of the topic you will cover, and (3) your intended audience. With some fine-tuning you develop your thesis statement, which includes the major points of your speech.

Analyzing the audience bridges the gap between selecting your topic and developing your speech. You can increase your understanding of the audience by assessing such things as audience demographics, including age, sex, and socioreligious background, and the additional characteristics of size, knowledge, attitudes, and needs. What you learn from your assessment can help you to adapt your topic to fit the particular audience.

How do you gather these data? Basically, there are three methods: observation, interviews, and questionnaires. Questionnaires can include closed questions, open questions, or those on a graduated scale (or combinations of all three). Your observations, interviews, and questionnaires provide a great deal of information about your audience which you must now use to adapt the topic selected at the beginning of this process to the audience you have come to better understand as a result of the assessment process. As you turn to the task of developing your speech, attempt to use the communication technique known as empathy. The results will be rewarding.

REVIEW QUESTIONS

1. What factors in your own background can assist you in choosing a topic?
2. Differentiate between individual and group brainstorming.

3. What factors should be included in your specific-purpose statement?
4. How can the audience's knowledge of the topic affect the way you develop your speech?
5. How would you incorporate an audience's need for esteem in a speech on corporate advancement?
6. Describe three types of questionnaires you can construct to gather information from the audience.
7. Why is it desirable to adapt your topic to the audience?

NOTES

1. Alex F. Osborn, *Applied Imagination: Principles and Procedures of Creative Problem-Solving*, 3d Ed. (New York: Scribners, 1979), p. 141.

2. For further discussion of the specific-purpose statement, see Stephen E. Lucas, *The Art of Public Speaking*, 2d Ed. (New York: Random House, 1986), pp. 49–55.

3. *Accident Facts: 1986 Edition* (Chicago: National Safety Council, 1986), p. 6.

4. Ed Magnuson et al., "Drama and Passion Galore," *Time*, July 30, 1984, p. 26.

5. For a discussion of Maslow's theory, see Abraham H. Maslow, *Motivation and Personality*, 2d Ed. (New York: Harper & Row, 1970), pp. 35–58.

ADDITIONAL READINGS

Bowers, J. W., and Courtright, J. A. *Communication Research Methods.* Glenview, Ill.: Scott, Foresman, 1984. Pp. 53–9.
    This book provides an excellent discussion on constructing questionnaires.

Lucas, S. E. *The Art of Public Speaking*, 2nd Ed. New York: Random House, 1986.
    Chapter 3 provides valuable information on selecting a topic and developing a speech purpose.

11

Gathering and Using Supporting Material for Your Speech

Learning Objectives

At the conclusion of this chapter you should be able to

1. Identify at least six potential sources of information for your speech.

2. Locate reference and periodical sources at the library to use in your speech.

3. Properly footnote sources used in your speech.

4. Briefly describe six forms of supporting material that may be used in your speech.

5. Briefly describe five different types of visual aids.

6. Explain three special problems associated with the use of visual aids.

Kathy's speech instructor has just announced that the assignment for the next class will be the presentation of a seven-minute informative speech, and he has allotted classroom time for students to work in groups to brainstorm for suitable topics. Since many of Kathy's classmates know that she is interested in MTV (she regularly watches its programs), many think this would be an ideal topic for her. Kathy agrees, but she wants to do more than a superficial analysis. Her goal is to trace the roots of MTV in order to better understand the prevailing themes often found in its productions. Although Kathy is enthusiastic about the topic, she realizes that she has a lot of work to do.

Regardless of your topic, integrating evidence into your presentation helps you to construct and develop your ideas more logically. Further, the added documentation helps you to inform your audience more accurately and thoroughly and increases the credibility of your arguments. In the preceding example, Kathy will undoubtedly need to do some research in order to uncover supporting material for her speech topic. In this chapter we shall take a look at the types of information available to you, where to look for these sources, how to cite them in a speech, and the kinds of supporting material you can use as a speaker.

SOURCES OF INFORMATION

When contemplating supporting material for a speech, it is important to know the kinds of materials available and where they can be found. In this section we shall discuss such important sources as personal experiences, interviews, newspapers, periodicals, books, and other media (that is, radio and television).

Personal Experiences

Speeches that relay personal experiences add a special dimension to public presentations. Whether the speech topic is a personal experience—winning a three-week vacation to France, your first day on a new job, delivering a child at home, being robbed—or whether personal experiences are included to augment an aspect of the topic (that is, interjecting a brief story about our effort to stop smoking as a way to reduce hypertension), the overall effect is one of adding "life" to the talk. No one knows better than you the significance of a particular experience, and the public speech provides you with an opportunity to successfully communicate these personal feelings.

The speech that focuses on personal experiences is ideal for the novice speaker. Being intimately acquainted with the subject, the individual can avoid some of the anxiety associated with public speaking; in its place is the feeling of confidence that comes from knowing the subject.

Interviews

While searching for sources of information for your speech, remember that the experiences and knowledge of other people can enhance almost any topic. These people may range from professionals, to researchers, to practitioners, to victims. Look for someone who has something special to bring to your topic—an individual who possesses some unique knowledge that can be used to enhance the quality of your presentation.

How do you decide who would make a good interviewee? First, take a serious look at your topic. What are some of the individual ideas you want to explore? Are there experts or individuals with experience you can contact for an interview? For example, if you have selected diabetes as your topic, you may wish to interview a physician who specializes in the treatment of the disease, someone who is conducting research on a new method of treatment (if such a person is available), or a person who has had diabetes since childhood. Naturally, different questions would be asked of each individual; in turn, their responses would help refine your topic, perhaps changing its focus. The information provided by the physician, for instance, might include both widely practiced treatments of the past and treatments used today. After sorting through your notes, you might decide that you want to focus your talk on current treatments and those treatments which look promising for the future.

There are several steps to keep in mind if you decide to interview someone: (1) come to the interview with prepared questions, (2) use concrete language to phrase your questions, and (3) listen carefully.

Come to the Interview with Prepared Questions   Before you go to the interview, think about the purpose of your speech and the kind of information you want to obtain from the interview. Do you want statistics? Do you want facts or opinions? Prepare and write down specific questions in advance that will help you to get the information you need.

Use Concrete Language to Phrase Your Questions   Your questions should be phrased using language that is concrete (that is, specific enough to be easily understood). Try to keep in mind the interpersonal skills discussed earlier in this book. Questions that place interviewees on the defensive may cause them to become hostile or, worse, leave the interview. Instead, word your questions so that they promote trust and openness. Why risk losing out on valuable information if you can take the necessary steps to avoid this situation? Consider the following:

> Kelly wants to find out if a particular company adheres to affirmative action regulations, so she arranges an interview with the chief of personnel. After the initial social dialogue, she asks this loaded question: "Why don't you have any women working here?" The personnel director becomes defensive and announces that the interview is over.

While penetrating questions can provide interesting information, you need to display some sensitivity when formulating your queries. For example,

> James was granted an interview with the chief of police after a shooting at the local shopping center. Realizing that the chief was likely to be sensitive (and possibly defensive) about the issue, James very wisely avoided questions that might be construed as an attack against the department's handling of the situation. Instead, he tried to keep his questions focused

on the impact the shooting had on the community. First, he asked the police chief to relay the sequence of events, thereby giving the chief an opportunity to describe the situation in detail. He followed up by asking the chief what steps were being taken to prevent any similar incidences in the future.

In this example James was able to gain valuable information without placing the interviewee on the defensive.

Listen Carefully   The main purpose of the interview is to gain information from the interviewee. Consequently, it is important to practice effective listening skills. Try to stay focused on the statements of the interviewee rather than concentrating on your own role in the interaction. If you are unclear about something that has been stated, make sure that you ask for clarification. If necessary, paraphrase the interviewee's statement so that he or she can confirm that you understood the point. Consider the following:

> Billy Joe was interviewing Ross McKenney, a prominent television critic, about McKenney's attitude toward prime-time sitcoms. In his discussion, McKenney alluded to the "puerile nature" of many of the programs now on the air. Billy Joe was not certain about the meaning of the word *puerile*. Although somewhat intimidated by the critic, Billy Joe's overriding concern for accuracy motivated him to ask McKenney to elaborate on this particular point. He then paraphrased the critic's words to ensure his own understanding of the term's meaning. "What you're saying, basically, is that many of today's programs are childish." Thus Billy Joe was able to clarify the critic's position by actively listening to McKenney's comments and responses to questions.

Newspapers

An excellent source of supporting material for current topics is the newspaper. Articles tend to be brief, but focused. Daily newspapers routinely include detailed accounts of events and reactions to those events, as well as factual and statistical information. For example, in the December 9, 1987 issue of the *New York Times* there are dozens of articles on the Washington summit between Ronald Reagan and Mikhail Gorbachev—ranging from accounts on the signing of the treaty to reduce the size of both nations' nuclear arsenals, to the text

This woman is doing research in the periodicals section of the library.

of the INF Treaty, to excerpts of remarks made by Reagan and Gorbachev at the welcoming ceremonies (their remarks before the signing and their remarks after the signing), to articles explaining how the Soviets and the United States will ensure that 2611 missiles are destroyed, to editorials on the treaty signing, to reactions in Moscow.

Because most major news stories require a second source to verify the position taken in the article, there is a great deal of pressure to describe the situation accurately. Even so, newspapers often have a bias, a fact that public speakers should be aware of.

Periodicals

Periodicals, written sources published at regular intervals (that is, weekly, monthly, quarterly, or semiannually), provide a wealth of factual and interpretive information on hundreds of topics. Speakers can rely on these sources to add substance to their presentations.

Magazines have a longer interval between issues than daily newspapers, which allows the writers to devote more time to researching the topic and to put into perspective the circumstances surrounding a particular event. Generally, magazine articles are more indepth than newspaper articles because of the additional time provided for research and because of the greater amount of space allotted to these stories.

As you consult magazines for information, keep in mind that many magazines (like newspapers) have a particular bias. For instance, to get varying perspectives on the subject of mothers who work outside the home, you might read articles in *McCalls,* a traditional women's magazine; *Newsweek,* where the approach is likely to be neutral and matter-of-fact; and *Ms.,* with its more feminist leanings. This approach allows a more thorough examination of your subject.

Journals contain research findings carried out in a particular field, such as medicine, social welfare, electrical engineering, or communication. They are also valuable resources for supporting material to enhance your speech. You might look at journal articles for several reasons: to get data and statistics provided by research studies, to get commentary on a subject by specialists, or to get more indepth coverage of a topic. For example, you might consult psychology journals to find studies documenting the effects of MTV on preadolescents.

Books

Because of the amount of space books provide, treatment of a topic is frequently more indepth than that found in newspaper, magazine, or journal articles. Rarely, however, does a speaker have time to read an entire book to get information about a topic; more commonly, a section or chapter of a book is used for that purpose.

Books, like journal articles, are often written by specialists in a field. Because books take longer to publish, however, the information they contain may be more dated than what can be found in either periodicals or newspapers. When timeliness is not an important factor, books often make excellent sources of information.

Other Media

Audiovisual sources, including radio and television broadcasts, films, sound recordings, and videos, have both advantages and disadvantages for the public speech. First, we shall consider radio and television broadcasts. As information sources, the chief advantage of radio and television news broadcasts is their immediacy. When news stories receive considerable attention via television and radio (which is especially true for such crises as the crash of the *Challenger* space shuttle, natural disasters such as earthquakes and volcanoes, and the October 1987 stock market crash), vast audiences are reached. Therefore, when you incorporate information from the broadcast in your speech, several members of your audience will likely instantly recognize what you are saying. You and your audience share a common ground, which increases the audience's understanding of your message. Another advantage of these sources is their dramatic nature. For example, coverage of the same issue in such print media as newspapers and magazines cannot compete with the drama of a live broadcast.

Films and sound recordings are good sources for reflecting the moods and attitudes of a particular time. Consider, for example, the way popular/rock music, motion pictures, and television comedies and dramas all reflect what our society is like during a specific period. A song, a film clip, or a clip from a television program can portray a "slice of life" to your audience.

Finally, videos, especially commercially produced educational videos, also can provide useful background information, particularly

Most libraries provide carrels so that you can do some of your research on the spot.

for an informative speech in which your purpose is to educate your audience. Excerpts included in your presentation can effectively complement your verbal explanations.

This brings us to the disadvantages or drawbacks of using audiovisual sources. Incorporating material you gather from the types of media just discussed poses two problems: (1) having adequate time in your speech to "set up" or introduce the material, and (2) operating the necessary machinery (film projector, tape recorder, record player, or VCR). You must consider these special conditions when contemplating the use of audiovisual materials in your presentation.

FINDING SOURCES: THE LIBRARY

The academic or public library is usually the best starting point in the search for sources of information. Several areas of the library can help you research your topic in order to prepare a more thorough speech. These include the main catalog, the reference desk, and the periodicals room.

The Main Catalog

The main catalog lists all the library's holdings. In today's libraries, the catalog may be the standard card catalog (drawer after drawer filled with author, title, and subject references), a microform catalog (either microfiche or microfilm viewed on a screen), or a computer terminal. Usually, the best approach to researching your topic is to consult the subject headings in the catalog. This will give you an idea of what the library has that relates to your topic. For example, if you want to give a speech on the long-standing popularity of the television program *Star Trek*, you would search the subject headings in the catalog for "Star Trek" (see Figure 11.1).

The Reference Desk

A second place to go is the reference desk, where a professional librarian will assist you with finding additional sources on your subject. Depending on your topic, the librarian may direct you to specialized encyclopedias, biographical sources, or government publications, to name a few. In addition to the traditional printed resources, many libraries now offer online computer searches, which dramatically increase the amount of information available to you. Ask about this service at your college or public library.

FIGURE 11.1   Catalog Cards: Subject Card, Title Card, and Author Card

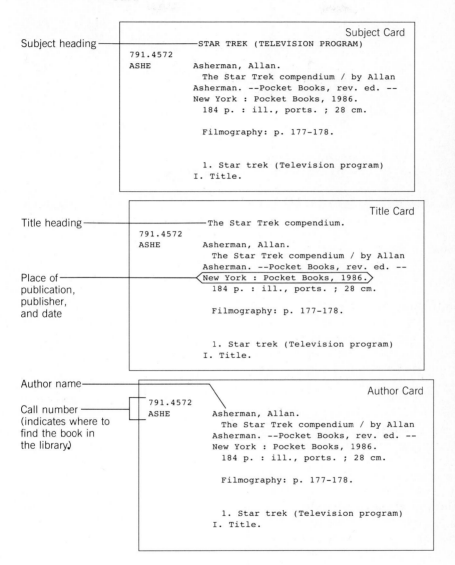

Subject heading

Subject Card

STAR TREK (TELEVISION PROGRAM)

791.4572
ASHE   Asherman, Allan.
            The Star Trek compendium / by Allan
      Asherman. --Pocket Books, rev. ed. --
      New York : Pocket Books, 1986.
            184 p. : ill., ports. ; 28 cm.

            Filmography: p. 177-178.

            1. Star trek (Television program)
      I. Title.

Title heading

Title Card

The Star Trek compendium.

791.4572
ASHE   Asherman, Allan.
            The Star Trek compendium / by Allan
      Asherman. --Pocket Books, rev. ed. --
      New York : Pocket Books, 1986.
            184 p. : ill., ports. ; 28 cm.

            Filmography: p. 177-178.

            1. Star trek (Television program)
      I. Title.

Place of
publication,
publisher,
and date

Author name

Author Card

791.4572
ASHE   Asherman, Allan.
            The Star Trek compendium / by Allan
      Asherman. --Pocket Books, rev. ed. --
      New York : Pocket Books, 1986.
            184 p. : ill., ports. ; 28 cm.

            Filmography: p. 177-178.

            1. Star trek (Television program)
      I. Title.

Call number
(indicates where to
find the book in
the library)

At the reference desk, a professional librarian will assist you with finding additional sources or hard-to-find sources on your subject.

Encyclopedias   Nearly everyone has had an occasion to look up information in a general encyclopedia, such as *World Book* or *Encyclopedia Britannica*. However, most libraries also own specialized encyclopedias published for numerous disciplines. Titles often found in the reference collection include *International Encyclopedia of the Social Sciences, McGraw-Hill Encyclopedia of Science and Technology, Encyclopedia of Education,* and *Dictionary of American History*. These sources include signed articles written by scholars in the field and are often accompanied by bibliographies or references to related works.

Biographical Sources   If your topic focuses on the accomplishments or fame achieved by a well-known individual, there are many biographical reference sources that await you. For example, *Biography Index*, published since 1949, contains citations to both periodical articles and books written about well-known people. *Current Biography* is a monthly publication with an annual cumulation called *Current Biography Yearbook*. This source includes biographical sketches of many living persons. The articles usually conclude with a brief list of additional references. Finally, there are several *Who's Who* biographical dictionaries that contain background information on thousands of individuals. Those considered standard reference sources include *Who's Who, Who's Who in America, Who's Who of American Women,* and *Who's Who in American Politics*.

Government Publications Perhaps your speech topic necessitates that you have current statistics to report to your audience. For example, are more men or women involved in fatal automobile accidents? How many Americans died of kidney disease in 1987? *Statistical Abstract of the United States* would be an excellent place to check for these figures. A few others worth mentioning include (1) *Business Statistics*, published annually by the U.S. Department of Commerce; (2) *Uniform Crime Reports*, an annual publication of the Federal Bureau of Investigation, U.S. Department of Justice; and (3) *Congressional Record*, the proceedings of the daily sessions of both houses of Congress. This source is particularly useful when researching how an issue was debated on the floor of the House of Representatives or the Senate. Which members of Congress spoke in favor of a proposed piece of legislation? Who opposed it?

To track down the thousands of government documents printed each year, check *Monthly Catalog of United States Government Publications*. Each monthly issue includes title, author, and subject indexes, and these are cumulated into semiannual and annual indexes.

Periodicals Room

The periodicals room is another storehouse of information. It contains newspapers, magazines, and journals, along with the accompanying indexes. Virtually every library owns either *Readers' Guide to Periodical Literature* or *Magazine Index*, or both. *Magazine Index* indexes over 400 popular periodicals. Its five-year cumulations are updated monthly on 16-mm film, which is viewed on a microfilm reader.

Reader's Guide to Periodical Literature indexes over 180 magazines with an alphabetical, topical arrangement. Also published by the H. W. Wilson Company are specialized periodical indexes, such as *Business Periodicals Index, Education Index, Social Sciences Index*, and *Humanities Index*, to name a few.

Large libraries also will have newspaper indexes on hand, most notably the *New York Times Index, Wall Street Journal Index, Washington Post Index*, or *National Newspaper Index*. At many libraries you can expect to find copies of these newspapers on microfilm. Furthermore, all the indexes mentioned here are available online. Other data bases available online include *Newspaper Abstracts*, indexing and abstracts for nineteen major newspapers; *AP News*, the full text of news articles from the AP (Associated Press) Data Stream service; and *UPI News*, the full text of news stories carried on the United Press International wire. Table 11.1 summarizes the types of sources available at the library.

TABLE 11.1   Selected Library Resources

Reference Desk:

Encyclopedias	*International Encyclopedia of the Social Sciences*
	Dictionary of American History
Biographical sources	*Biography Index*
	Current Biography
	Who's Who in American Politics
Government publications	*Statistical Abstract of the United States*
	Congressional Record
	Uniform Crime Reports

Periodicals Room:

	Readers' Guide to Periodical Literature
	Magazine Index
	Education Index
	New York Times Index

CITING SOURCES

An important part of constructing your speech is to indicate your sources of information. This process should enhance your credibility, especially if you are planning to present a controversial argument. More important, it is unethical to omit mentioning whose ideas you are borrowing for your speech. When you use the ideas of another and do not indicate where those ideas come from, you are **plagiarizing.**

In written material, the process of citing a source is called **footnoting.** Its purpose is to indicate where someone else could find the data you used. A footnote should indicate whose idea is being used and the source from which it was obtained. In order to give proper credit to others, you should include footnotes after every direct quote, as well as for those times when you paraphrase someone else's ideas. Several stylebooks describe the proper format for footnotes. Your instructor may require that you use a specific style manual for citing sources in your speech outline (see Chapter 12).

It is possible (and acceptable) to give credit orally to a source you have used. This is known simply as the **oral footnote.** For example, in his speech about courage, Bradley included the following oral footnote: "Nancy Cooper, in a recent *Newsweek* article, chronicled Philippine President Corazon Aquino's tremendous inner strength and courage as a political leader."[1] This statement lets Bradley's audience know that the idea originated with someone else.

Application Activity

USING THE LIBRARY

1. Find three citations to magazine articles on Soviet leader Mikhail Gorbachev's rise to power. Use *Readers' Guide to Periodical Literature, Magazine Index,* or *Biography Index* to locate these articles.

2. Check the catalog to see whether the library owns any books about Gorbachev. If so, write down the bibliographic citation (author, title, place of publication, publisher, date of publication).

As you gather information for your speech, you may wish to prepare a bibliography of all your sources. The bibliography should include all the sources you use, even if they are not directly cited in the text of the speech. The style manuals used for footnotes also should be used for these bibliographic citations. Whenever questions arise about the information you have presented in your speech, you can refer to your bibliography to direct the questioner to particular magazines, books, and films. A thorough bibliography, appended to your speech outline, usually indicates a well-researched speech.

FORMS OF SUPPORT FOR YOUR SPEECH

In an effort to present your ideas clearly and convincingly, it is important to include evidence to support those ideas. The purpose of using supportive material is to supplement your major ideas, and this, in turn, adds credibility to your position. An added benefit is increased self-confidence, because you know that the argument you are presenting is thorough and well documented. Several different types of supporting material are discussed in the following subsections.

Examples

One of the strongest types of support is the use of examples. **Examples** are statements that attempt to illuminate the facts. They can be very effective in your effort to involve the audience in your presentation. Moreover, they help to clarify your presentation by reinforcing the points in your arguments. This assists the audience in following the progression of your ideas. A properly used example is one that is relevant and relates to the major ideas of your presentation. Let's take a look at two types of examples.

Factual Example   A **factual example** is something that you have observed. It grows out of your own experience, and as with any good example, it helps to reinforce a point. When the example is believable, it keeps the audience involved in your presentation and can lead to greater interest on their part. Consider the following:

> Dave's speech topic, emotional pain, needed the focus of a specific example to illustrate one type of emotional pain. He recalled attending the funeral of a friend's teenage daughter and the pain he witnessed there. The language Dave used to describe the situation—people sobbing uncontrollably, the parents needing to be supported by other family members, and so on—captured the emotional pain this family was experiencing and earned the attention of the audience as well.

Hypothetical Example   A **hypothetical example** is one that invites the audience to imagine a situation created expressly for the speech they are listening to. It is an effective way to capture the audience's interest, because it involves them directly in the process. Consider the following:

> Denise, a member of the local election board, was addressing a civic group. Her purpose was to inform the audience of the procedure for registering voters. She believed her speech was crucial to increasing voter turnout in the upcoming off-year election. To emphasize her point, she created a hypothetical situation—she asked the audience to imagine that they were Soviet citizens known as "Refuseniks" who were being denied their rights. In her story she spoke of Rebecca and Aaron, separated for nearly nine years. Rebecca was allowed to emigrate to Israel in 1977, but her husband has been denied emigration since then. In addition, Aaron has never seen his son Zvi, who was born six months after Rebecca arrived in Israel. While not an actual case, Denise's example dramatically expressed her feelings that our freedom should not be taken lightly. She then moved back to her original theme—we need to be aware of the registration process and exercise our right to vote.

FIGURE 11.5 The Difference Between a New Spark Plug and a Worn One

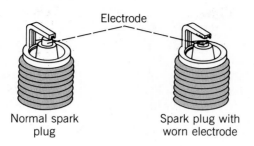

Electrode

Normal spark plug

Spark plug with worn electrode

FIGURE 11.6 Proper Spark Plug Wiring

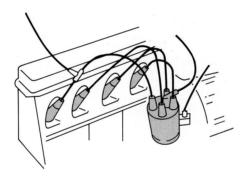

Keith belongs to a self-awareness group from his church. Currently, members of the group are discussing the importance of family communication. Each member is reading Judith Guest's novel *Ordinary People*. In addition, Keith has been asked to speak before the group on some aspect of family dynamics. He decides to talk about the importance of male family members' expressing their feelings. He recalls how stirring and powerful the movie *Ordinary People* was and decides to show the concluding scene between the father and son. It brings several members of his audience to tears.

Slides and movies present a special kind of difficulty, however, because of the mechanics involved in operating the necessary equipment. If you choose to include slides or a movie, make sure you understand how to operate the machinery. Take some extra time to practice before your actual presentation.

Photographs   Well-chosen photographs can capture an emotion, an attitude, or a special image. Further, photographs that are directly related to your topic can have a powerful impact on your audience. Imagine, for example, the impact of a set of before-and-after pictures, the first depicting a child on the verge of starvation, the second showing the same child three months after having received food and medical attention.

Your Body   You may wish to demonstrate or explain an important point in your speech by using your body. The movement of your body also can have an additional benefit—it helps reduce excess tension. Consider the following:

> Michael wants to enlighten his audience about the relationship between dance and culture. Specifically, he wants to demonstrate how the twist, disco dancing, and break dancing grew out of the cultures of particular time periods. In order to make sure that the audience is familiar with these dances, Michael briefly demonstrates each one. Michael's "performance" adds a special quality to the presentation and assists him in advancing his theme.

Using Visual Aids   It is important that your visual aids enhance your presentation, but that they do not become the center of your presentation. On the contrary, they should *support* the points you wish to make. If, for example, your audience becomes preoccupied with a visual aid (that is, a graphic picture or a breathtaking photograph), your message may get lost.

Too often speakers pay so much attention to a visual aid that they forget to talk to the audience. It is crucial that you not speak directly to your visual aid; instead, glance at it and then establish direct eye contact with the audience. By focusing exclusively on the visual aid, you risk losing contact with the audience.

For your visual aid to complement and enhance your presentation, all members of your audience need to be able to see it. Avoid making the audience squint or strain their eyes in an effort to see your visual aid. Also, when selecting your visual aid, keep the size of the room in mind. What is the length of the room? How are the

Application Activity

USING VISUAL AIDS

1. Your topic is "redesigning the town hall." How might you incorporate each of the following visual aids in your speech?

   a. Graphs

   b. Drawings

   c. Slides or movies

   d. Photographs

2. What precautions would you use with each type of visual aid?

seats arranged? Ask yourself these questions to help you determine the appropriate size for your visual aids. If you have difficulty seeing the visual aid when standing in the back of the room, chances are the audience will too. Here are three additional pointers: (1) use extra wide markers in preparing graphs or drawings, (2) use dark colors which show up better from a distance, and (3) make the characters large enough to see from a distance.

SUMMARY

An arsenal of supporting materials will help to make your speech clearer, more credible, and more accurate. In this chapter we identified several sources of information for your speech, including personal experiences, interviews, newspapers, periodicals, books, and other media such as radio and television broadcasts.

In order to use these various sources, you must know how to find them in the library. The reference collection includes such helpful sources as encyclopedias, biographical materials, and government documents. The periodicals room has a variety of magazine, journal, and newspaper articles accessible by means of such indexes as *Readers' Guide to Periodical Literature*, *Magazine Index*, and *The New York Times Index*.

After locating supportive material and deciding what to incorporate in your speech, you begin the process of developing the ideas in your speech. You are responsible for giving credit to others for any ideas of theirs that you use. This is done through oral foot-notes during the delivery and in your bibliography.

Your efforts to find supporting materials for a speech generally produce a number of possibilities. Depending on your topic, you will want to include one or more of these types of supporting material: examples, both factual and hypothetical; statistics; authoritative opinions; analogies; definitions; and visual aids, including graphs, drawings, slides and movies, photographs, and your body. Knowing how to incorporate appropriate forms of support increases your confidence during your speech. Further, knowing how to support your ideas with examples, statistics, and other materials assists you in developing your ideas more completely, which is the purpose of using supporting materials.

REVIEW QUESTIONS

1. List six sources of information that provide supporting material for your speech.
2. What three steps are important to remember when interviewing someone?
3. List three resources you can find in the periodicals room.
4. Why is it important to cite your sources?
5. Explain the benefit of using examples in a speech.
6. Explain the difference between median, mean, and mode.
7. What guidelines should you keep in mind when you plan to use statistics in your presentation?
8. Under what circumstances would you incorporate these visual aids in your speech:
   a. Line graph
   b. Pie graph
   c. Bar graph
9. What guidelines should you keep in mind when using visual aids?

NOTES

1. Nancy Cooper et al., "The Remarkable Rise of a Widow in Yellow," *Newsweek*, March 10, 1986, p. 32.

2. Tom Morganthau et al., "Future Shock," *Newsweek*, November 24, 1986, p. 30.

ADDITIONAL READINGS

An asterisk indicates an advanced reading.

Rottenberg, A. T. *Elements of Argument*. New York: St. Martin's Press, 1985. Pp. 54–64.
> This book provides an illuminating discussion of definition as a means of supporting an argument.

Rubin, R. B., Rubin, A. M., and Piele, L. J. *Communication Research: Strategies and Sources*. Belmont, Calif.: Wadsworth, 1986.
> Chapter 5 provides information on bibliographic data base searching.

Sproule, J. M. *Argument: Language and Its Influence*. New York: McGraw-Hill, 1980. Pp. 103–8.
> This book discusses the use of examples in constructing arguments.

*Williams, F. *Reasoning with Statistics: How To Read Quantitative Research*, 3d Ed. New York: Holt, Rinehart and Winston, 1986.
> This book is designed to increase your understanding of statistics.

12

Organizing
Your Speech

Learning Objectives

At the conclusion of this chapter you should be able to

1. Name and describe the three major parts of a speech.
2. Describe five patterns that are useful for organizing the body of your speech.
3. Develop the body of your speech.
4. Construct the introduction of your speech.
5. Construct the conclusion of your speech.
6. Compose transitions, including transitional previews and summaries, for your speech.
7. Compose a full-sentence outline for your speech.
8. Develop a key-phrase outline for your speech.

Chapter 10 concentrated on selecting a speech topic, determining the purpose of your speech, and analyzing the audience. Chapter 11 focused on gathering supporting materials for your topic. This chapter builds on the discussions of the previous two chapters.

As a speaker, you want your audience to find your speech not only informative and interesting, but easy to follow. You are responsible for ensuring that members of the audience understand your speech. To do this, you need to make sure that your speech is well organized. A well-organized speech will take your audience from a position of unfamiliarity with your treatment of a topic to a position of enlightenment.

Traditionally, a speech has three major parts: a beginning, a middle, and an end. These parts are known, respectively, as the introduction, the body, and the conclusion of a speech. Transitions between the major parts of the speech further clarify your presentation.

THE BODY

The **body** is the main part of your speech; as such, you begin your work here. Those ideas expressed in your thesis statement are fully developed in the body. For example, a speech on situation comedies might include the development of those factors which contribute to a successful show: good scripts, appealing characters, and a degree of social commentary. Further, it is in the body of your speech that you incorporate the supporting material gathered from personal experiences, interviews, or sources of information found at the library. The ideas you wish to express in your speech can be shaped into logical, observable patterns. In fact, logically developed ideas contribute to a speaker's confidence and at the same time make it easier for the audience to follow the presentation. Two helpful steps in preparing the body include organizing your ideas and outlining.

Organizing Your Ideas

An element that helps create a logical flow of ideas is **sequence,** or order. Ideas that are organized in a definite pattern or progression help your audience follow the development of your talk. Generally speaking, certain topics are better suited for a particular organizational pattern, although there are no ironclad rules for selecting one

Organizing your speech properly takes a great deal of time and effort.

over another. Ultimately, you must decide which pattern seems most appropriate for the development of your topic and the audience you will be speaking to. Five organizational patterns that you can choose from in deciding what type of order would be most appropriate for your speech include causal order, problem solution, spatial order, time order, and topic order.

Causal Order   **Causal order** establishes the fact that certain events are linked to other events that have precipitated them. When using a cause-and-effect format, first define the cause and then follow up by discussing effects. For example, if the basis of your speech is, "If the U.S. Senate fails to ratify the 1987 INF Treaty, the relationship between the Soviet Union and the United States will suffer," then the body of your speech would need to address either the adverse effects of a failure to ratify or the positive effects of the treaty's ratification.

We can skip

Problem Solution   The **problem solution** approach to organizing a speech involves identifying a conflict and then offering a potential course of action that will correct the problem. In most instances, the first part of the speech is reserved for discussing the problem; in the second part of the speech the speaker offers a solution to that problem. In most cases, the speaker is attempting to persuade the audience to follow the solution offered in the speech. This organizational pattern would be appropriate for the following topic: "Thousands of Americans suffer from hypertension [problem], but there are proven ways to reduce this condition, namely, controlling your diet, exercise, and medication [solution]."

Spatial Order   **Spatial order** refers to organizing the parts of a topic according to the relationship of their positions. This relationship can be geographic (the different wine producing regions of France), rank-ordered (the degrees of proficiency in karate), or directional (the exterior, then interior features of a house, car, boat). In the case of karate, the body of your speech might be organized around describing the specific techniques required for each rank from beginners (white belt) to experts (black belt).

Time Order   **Time order** arranges ideas in a chronological framework. This pattern of organization is best suited to topics that present a step-by-step explanation (how to wallpaper a kitchen, how to cook a turkey) or a historical development. For example, a speech

Application Activity

IDENTIFYING ORGANIZATIONAL PATTERNS OF A SPEECH

Name the organizational pattern illustrated in each of the following descriptions:

1. There are several Hollywood celebrities who have gone into public office:

    a. George Murphy served as a U.S. Senator during the 1960s.

    b. In 1986, Clint Eastwood was elected mayor of Carmel, California.

    c. Ronald Reagan has served as both Governor of California and President of the United States.

2. In an effort to curb campaign funding abuses, the U.S. government established new regulations.

3. Society is putting fewer resources into our large urban cities. If this trend continues, these cities will continue to decay.

4. The following steps are helpful when buying a new car:

    a. Research the different models available in the size and price you can afford.

    b. Select the model that best suits your needs and pocketbook, based on your research.

    c. Go to several dealerships that sell the car.

    d. Purchase the car at the dealership where you feel you received the best treatment.

5. Highway 1 along the coast of California is known for its scenic beauty and vacation spots. In 1986, I visited the following places along that route: (a) San Francisco, (b) Carmel, (c) Big Sur, (d) the Hearst Castle at San Simeon, and (e) Los Angeles.

Answers: 1. Topical order, 2. Problem solution, 3. Causal order, 4. Time order, 5. Spatial order on Vanna White's climb to "stardom" could chart the course of her career, including dates and specific achievements—the year she began turning letters on *Wheel of Fortune*, the year her autobiography was published, and so on. These points would be treated chronologically; to do otherwise would be confusing for both the audience and the speaker.

Topic Order   **Topic order** involves breaking down your main topic into smaller points that are pertinent to the main idea. For example, if the purpose of your speech is to define what a teacher is, you might discuss each of the following subtopics: (1) a teacher is someone who educates others, (2) a teacher is a role model, and (3) a teacher is someone who instills a love of learning. The order of the discussion may be unimportant, or you may view one subtopic as more important and want to address it first. That is something you must determine.

Outlining the Body

Why should you outline the body of your speech next? Is not selection of an organizational pattern enough to develop your speech? The answer is *no*. Your decision to adhere to a particular organizational structure is based on the way you view your total topic, including both its general and specific purposes. Outlining the body of your speech helps you to develop fully the points made in your thesis statement. Outlining is simply another step in the process of preparing a speech. To summarize what has happened so far, consider the following:

General purpose: To inform.

Specific purpose: To inform my classroom audience about the benefits of being fit.

Thesis statement: Three benefits of being fit are your physical appearance, an improved cardiovascular system, and a healthy mental attitude.

Organizational structure: Topic order

The next step is the outline:

  I. Physical appearance
 II. Cardiovascular system
III. Mental attitude

In other words, the task that awaits you is to construct an outline that develops the three ideas mentioned in your thesis sentence.

The main purpose of outlining is to help both the speaker and the audience follow the development of ideas in the speech. When constructing an outline for the body of your speech, it is helpful to use full sentences. Specific outlining rules follow, and each is related to the body of the speech.

An Outline Consists of Coordinate and Subordinate Points   **Coordinate points** are the major ideas in a speech that grow out of the thesis statement. It is essential for the speaker to clearly identify the major points, because this helps clarify the direction of the talk for the audience.

Subordinate points are minor points that grow out of the major ideas. It is equally important to realize that your subordinate points should at all times support your major ideas. When analyzing and developing your presentation, be sure that a clear connection exists between your major and minor points. Further, make sure you include at least two subordinate points for each coordinate point.

In the following example, the coordinate points (Roman numerals) represent the major ideas of the talk, while the subordinate points (letters) are minor points whose function is to support the major ideas:

   I. There are three different levels of friendship.

      A. There are acquaintances.

      B. There are social friends.

      C. There are close friends.

  II. Friendships dissolve for several reasons.

      A. Misunderstandings are one cause.

      B. Defensiveness can invade friendships.

 III. It takes an effort to build a meaningful friendship.

      A. Take time to be a good listener.

      B. Take time to share openly with a friend.

Each Idea in an Outline Is Discrete   **Discreteness** is the quality of being separate. Your ideas are said to be discrete if they have the ability to stand on their own. For your outline, this means making sure that only *one* idea is contained in each sentence. The two subordinate points in the following example are discrete, separate ideas. Each one achieves its goal of supporting the coordinate point.

Friends need to listen to each other in order to understand each other.

1. It is helpful to paraphrase the statement of your friend when you wish to clarify a point.
2. Asking questions about a statement helps to promote understanding.

What is the problem in this next example?

Friends need to listen to each other in order to understand each other.

1. It is helpful to paraphrase the statement of your friend when you wish to clarify a point.
2. It is helpful to repeat your friend's ideas.

The preceding points are not an example of discreteness; they are similar rather than distinct ideas.

Limit the Number of Major Ideas   It is wise to limit the number of major points you choose to include in a classroom speech. Your speech will be too lengthy or cumbersome if you include more than five major points; with too many main ideas you run the risk of treating your topic superficially. Table 12.1 provides a checklist for outlining the body of your speech.

TABLE 12.1   Checklist for Outlining the Body of Your Speech

✓ Include coordinate and subordinate points	Do your coordinate points represent your main ideas? Do your subordinate points support your coordinate points?
✓ Make each idea discrete	Is each idea distinct?
✓ Limit the number of major ideas	Did you include too many major ideas?

Application Activity

DEVELOPING A SPEECH BODY

1. Choose a topic for a speech.

2. Create a speech body that contains three coordinate points and two subordinate points under each coordinate point.

3. Use full sentences in completing this task.

THE INTRODUCTION

The **introduction** is the place where you strive to create a "need to know" on the audience's part. What motivates an audience to listen to the development of your ideas during the body of your speech? Hopefully, your introduction. An effectively constructed introduction can elicit support from your audience. As a speaker, it is both exciting and encouraging to see an audience show signs of interest and involvement in the first minute of your talk. The objectives for your introduction, then, are threefold: (1) to capture the audience's attention, (2) to establish your credibility, and (3) to communicate the nature of your topic to the audience.

Drawing the Audience's Attention

Drawing the attention of your audience in the introduction is crucial if you expect to maintain their interest during the body of your speech. There are a number of ways to achieve this goal, including the use of one of the following: a narrative, a startling statement, a rhetorical question, or a quotation.

Determining a suitable format for your introduction requires that you analyze both your topic and what you consider to be the needs of your audience. In Chapter 10 we addressed the subject of topic selection and adapting to the needs of the audience. At this time you may find it helpful to review that discussion. Each of the following introductions appeals to the audience's need to belong (review the discussion on Maslow in Chapter 10).

Narrative   An effective way to introduce a speech is to use a **narrative,** or story. It can enable the speaker to create a feeling of understanding with the audience. Because narratives are often based on personal experiences that the audience can easily identify with, they can capture the audience's interest right away. A narrative can be either factual or hypothetical as long as it relates to the central theme of the talk. Consider the following:

I want to tell you about my friend Julia. We met twelve years ago when I was a sophomore in college. Our relationship experienced many ups and downs as it changed from a platonic one to a romantic one. We struggled through a three-year engagement which culminated in marriage. Our first year of married life was a challenge; adjusting to our new roles and the added strain of financial difficulties created stress for both of us. We survived these early years, however, and supported each other in our careers.

    When we moved out of state four years later, our relationship changed. We seemed less dependent on outsiders, and therefore, we grew closer to each other. My wife became my best friend. Today I would like to share the stages of change our relationship underwent in the hope that my experience may be applicable to your lives.

Startling Statement A **startling statement,** one that shocks, arouses, or surprises an audience, will certainly capture their attention. Remember, however, that this statement must relate to the topic. If not, you may gain the audience's attention, but for the wrong reasons, making it difficult to bring the audience back to the topic later on. This is particularly true if you incorporate something gimmicky or humorous and then attempt to speak on a serious topic. The startling statement can be very effective if it is used properly. Consider this opening statement: "It took the suicide of a former college roommate to bring us together." The speaker's attempt to startle the audience was done for the express purpose of gaining interest in the topic, "Why we lose contact with our old friends."

Rhetorical Question Try asking a rhetorical question to introduce your speech. A **rhetorical question** is one that is posed to the audience and later developed or answered in the talk. The speaker does not expect the audience to answer a rhetorical question; its purpose is to motivate the audience to think about the topic. If the speaker is successful, the audience will want to hear more. Consider the following:

Do you know what it's like to lose a close friend—someone you've counted on to listen to you and share your feel-

> ings? Close friends are hard to find, which is why I feel
> particularly sad that my friendship with Paul has eroded.
> I want to share this experience with you in the hope that
> you will conclude that friendships are worth maintaining.

In this example, the speaker asks the audience to think about
their own relationships. This is accomplished by including a question that the audience can easily relate to—certainly most people
can recall friendships that have drifted apart.

Quotation   Using a **quotation** to introduce a speech involves taking
someone else's exact words to support the ideas covered in your
speech. Quotations are often dramatic in nature and can therefore
elicit the audience's interest. After stating the quote, follow up by
drawing a connection between the quote and the topic for the audience. Occasionally you may be forced to take excerpts from a
lengthy quotation. When this occurs, be sure you are capturing the
essence of the quote. The following quotation relates to the topic of
friendship:

> "Friendship adds a brighter radiance to prosperity and
> lightens the burden of adversity by dividing and sharing
> it."[1] Sometimes we get involved in an intense relationship
> that undergoes a dramatic change. However, a good friend
> can see you through these difficult times. Today I want to
> share my feelings about developing a strong relationship
> with a friend.

In this example, the speaker uses a quote as a springboard for
his speech, and it is successful because it is directly related to the
topic. Note the brevity of the quote; with a lengthy quote you risk
losing the audience's attention. Also, it is more difficult to deliver a
quote because you are stating someone else's words and the speech
patterns are likely to be unnatural to you. Because of these factors,
a quote that is short and to the point will work better for most circumstances.

Establishing Your Credibility

After capturing your audience's attention, you must still address two
remaining goals before moving to the body of your speech: (1) to
establish your credibility and concern, and (2) to communicate the
nature of your topic. Establishing your credibility as a speaker for a
particular topic involves conveying your knowledge about the topic

(that is, mentioning personal experiences or recently conducted research), as well as your concern. In the previous example of an introduction using a rhetorical question, the speaker relies on his or her own experience of letting a friendship slip away as proof of credibility.

When constructing your introduction, you want to communicate that your topic is important and that you are committed to sharing it. Ask yourself a few questions, such as "How does this topic relate to my needs?" and "Why do I want to share my views with this audience?" The answers to these questions will help you to communicate your involvement in the topic.

Providing Information about Your Topic

In the last phase of your introduction, indicate what the body of your speech will include, stopping short of actually developing your ideas. Save that discussion for the body. What you should reveal to your audience is the purpose of your speech. For example, you

Application Activity

DEVELOPING AN INTRODUCTION

1. Earlier in this chapter you developed your speech body. Using the same topic, write four different types of introductions.

   a. Narrative

   b. Startling statement

   c. Rhetorical question

   d. Quotation

2. As you write these introductions, ask yourself how you can capture the audience's attention.

3. How could you demonstrate your credibility as a speaker on this subject?

4. Share your introductions by forming small groups.

5. Elicit the feedback of your peers on how involved they become in your talk.

could mention that you intend to talk about three levels of friendship: acquaintances, social friends, and close friends. Your actual
discussion of these subjects would follow in the body.

THE CONCLUSION

The functions of the **conclusion** are (1) to draw your speech to an
end, (2) to reiterate the central theme of your presentation (especially in an informative speech), and (3) to indicate to the members
of your audience what you would like them to do (especially in a
persuasive speech).

As you begin your conclusion, give your audience a cue so that
they can refocus their attention. Phrases such as "in conclusion" or
"in closing" generally work. Now use your remaining time to reinforce your speech's purpose or to ask something of your audience—
either that they change the way they look at an issue or that they
take some action. There are different techniques to achieve this

"IN CONCLUSION, I WILL NOW READ
THE SECOND DRAFT OF THIS SPEECH."

goal, including the summation, the challenge, and the call for action.

The Summation

One way you can conclude your talk is with the **summation,** which reinforces the main points in your speech. For example, the following statement could be a meaningful close for a talk that centers around the importance of friendship:

To me there are few things in life as special as a close friend. I hope you remember, as a result of my presentation today, that a meaningful friendship requires commitment, unselfish behavior, and empathy.

The Challenge

Another way to end your speech is by **challenging** the audience. This occurs when the speaker calls on the audience to think further about the topic. After speaking about losing her best friend, Amy concludes with the following:

Good friends are hard to find. Think about the important relationships in your life and don't take people for granted. Don't make the same mistake that I did!

The Call for Action

There are times when you want to persuade your audience to act. This is known as a **call for action.** Such a call necessitates going a step further than presenting information. Although the conclusion still grows out of the presentation's central purpose, you make an effort to inspire, motivate, or move the members of your audience to take a stand, change their behavior, or act on their beliefs. Consider the following:

In keeping with her theme on the importance of close friendships, Amy concluded her speech by telling the audience how much her friend Susan's presence meant to her during her mother's long illness. At the conclusion of this emotional narrative, she looked directly at her audience and said, "You can be just as important to one of your friends. Don't let the person down!"

Application Activity

PRACTICE WRITING CONCLUSIONS

1. Use the same topic from the last two Application Activities to create two conclusions.

    a. Make sure each conclusion summarizes your thesis statement.

    b. Have one conclusion challenge the audience.

    c. Have the second conclusion call the audience to action.

2. Share your conclusions with other members of the class.

3. Use the feedback you receive to revise your conclusions.

TRANSITIONS

A **transition** provides a link between the main parts of your speech. It helps to have a transitional preview after the introduction (to give your audience an idea of what is to come), to have transitions between the coordinate points in the body of your speech ("Now that I've explained the importance of the primaries, I'll move next to the nominating conventions"), and to have a transitional summary before the conclusion (to recap all the coordinate points). Transitions show the relationships between the ideas in your speech, while transitional previews and summaries allow the audience to hear the main ideas several times. Because the audience can miss a point during your presentation, previews and summaries provide an additional chance for them to follow and understand your speech.

PREPARING A SPEECH OUTLINE

For help in preparing and delivering your speech, use a speech outline. There are two types of speech outlines: the full-sentence outline helps you construct or develop your topic (see the earlier section entitled "Outlining the Body" for more discussion); the key-phrase outline helps ready you for your presentation to the audience.

Full-Sentence Outline

The first step in constructing your speech is to prepare a **full-sentence outline**—one that uses full sentences to list the major and minor points, as well as the different forms of support in your talk. This process helps you to clearly delineate the different parts of your speech. An added benefit of this exercise is that you will feel more confident that you are presenting a well-thought-out speech. As you develop your full-sentence speech outline, keep these techniques in mind: (1) label the different parts of the speech, (2) use a consistent symbol system, and (3) attach a bibliography.

Your outline will be more effective if you take the time to label the different parts of your speech (introduction, transitional preview, body, transitional summary, conclusion). Make these labels in bold print so that the different parts stand out. You can write these headings in the center of the page or place them off to the side.

As you construct your speech outline, it also is helpful to use a symbol system that follows standard outlining procedures. Those ideas of greater importance are placed further to the left in the outline than ideas of lesser importance. The symbol system used in the following example shows the relationship between ideas. Major points are indicated by Roman numerals, subordinate points are designated by capital letters, followed by Arabic numerals for sub-subpoints.

I. One of the purposes of friendship is to provide comfort in times of need.

   A. When my son died, Jane was a tremendous support.

      1. She telephoned several people to let them know about the funeral arrangements.

      2. She spent hours by my side during those difficult weeks following the funeral.

When you develop a talk for a classroom presentation, you may be required to show the instructor the sources you used in gathering your information. These sources, including books, magazines, journals, newspapers, interviews, or audiovisual materials, should be listed in a bibliography which is attached to your full-sentence outline. There are several style manuals that include accepted bibliography formats. Check with your instructor to see if there is a preferred one for your class. (See Chapter 11 for a more detailed treatment of this topic.)

Example

I. I would wager that all of you have encountered individuals who are difficult to communicate with.

II. These individuals display defensive communication behaviors.

    A. Distancing is a commonly used defense mechanism.

    B. Sarcasm is another form of defensive communication.

III. Because I have encountered such behavior and have read extensively on the subject, I would like to share what I have found to be successful ways of coping with defensive people.

IV. In this speech I will explain the nature of defensive communication, describe two types of defense mechanisms, and tell you how to cope with defensive communication.

I. What do we mean by defensive communication?

    A. Defensive communication is our response to a threatening communication environment.

        1. We may be uncomfortable in social gatherings.

        2. Perhaps we are terrified to speak in public.

    B. Defensive communication is a means of self-protection.

        1. When we are uncomfortable, we erect walls to insulate ourselves from others.

        2. As part of our protective shield, we display defense mechanisms.

Let's turn now to our next point.

II. Defense mechanisms can be either nonverbal or verbal forms of communication. I will describe one of each.

    A. Distancing is one type of nonverbal defensive communication.

1. Distancing is a conscious decision to minimize verbal communication with others.

2. Distancing occurs when an individual erects a wall that communicates, "Don't get close to me."

3. The individual who distances himself or herself from others appears to be aloof.

   a. Closer examination shows that this assumption is often false.

   b. The person who uses distancing is shy.

4. My personal relationship with Fred is a good example of distancing.

B. One type of verbal defensiveness is sarcasm.

1. The sarcastic person uses a biting sense of humor to put others down.

2. Sarcasm verbally keeps others at a distance.

3. Stuart is a good example of a sarcastic person.

Transition
Having described two defense mechanisms, let's turn our attention to how we can cope with the defensive communication of others.

III. While there are several techniques for coping with defensive communication, I will focus my discussion on two of them.

A. Make a conscious effort not to internalize the other person's defensiveness.

1. You are not responsible for the defensiveness generated by others.

2. Do not be trapped into blaming yourself for the way others communicate.

B. Attempt to provide supportive feedback for the other person in an effort to improve the communication climate.

1. Try to empathize with the difficulty being experienced by the other person.

2. Be nonjudgmental in the feedback you give.

Application Activity

DEVELOPING A FULL-SENTENCE OUTLINE

1. Using the principles of effective outlining, create a full-sentence outline for one of the following topics:

   a. Human rights

   b. Divorce

   c. 1988 Olympic Games

   d. Exercise

   e. Child abuse

2. Be sure to include sections for the introduction, body, conclusion, and transitions.

Transitional summary

Now that I have talked about what defensive communication is, described both a nonverbal and a verbal defense mechanism, and told you about two techniques for coping with defensive communication, I would like to leave you with these thoughts.

Conclusion

I. You now have an expanded view of defensive communication.

   A. You know what causes individuals to behave defensively.

   B. You can recognize defensiveness in others.

II. Next time you encounter a defensive individual, I would like to think you will practice the techniques I discussed with you today. You will be pleased with the results.

Key-Phrase Outline

While the intent of a full-sentence outline is to help you develop the ideas in your speech, the purpose of a key-phrase outline is to help you to prepare your delivery. The **key-phrase outline** is an abbreviated version of the full-sentence outline that is intended as a cue to each point in your presentation. Use it to practice your delivery.

Consider these points as you develop this outline: First, convert the major points in your full-sentence outline from full sentences to key phrases. Second, use standard outlining procedures— Roman numerals, letters, Arabic numbers. Third, space generously between the lines (key phrases) in your outline so that you can easily follow along during the delivery of your speech. It is easy to lose your place during the delivery when the outline is crowded or cluttered. Finally, insert directions or cues regarding delivery, such as *pause, slow down, eye contact.* The necessity for these notes will become apparent as you practice your delivery.

Example

Introduction

   I. Encounter difficult individuals

        (Calm down!)

  II. Defensive behaviors

     A. Distancing

     B. Sarcasm

 III. Share how to cope with defensiveness

Transitional preview

 IV. Cover nature of defensiveness, two defense mechanisms, how to cope

        (Pause)

Body

   I. Define defensive communication

     A. Reponse to threatening environment

       1. Uncomfortable in social gatherings

       2. Terrified of public speaking

     B. Means of self-protection

       1. Erect walls to insulate self

       2. Display defense mechanisms

Transition

     Turn to next point

  II. Defense mechanisms, nonverbal or verbal

     A. Nonverbal distancing

(Look directly at audience)

1. Minimal verbal communication

2. Don't get close-wall

3. Appear aloof

   a. False assumption

   b. Actually shy

4. Example of Fred

B. Verbal sarcasm

   1. Biting sense of humor

   2. Keep others away

   3. Stuart good example

Transition   Turn next to coping techniques

(Pause)

III. Two techniques to discuss

A. Don't internalize others' defensiveness

   1. You're not responsible

   2. Don't blame yourself for their communication

B. Give supportive feedback

   1. Empathize with other person

   2. Give nonjudgmental feedback

(Direct eye contact again)

Transitional summary   Discussed defensiveness, defense mechanisms, coping techniques—leave you with these thoughts

Conclusion   I. Expanded view of defensive communication

A. Causes

B. How to recognize defensiveness in others

(Pause)

II. Next encounter with difficult individual, use coping techniques

Application Activity

DEVELOPING A KEY-PHRASE OUTLINE

1. Use the same topic you selected from the preceding Application Activity. Convert it from full sentences to key phrases.

2. Use the key phrases to practice delivering this speech.

3. Insert notes to yourself at appropriate points to make your delivery more effective.

SUMMARY

This chapter provided discussions on the major parts of your speech and how to prepare a speech outline. The body is the main part of your speech. The ideas in that body often form patterns that provide a framework for arranging your speech more effectively; these patterns include causal order, problem solution, spatial order, time order, and topic order.

The chapter also promoted outlining the body to help with your speech's development. Among the outlining principles discussed were the following: (1) an outline consists of coordinate and subordinate points, (2) each idea in an outline is discrete, and (3) the number of major ideas should be limited.

The introduction serves three purposes: to draw the audience's attention, to establish your credibility as a speaker, and to provide information about the topic. You can use a narrative, a startling statement, a rhetorical question, or a quotation to introduce your speech.

The conclusion signals the end of your speech. It also reinforces the central ideas in the speech and indicates what you would like the audience to do after the speech has ended. The conclusion can take various forms, including the summation, the challenge, and the call for action.

Transitions provide a link between the main parts of your speech. By previewing and summarizing ideas, they provide an additional opportunity for the audience to follow the speech.

Ideally, as a speaker you should use two outlines to prepare your speech. The first, a full-sentence outline, is meant to assist you

13

Delivering Your Speech

Learning Objectives

At the conclusion of this chapter you should be able to

1. Identify four factors that help control speech anxiety.

2. Recognize the four types of delivery.

3. Understand the importance of spontaneity and sincerity in speech delivery.

4. Discuss six ways to use your body to enhance your delivery.

5. Identify five ways that your voice can improve your delivery.

An important aspect of the speech-making process is the delivery, since the way you present your ideas will affect the way your audience responds to them. While the content of your speech is highly important, a poorly delivered speech can undercut even a well-prepared message.

Delivery is usually the most dreaded aspect of the speaking situation. Understandably, people feel self-conscious when they are standing in front of an audience. Fear of rejection is an overwhelming factor in public speaking; however, learning what to do in order to feel comfortable during speech delivery can lead to improved self-confidence. An audience views a composed public speaker as a confident communicator with a message worth listening to. Furthermore, the positive feedback received from the audience reinforces your self-confidence.

How do you overcome a fear of speaking in public? There are specific techniques you can use to improve the effectiveness of your delivery and to diminish your speech anxiety. To that end, this chapter will focus on the different types of delivery, sharing ideas, bodily action, and voice quality and control. Incorporating the techniques that are natural to you will help you to deliver your speech more effectively and, in turn, lead to greater confidence when you are giving a speech.

UNDERSTANDING SPEECH ANXIETY

Although most people like to talk in informal settings, many have a genuine fear of delivering a public speech. Personal concerns about how others perceive us are intensified when we speak in public.

The internal tension is understandable; no one likes being rejected—the greatest fear associated with public speaking. Unlike writing in a diary or turning in a project to an instructor, our public speeches are visible to an entire audience.

While there is no magic formula to dispel your fear of public speaking, you can take comfort in knowing that your nervousness can be significantly reduced by following a plan. This plan requires that you follow several of the points mentioned in Chapters 10, 11, and 12: select an appropriate topic, analyze your audience, find supporting materials to incorporate in your speech, and organize your ideas and support into a logical presentation. As a result of doing this extensive preparation, you will know where your speech is going and what you are about. You will have become the expert on your topic. All your hard work will pay off by translating into a feeling of confidence that you are well prepared and that you will not be caught off guard.

There are a few additional pointers that can help you deliver your speech with less apprehension: control excess tension, focus on the topic, remember that you are not alone, and develop a positive attitude.

Control Excess Tension

When told that they must deliver a speech, most people generally feel nervous. It's as if the word *speech* triggers an alarm. Nervousness often manifests itself in tension; it is possible, however, to use your body in a way that allows you to reduce the excess energy caused by tension. Merely taking a deep breath or a few steps away from the lectern may help free your body of extra energy. These small efforts will help you feel more relaxed when delivering your speech.

Focus on the Topic

Concentrating on what you are talking about, rather than thinking about the fact that you are standing in front of an audience, is an important step in reducing speech apprehension. Concentrating on your message helps reduce your anxiety because you stop focusing on your role and instead direct your energy toward the treatment of your topic. Once you take the focus off yourself, you will be able to share your ideas with the audience. These ideas need to be the center of attention—not you! A second important factor, then, is to select a topic in which you are genuinely interested (see Chapter 10 for a more complete discussion of selecting a topic). Consider the following:

> Bob, who has an extensive collection of *Late Night with David Letterman* videotapes (David Letterman's show), decides to speak on some of the comic routines made popular on that show (that is, stupid pet tricks, viewer mail, daily "top 10" list from the home office in Milwaukee, Wisconsin, then Scottsdale, Arizona, then Lincoln, Nebraska). Because Bob both knows and enjoys his topic, he becomes thoroughly involved in his presentation. As a result, he forgets about being nervous in front of his audience.

Remember that You Are Not Alone

Try to place the speech experience in its proper perspective. It is likely that several members of your audience have been in your shoes before, so they can empathize with your nervousness over speaking in public. People are basically kind. They do not want to see you fail. Perhaps this example will demonstrate my point: Have you ever been backstage in a theater when an actor forgot his or her lines? The audience did not laugh or ridicule the actor; instead, they remained quiet and probably empathized with the performer.

Develop a Positive Attitude

When you get up in front of your audience, it helps to remember that you have prepared something worthwhile to say to them. Since *you* are the person who has researched, developed, and organized your subject, no one will know your topic as well as you. In addition, the way you have decided to handle your topic probably depends on your values, attitudes, and past experiences. Even a simple assignment gives you an opportunity to bring your own rich background to the speaking experience. Condition yourself to think, "I have something interesting to share with others."

This positive attitude can carry over to your audience. Being involved in your presentation communicates a feeling of confidence to the audience. In turn, you should feel more comfortable because you will be able to observe the audience's involvement in your presentation. Remember that you are a unique individual who has something special to share with the audience. Believe in your ability to share ideas—you do it all the time with your friends, work associates, and family. Table 13.1 provides a checklist for understanding speech anxiety.

TABLE 13.1   Checklist for Understanding Speech Anxiety

✓ Control excess tension	Take a deep breath; take a few small steps away from the lectern.
✓ Focus on the topic	Think about what you are sharing with the audience.
✓ Remember that you are not alone	Others can understand your nervousness.
✓ Develop a positive attitude	Remember that you have something to share with your audience.

TYPES OF DELIVERY

Four methods of delivery can be used to share information in public. Each, of course, has its own place in a communication situation. However, certain methods appear to be more advantageous than others. Described below are the different methods of delivery.

The Impromptu Speech

Adv.
Natural
No time to get nervous

What is the usual response when someone is asked to deliver an impromptu speech? Panic comes to mind! An **impromptu speech** is delivered without advance preparation or practice. Although diffi-

(warning)

Dis.
Repitition

Application Activity

SPEECH ANXIETY

Jackie is a student in your communication class. The thought of having to deliver a speech is so threatening to her that she is seriously thinking about dropping the class.

1. Discuss this problem in small groups.

2. In what ways can Jackie control some of the anxiety she feels?

3. What can you suggest from your own experiences to help Jackie cope with this problem?

4. What have you learned from this activity that applies to your own fears about public speaking?

cult for the student, the impromptu speech has its benefits. An instructor may want to give his or her students an opportunity to "think on their feet" and at the same time expose them to being in front of the class. The typical introductory speech on the first day of class helps fulfill this goal. In this context, the impromptu delivery represents a useful tool. On a more practical level, business seminars or meetings frequently give rise to impromptu speeches. For example, the assistant director of the botanic garden asks Jerry to summarize his findings on the viability of instituting a continuing education program for the community. Although Jerry has no advance notice, he talks about the program to the staff members at the meeting. In this situation, the impromptu speech came about as a natural part of the meeting.

Despite Jerry's success in the preceding example, the impromptu speech generally does little to bolster a speaker's confidence. After just a few minutes, the presentation commonly becomes repetitive, which causes the speaker to become self-conscious and nervous.

To give an impromptu speech simply because you have failed to prepare comments ahead of time communicates to your audience that you really did not care about your responsibility enough to adequately prepare for your talk. An ill-prepared speaker does not gain the respect of the audience. As a speaker, your credibility and confidence will be diminished if the audience perceives you as either unprepared or uncaring.

The Manuscript Speech

If you were in a position of authority, like the President, it would be appropriate for you to use a **manuscript speech**, one delivered from a prepared script. Consider President Kennedy's delicate position during the 1962 Cuban Missile Crisis. After preparing several drafts of what was one of his most important speeches, Kennedy addressed the world. He needed to communicate the position of the United States regarding the Soviet Union's placement of offensive ballistic missiles in Cuba. It was imperative that he deliver the exact words of the final speech draft to ensure that the intentions of our nation would not be misinterpreted by the rest of the world.[1] The gravity of the situation required that he use a manuscript in which each word was painstakingly selected.

It is unlikely that you would find yourself in a situation of such magnitude; however, there are circumstances where a manuscript speech is appropriate, even desirable. If, for example, you are asked to explain new company procedures or describe the steps used in cardiopulmonary resuscitation (CPR), where accuracy is essential, a prepared manuscript is beneficial. What the manuscript does is to keep you focused on your speech.

There are drawbacks, however. Because the manuscript speech is extremely precise, it is apt to be mechanical, lack spontaneity, and stifle interaction with the audience. Some speakers even plan their gestures in advance. Indeed, it is a rare individual who can appear fresh when such minute details are orchestrated beforehand. If you must use a manuscript, make every effort to appear to be talking to your audience instead of reading lines to them. Consider the following:

> Lisa Crandall is the newly elected president of the Biochemical Engineering Society of Pittsburgh. She is nervous about the acceptance address she must deliver at her installation because she doubts her ability to speak in public. She writes out her entire speech ahead of time and essentially reads it to the group. When she looks at the audience, she sees people gazing around the room—a sure sign of boredom.

Manuscript delivery is undoubtedly difficult to master. Obviously, it was not done well by the speaker in the preceding illustration. It takes considerable time, practice, and familiarity with the types of situations that necessitate its use.

The Memorized Speech

Adv.
Look at
audience

The type of delivery that requires the greatest investment of time is the **memorized speech**. The speaker not only develops the complete manuscript, he or she spends additional time memorizing it word for word. When would a speaker choose to memorize a speech? Perhaps in these cases: when delivering a eulogy, making a sales pitch (especially if it has proven to be successful in the past), or toasting the bride and groom at a wedding. In each of these situations, considerable effort has gone into preparing the message and selecting appropriate words; the speaker wants to communicate his or her thoughts exactly as planned.

Dis.
Mechanical,
Might lose
your place,
Time

Delivering a memorized speech has its drawbacks—most notably, the difficulty in maintaining spontaneity. There is an additional pitfall to the memorized presentation, one that most experienced instructors have seen snare the inexperienced speaker: Countless students forget a word or a phrase midway through their speech, lose their composure, and out of desperation return to the beginning of the speech to start again.

If you practice a speech sufficiently before giving it to your audience, a certain degree of familiarity results. Because you are now familiar with the ideas in your speech, you probably will not be shaken if a particular word or phrase escapes you during the pressure of the speaking situation. Unless your instructor asks you to memorize a speech for a specific assignment, try to avoid doing so.

Let us say that you need to memorize a phone number as part of a message you will later relay to a friend. Since you do not have a pencil and paper, you recite the numbers until they are committed to memory. While engaged in this task, you try your best to visualize the numbers. This seemingly simple task requires a great deal of concentration. When considered on these terms, the business of memorizing a speech suddenly becomes enormous. Nearly all the speaker's energy in this type of delivery is focused on *remembering* words, rather than on *sharing* ideas with an audience. The process of memorizing leaves little or no time for concentrating on how you deliver the speech to your audience.

The Extemporaneous Speech

The type of delivery that combines the best features of the preceding methods is the extemporaneous delivery. An **extemporaneous speech** is thoroughly prepared and practiced, but it is delivered in a conversational style. In an extemporaneous delivery, the emphasis is placed on sharing ideas that have been researched and analyzed. The speaker often uses note cards or an outline while delivering the talk and can enjoy some flexibility with the audience because he or she has prepared, organized, and practiced his or her thoughts in advance. This allows the speaker to respond to the feedback he or she receives from the audience.

Adv. Involve Audience, Full understanding of the thought, Alot of flexibility, Spontaneous

Extemporaneous delivery implies that the speaker has a thorough knowledge and understanding of the topic and an intelligent plan to present it. It avoids the stilted, formal presentation inherent in the manuscript speech or memorized speech. In addition, it suggests to the audience that the speaker is trying to interact with them, because the speaker's language is more spontaneous and the response to audience feedback is more immediate. This feeling helps keep the audience involved, which, in turn, promotes confidence in the speaker.

Perhaps one of the most successful moments in speechmaking in recent history occurred when Martin Luther King, Jr., spoke extemporaneously at the Lincoln Memorial in 1963. His ringing words proclaimed "I have a dream." The moment is captured by Reverend Ralph Abernathy:

It is the usual custom of a preacher as he finishes a prepared text to say some other words. Here he establishes eye contact with his audience. On this day, Martin Luther King's speech really began when he left his text. He said, "I have a dream," in a very musical voice, and he lifted his hands in oration. As he lifted his hands, the people lifted theirs, and he went on.

"I have a dream that one day on the red hills of Georgia, the sons of former slaves and the sons of former slave owners will be able to sit down together at the table of brotherhood. . . . I have a dream that my four little children will one day live in a nation where they will not be judged by the color of their skin, but by the content of their character. . . ." People were standing on their seats, yelling "Amen!" and those who were not standing began to applaud. He was calling for integration at its best, for the tearing down of walls of an unjust system. He was expressing the longings, hopes and dreams of every person in that assembly of 250,000 people. He took the audience higher and higher, and as he left, the entire group rose to its feet. It was one of the greatest moments in the history of our nation.[2]

In Abernathy's words, the key moment in King's speech was the point where he began to extemporize. His attempts at audience involvement were an immediate success.

On a lesser scale, King's skills as a public speaker can be compared to others you may know. Please consider the following:

Harriet Gaynor teaches Economics 200, a required course for all liberal arts and sciences students at Western University. Over the years, Harriet has developed a reputation on campus as a superior lecturer. She teaches multiple sections of this course. Much of her success is a result of the tremendous amount of time she spends preparing her material. She practices each lecture to become familiar with the *ideas* she wishes to present. Although she brings the same outline to each section of Economics 200, the words she delivers to each class differ. Her choice of words grows out of her relationship with each class. The humor, pace, and movement in each lecture depends on the feedback she receives from her class.

Application Activity

DEVELOPING AN AWARENESS OF THE QUALITIES OF GOOD SPEECH DELIVERY

1. Name the speaker you most admire.

2. List several of his or her positive speaking behaviors.

3. Which type of delivery best reflects the speaking characteristics of this person?

Professor Gaynor's ability to rely on the extemporaneous delivery has contributed to her success as a speaker and teacher. The flexibility and adaptability inherent in the extemporaneous delivery allow for a degree of give and take between speaker and audience.

SHARING IDEAS

Every speech delivery is enhanced by the speaker's ability to share ideas. The more a speaker can concentrate on the ideas in the speech rather than on himself or herself or the speaking situation, the more likely the receiver also will concentrate on those ideas. In other words, the speaker's goal is to get his or her audience just as involved in the subject as he or she is. This objective is possible only if the speaker is genuinely interested in the topic. A lukewarm attitude will not get the audience's attention.

The individual who is able to concentrate on sharing his or her ideas will develop into a more confident, effective speaker. Several factors discussed in this section will aid the speaker in communicating with confidence to the audience.

Spontaneity

Just as involvement leads to greater sharing of ideas, so too does a feeling of spontaneity with the audience. **Spontaneity** refers to a speaker's apparent natural behavior at the time of delivery. As a speaker's involvement with the topic increases and his or her concentration becomes focused on ideas, he or she sends signals of spontaneity and immediacy that are absent from memorized and manuscript deliveries. Words chosen spontaneously convey to an audience that the sender both is interested in the topic and wants to share his or her ideas. Not only are the words more appropriate to the audience, but the accompanying vocal inflections add to the interest, further capturing the attention of the audience.

The same is true of movements and gestures. The speaker may not be aware of facial expressions, gestures, or bodily movements, but when spontaneous, these reiterate the desire to share. For example, a preplanned gesture, such as mechanically pointing a finger when a certain word is said, can communicate an aura of superficiality. However, the same gesture made spontaneously will help draw the audience more completely into the talk.

Sincerity

Another key component to sharing ideas is the incorporation of **sincerity** into the presentation; that is, a speaker wants to show the audience that he or she cares about the topic and its presentation. By doing so, the speaker may capture the audience's interest in the topic. The speaker wants to start a chain reaction from speaker to audience. In turn, the positive feedback he or she gets from the

The "Bizarro" cartoon by Dan Piraro is reprinted by permission of Chronicle Features, San Francisco.

audience will help the speaker feel more confident during the speech and in subsequent speeches as well. Audience support builds confidence.

Using Your Body

Effective use of your body is another way to enhance your speech. Your nonverbal communication can convey as much to the audience as the words in your speech. In fact, your bodily actions can reinforce the major ideas in the presentation. Becoming aware of some of the ways to use your body to increase audience involvement and understanding is highly desirable. Many components contribute to the role your body plays in delivering a speech, including gestures, facial expressions, walking transitions, appearance, posture, and eye contact.

Gestures   Hand movement in a speech delivery should be spontaneous; in other words, it should *naturally* stem from the speaker's involvement with the subject. Your hands can be used to emphasize or clarify your ideas.

Gestures are useful only as long as they remain natural. Adding gestures for the sake of incorporating movement into the delivery will detract from, not enhance, your presentation. John Kennedy, for example, would point his finger aggressively in an effort to drive home his points. This technique was successful in conveying his *commitment* to the ideas he was presenting. As he delivered his ideas, he felt the *need* to emphasize a point; therefore, his gesture was natural and appeared to be spontaneous.

Facial Expressions   Your face usually communicates your feelings, so use it to help communicate your message to the audience. As with gestures, your facial expressions should be spontaneous, arising naturally from your involvement with your topic. Allowing the audience to see your commitment to your topic also may elicit their interest; knowing that you have the audience's attention gives your confidence as a public speaker a welcome boost. Good technique obviously has its rewards.

We can look to the 1984 Presidential primary race for an example of inappropriate use of facial expression. Walter Mondale, the early frontrunner for the Democratic nomination, experienced several upsets during the campaign, especially his losses to Senator Gary Hart in New Hampshire, Florida, and Massachusetts. In interviews following these defeats, Mondale claimed he was still confident that he would be the party's nominee, yet his smile on camera appeared forced and unnatural. His uneasiness was apparent to the viewing audience. In contrast, consider the following example, in which a natural expression of emotion is displayed to the audience:

> Susan was a student in Communication 101. She decided to draw from her experiences as an aide at the Bollingstone Nursing Home as the basis for her speech. Specifically, she focused on the relationship she had developed with one of her patients. Over the course of a few months, Susan had come to know Mrs. Steele. This bright woman had been in the nursing home for two years, and she deeply resented what her life had become. In their frequent conversations Susan was successful in getting Mrs. Steele to let her guard down. What this woman feared most was slipping into senility, as so many of the other nursing home residents had already done. For both

Good speakers make effective use of body actions.

women, this admission was charged with emotion. Susan's insight into the elderly was deepened by this experience, and she focused her speech on this important event. While describing the situation to her audience, Susan's tear-filled eyes clearly expressed her emotions. This natural expression captured the attention and support of the class.

Walking Transitions   Foot movement can also be used to enhance your talk. More important, foot movement can help the speaker decrease the amount of physical distance between himself or herself and the audience. Foot movement has the benefit of reducing the speaker's dependency on the lectern. It also allows the speaker to divert some of his or her excess energy, thereby relieving the mental anxiety associated with talking before an audience. Taking a step or two forward to emphasize a point or turning slightly during a transition captures the group's attention and shows your involvement with the presentation.

When incorporating walking transitions, make sure that they grow out of your involvement with the presentation. They should not detract from your speech. If you have a reason to move about, you will avoid overuse. When you appear relaxed enough to move about in front of your audience, your efforts will contribute to a greater sense of confidence on your part.

Appearance   The speaker's appearance also communicates a message to the audience. The members of the audience *see* you before they *hear* you speak; consequently, their first impression of you can be shaped by your appearance. In formal settings we see political

Application Activity

LEARN TO INCORPORATE MOVEMENT IN YOUR SPEECH

1. In small groups develop short skits to present to the rest of the class. During these pantomimes, only bodily actions should be used to communicate your ideas to the class. One further stipulation applies: *All* members of the group should participate in the movement so that they gain practical experience before an audience.

2. How did your classmates use their bodies to communicate their ideas?

Appearance was one of the determining factors in the Kennedy-Nixon debate in 1959.

speakers paying particular attention to their appearance. The impact of Richard Nixon's appearance in his historic debate with John Kennedy dramatically illustrates this point.[3] Many politicians recall Nixon's haggard image during the televised debates; his light-colored suit looked dull under studio lighting, and his five o'clock shadow made an especially bad impression. Nixon's painful experience provided a lesson for other political candidates. In more recent presidential debates, the candidates have paid particular attention to the way they look on camera.

Although personal attire does not play a significant role in classroom speeches, you should make sure that your appearance does not draw the audience away from your intended message. For example, a wild hairdo will surely distract the audience. You do not want the audience to pay more attention to what you are wearing than to what you are saying to them. In fact, if your audience's attention is focused on your appearance, it is probably safe to say that your appearance is doing you a disservice. In deciding what to wear, consider both the audience and the nature of the speaking situation. For example, a talk with high-school students about drug abuse would call for casual attire (no suits), while a presentation to a group of business managers would call for a suit (no jeans with sweaters). Both audiences would likely be uncomfortable if the speakers dressed differently.

Posture   Good posture is one aspect of bodily action that commands the attention of your audience. When speaking in front of a group, avoid slouching over or bending your knees; keep your spine straight, your shoulders back, and your feet a comfortable distance apart. You do not, however, want to look like a soldier standing at attention. Avoid a rigid stance because it communicates that you are tense and inhibits any other natural movement. Avoid, too, appearing so loose and casual that you find yourself leaning against the blackboard or sprawling over the lectern. Finally, avoid shifting your weight from foot to foot as you speak.

Good posture can enhance your presentation because you will appear more confident and involved in the topic. You want the audience to concentrate on what you are sharing; proper posture will not detract from this goal. Instead, it will reinforce your image as a well-prepared, confident public speaker.

Eye Contact   Perhaps one of the most difficult skills for the public speaker to master is direct eye contact. As mentioned earlier, your eyes are one of your most revealing features; therefore, a conscious effort to establish direct eye contact acknowledges that you wish to draw the audience in. Understandably, many speakers feel anxious about this task. However, the rewards are gratifying—your audience will feel more involved in your presentation, and you will be able to see it on their faces and in their eyes.

For many it is easier to establish direct eye contact with a small audience, because the size of the group is less threatening. Even with a small group, however, it is difficult to establish direct eye contact with every member of the audience; an attempt to do so will result in little more than scanning the audience. This is not direct eye contact; rather, it is a mechanical back-and-forth motion. Some speakers tend to look above the heads of those in the audience in an effort to appear to be looking at everyone. Still others simply stare out a window or keep their eyes glued to their notes. These techniques prohibit the speaker from responding to any feedback the audience sends.

What the speaker needs to do is establish direct eye contact with certain members of the audience. I suggest picking individuals who are scattered in different parts of the room. For your first speeches, try to include people with whom you feel comfortable or those who you believe will be supportive. Doing so will make it

Application Activity

PRACTICING EYE CONTACT

1. Practice establishing direct eye contact with people you are comfortable with, such as close friends and family members.

2. Practice this skill while participating in small groups.

3. Next, establish direct eye contact with members of an audience.

easier for you to practice this technique and to respond to any feedback they might give you. As you gain experience and confidence, you will be able to gradually include members of the audience whom you do not know, as well as those who give negative feedback. You need to respond to both positive and negative feedback in order to make your speech more effective.

In our culture, direct eye contact is extremely important because it communicates confidence and the appearance of a strong self-image. In addition, it shows concern about communicating with others. An audience can sense when a speaker is in control and usually reacts favorably as a result. Naturally, a boost to one's self-image will provide greater confidence for subsequent speeches. This "snowball" effect leads to growth and maturity for the public speaker.

Learning to use direct eye contact is like learning any other skill: practice is the key ingredient. At first, your attempts may seem mechanical. You may feel uncomfortable because you are self-conscious about your behavior. With time and practice, however, direct eye contact can become a natural part of your communication behavior. Know in advance that many people in the audience will be unable to establish direct eye contact with you; this does not mean that they are rejecting you.

Using Your Voice

Your voice gives meaning to the words in your speech. Your voice can reflect the way you feel about your topic; therefore, you can use it to emphasize points. For example, a voice that quivers during the eulogy at a friend's funeral expresses the speaker's sorrow and pain. Likewise, a voice that grows louder reflects anger or passion about some issue, for example, a speaker's outrage over the number of homeless people in the United States and the lack of assistance governmental agencies provide. It is equally important that you pronounce words clearly and precisely so that the audience will understand your message. Several vocal aspects of delivery are discussed below, including volume, rate, inflection, pause, and pronunciation and articulation.

Volume **Volume** refers to the loudness of a speaker's voice. Before the use of electronic devices, it was essential for an individual to speak in a loud and powerful voice. This holds true in the classroom as well, since it is not likely that you will have the opportunity to use a microphone. Consequently, you will find it necessary to adjust your voice so that all members of the audience will be able to hear your message. If your audience must strain to hear you, they will probably miss a large part of your message. In fact, you run the risk of losing them altogether as responsive members. Additionally, if you speak very softly, you may appear to lack confidence.

By the same token, you do not want to shout or scream at your audience in order to capture their attention. Shouting can be construed as overdramatization and may communicate to your audience that you are not sincere about the ideas you are sharing with them. Instead, it appears that you are acting a part in a play.

The level of your voice should correspond to the way you treat your topic. There will be times when you will want to raise or lower your voice based on your feelings about the subject. Let the volume of your voice change as a result of your enthusiasm for the topic.

Rate The **rate** of your speech is dependent on the number of words you deliver in a given amount of time. Most Americans deliver between 120 and 150 words per minute. Your rate should vary, depending on the speaking situation. The appropriate rate will grow out of the relationship among the audience, the message, and the speaker. Furthermore, the rate will fluctuate throughout the speech; there will be moments when you find it necessary to pick up the pace and other times when you find it more appropriate to slow down.

Although some beginning speakers talk too slowly, most novices experience the opposite problem—they tend to speak too rapidly. Anxiety usually causes this condition. When we get nervous, we tend to speak more rapidly owing to excess tension. The difficulty of the situation is compounded when the audience is unable to comprehend the message.

Special efforts are necessary first to identify and then to correct this problem. For instance, it is helpful to listen to your voice on a tape recorder. This gives you an opportunity to hear the speed at which you speak, thereby increasing your awareness of the problem. A friend or family member also can help by listening to you practice your speech. Ask that person to listen specifically to whether you deliver your speech too rapidly. Finally, indicate in italic print in your notes to *slow down* at particular points. Such reminders will keep you aware of your speaking rate during your delivery.

Inflection   Think of how boring it is to listen to a speech delivered in a monotone voice. **Inflection** is the tone of your voice. Lack of variety in vocal inflection has been known to put more than one audience to sleep. The inflection of your voice can and should change as you move to different points in the speech. As you try to stir your audience, for example, the pitch of your voice should rise.

Pause   It is virtually impossible to deliver a speech without inserting some pauses. There are a few places in a speech where pauses can be very effective. First, a pause is helpful as you shift from one idea to the next. This gives your audience a sense that you are about to move on to another point. Furthermore, it allows your audience time to assimilate new or complex ideas. Second, pauses are used effectively when you are striving for emphasis.

When President Reagan announced to the nation January 29, 1984, that he would seek a second term in office, his speech demonstrated the drama that can be stirred in an audience. After speaking about the problems that had plagued America when he took office in 1980, he moved on to discuss the accomplishments of his administration and his goals for the future. Finally, following an effective, suspenseful pause, he delivered his punch line—he would be seeking reelection. His well-placed pause enabled him to add some drama to the moment.

The technique of using well-placed pauses is developed with practice. As you become more adept at using pauses, you will achieve your goal of sustaining the audience's interest. An audience often responds to a pause by looking up at the speaker. They are waiting to hear more. You have got their attention—now proceed.

Vocalized pauses such as *ah*, *um*, and *you know* should not be confused with well-placed silent pauses. In fact, these interjections can be interpreted as signs of nervousness or lack of adequate preparation and will detract from your effectiveness and credibility as a speaker.

Pronunciation and Articulation   If your audience is to understand the words in your speech, you must say them correctly (**pronunciation**) and clearly (**articulation**). A common occurrence in speech is the mispronunciation of words. We have all done it at one time or another and have probably suffered a degree of embarrassment when the error was pointed out. For example, the following table illustrates four words that are frequently mispronounced:

WORD	COMMON MISPRONUNCIATION	CORRECT PRONUNCIATION
February	Feb-u-ary	Feb-ru-ary
disastrous	di-sas-ter-ous	di-sas-trous
burglar	bur-ga-lar	bur-glar
athlete	ath-a-lete	ath-lete

To ensure that your delivery is free of mispronunciations, consult a dictionary for those words you have any doubt about. Also, practicing your delivery in front of a friend or family member may help catch errors.

Articulation refers to the clear or distinct pronunciation of words. It is not identical to pronunciation, for you can say a word crisply but still mispronounce it (for example, saying the *w* in *sword* or the *l* in *salmon* is a mistake in pronunciation). A few general pointers may give you more confidence over the question of articulation. Avoid the following when delivering your speech: (1) run-

"NO 'ERS', NO 'Y'KNOWS', NO 'WHATCHAMACALLITS',
NO 'UMS' — AREN'T YOU EVER AT A LOSS FOR WORDS?"

Application Activity

PRACTICE USING YOUR VOICE

1. Select an emotionally charged "Letter to the Editor" from your local newspaper.

2. Try to read the letter as if you had written it. In other words, try to recreate the feelings of the writer as you recite it aloud.

3. As you read the letter, pay attention to volume, rate, inflection, pauses, and proper pronunciation and articulation. If there are any words that you are having difficulty pronouncing, consult your favorite dictionary.

4. Reflection: How do you think this procedure can help you practice using your voice for your own presentations?

ning words together, such as "wanna" for *want to* or "didja" for *did you*; (2) omitting word endings, such as "havin" for *having* or "runnin" for *running*; and (3) sloppy articulation, such as "git" for *get* or "fer" for *for*. This type of carelessness can contribute to a lack of understanding on the part of the audience. To improve your articulation, practice reading passages aloud at a slow pace. This will help you to emphasize each word, which in turn will increase your awareness of appropriate articulation.

PRACTICING YOUR SPEECH

I have discussed several steps that are designed to help you feel more confident when you are required to speak in public. Implementing the skills associated with these ideas will help you feel more self-assured and in control. The finishing touches for your presentation are achieved through practice. The following are several steps that will help you to prepare to speak in front of an audience:

1. Begin to practice the speech aloud. There are several techniques you can use to become comfortable with your material. First, try to become familiar with your ideas. This necessitates going through the speech completely several times. Even if you make a mistake, continue to go through the speech until you reach its conclusion. This will help you to grasp the ideas and keep you focused on the ideas when you actually deliver the speech.

Videotaping your practice speech will allow you to both see and hear your delivery.

2. Once you become comfortable with the ideas, you need to re-fine your delivery. Begin to practice your delivery in front of a mir-ror. Take note of your movement, and keep in mind that any move-ment should reflect your involvement with the ideas. If you notice any annoying mannerisms, try to refrain from repeating them. You also may choose to use a tape recorder to check the quality of your voice. This can be especially helpful if you are having a difficult time with pronunciation. Finally, if a video camera and recorder are available to you, consider taping your delivery. Video equipment has the advantage of combining the techniques just mentioned—in a single operation you can both see and hear your delivery.

3. Once you have practiced your speech in front of the mirror or have taped your delivery, you may wish to elicit feedback from friends and family. While you are delivering your speech to the au-dience at home, practice establishing direct eye contact with them. This will help you to incorporate direct eye contact with members of your actual audience.

4. Once you feel comfortable with your presentation at home, you also may wish to practice the speech in an empty classroom. Do so *before* the day that the speech is scheduled. This will give you an opportunity to become familiar with the setting of the speech.

Keep in mind that each individual's background brings a uniqueness to any topic he or she chooses to share with an audience. Believing that you have something special to share will give you a tremendous boost in confidence.

SUMMARY

This chapter provided information to help you deliver a more effective speech. Stage fright is a fear common to many people, but there are ways to cope with it. These include reducing excess tension, focusing on the topic, realizing that you are not alone, and developing a positive attitude. If you can remember to keep public speaking in its proper perspective, you will be less fearful of speaking in front of an audience.

There are four different types of speech delivery: impromptu, manuscript, memorized, and extemporaneous. Of these, the extemporaneous delivery has a major advantage; the speaker prepares the topic in advance, but the delivery is still flexible enough to allow the speaker to adapt to the audience.

There are several techniques you can learn to improve your ability to share ideas with an audience. Spontaneity and sincerity are two important aspects of delivery. In addition, you can use your body to its best advantage by incorporating the following into the delivery: natural gestures, facial expression, walking transitions, appropriate appearance, good posture, and direct eye contact. Still another way to enhance delivery involves the use of your voice. Volume, rate, inflection, appropriately placed pauses, and pronunciation and articulation are factors to consider when delivering your speech. Your confidence as a speaker will increase as you learn to effectively incorporate these techniques into your delivery.

Finally, there are suggested steps to follow when practicing your delivery. Once you feel comfortable with the material, begin practicing the speech aloud. Whether you do this in front of a mirror, a video camera, or your family, remember that you have something of value to share with the audience. Practicing your delivery should increase your confidence, because you will know that you have adequately prepared for your presentation.

REVIEW QUESTIONS

1. What steps can you take to help control speech anxiety?
2. Name the four methods of speech delivery and briefly describe each one.

3. Why is it important for your bodily movements to be spontaneous?
4. Why is it helpful for a speaker to establish direct eye contact with an audience?
5. What are the different ways in which you can use your voice to improve your delivery?
6. What steps can you use to practice your delivery?

NOTES

1. For the complete text of Kennedy's speech, see John F. Kennedy, "Cuba Quarantined and Khrushchev Challenged," in Allan Nevins (Ed.), *The Burden and the Glory* (New York: Harper & Row, 1964), pp. 89–96.
2. Ralph Abernathy, "Martin Luther King's Dream," in Lynda Rosen Obst (Ed.), *The Sixties: The Decade Remembered Now, By the People Who Lived it Then* (New York: Random House, Rolling Stone Press, 1977), p. 94.
3. *Newsweek*, October 10, 1960, p. 25.

ADDITIONAL READINGS

An asterisk indicates an advanced reading.

Kougl, K. M. "Dealing with Quiet Students in the Basic College Speech Course." *Communication Education* 29: 234–8, 1980.
    This is a sensitively written article dealing with the subject of shyness.

Mayer, L. V. *Fundamentals of Voice and Diction*, 8th Ed. Dubuque, Iowa: Wm. C. Brown, 1988.
    This book provides helpful information and exercises in pronunciation and articulation.

*Page, W. T. "Rhetoritherapy vs. Behavior Therapy: Issues and Evidence." *Communication Education* 29: 95–104, 1980.
    This article explores and evaluates two viewpoints on communication anxiety.

*Phillips, G. M. "Reticence: Pathology of the Normal Speaker." *Speech Monographs* 35: 39–49, 1968.
    This is an important early article that discusses reticence.

14

The Informative Speech

Learning Objectives

At the conclusion of this chapter you should be able to

1. Explain the purpose of an informative speech.

2. Describe three ways to make a topic relevant to the audience.

3. List several appropriate informative speech topics.

4. Structure an effective informative speech.

5. Use the methods of narration, description, definition, and demonstration to present an informative speech.

We have now come to a chapter on the informative speech. Before we begin our discussion about the special qualities of this type of speech, it might be helpful to review how we got to this point. You will soon discover that all the necessary tools for preparing and delivering an informative speech were provided in the previous four chapters on public speaking.

Chapter 10 provided you with the foundation for public speaking and gave you direction; armed with a topic, a purpose, and a sense of your audience, you were ready for the next step in preparing a public speech—gathering materials. In Chapter 11 you discovered that your credibility as a speaker, and your topic itself, could be enhanced by supporting materials gathered from such sources as interviews, newspapers, periodicals, and books. What did you do with this additional information? You incorporated it into the development of your speech. Chapter 12 showed you how, by ordering the ideas related to your topic, you could develop a logical, fluent speech. Outlining these ideas proved to be a systematic way to further develop your speech. At last you were ready for the delivery. Chapter 13 provided you with techniques for translating your written ideas into an effective oral presentation. Now let us put into practice all that you have learned, beginning with the informative speech.

THE NATURE OF THE INFORMATIVE SPEECH

The purpose of an informative speech is to educate an audience. "About what?" we might ask. Today we live in an information age that bombards us with new facts and ideas each day, yet we cannot

Governor Michael Dukakis of Massachusetts speaking against drugs.

possibly digest all this information, nor do we desire to. Rather, we make decisions about what interests us, and then we focus our attention on those issues and ideas. This becomes a key consideration when we select a topic for an informative speech and when we develop that topic.

Unlike the **persuasive speech,** whose purpose is to change an attitude, the overriding concern of the **informative speech** is to impart knowledge. Your appeal as a speaker is directed at the audience's desire for information that matters. In other words, you must operate on the premise that the members of your audience are eager to learn something new and that part of your function is to make the information relevant to them. How do you accomplish this?

Your first objective is to *engage your audience.* Ask yourself such questions as, "What do I know about the demographics of this audience?" and "What do I know about this group's attitudes and interests?" By making these data the basis for a topic that will appeal to the needs or interests of the audience, you will likely be successful at drawing the audience's attention and establishing the relevance of your topic. For example, at first glance, individual retirement accounts (IRAs) may not seem like an engaging issue for an audience between the ages of twenty and thirty-five. Look what happens, however, when you shift the focus of the subject: "By the time your generation reaches retirement age, the Social Security system will likely be bankrupt. For that reason, I would like to provide you with information about a viable alternative—individual retirement accounts."

The AIDS issue also illustrates the point about relevance and the audience's desire for information. When the first AIDS cases were reported in 1981, the American public saw little need for concern—after all, these cases were restricted to an isolated population of homosexual men and intravenous drug users.[1] By the mid '80s, however, over 1000 new cases were being reported in the United States each year.[2] The public craved information and was especially receptive to information presented in simple, clear terms.

This leads us to a second important quality of the informative speech—*simplicity.* If your audience is unfamiliar with your topic, yet you have succeeded in capturing their interest, it is crucial that you present your information so that it is easily digested. A sure way to lose an audience is to present information that is too complex or sophisticated for them to comprehend as you are speaking. This is not to say that the development of your topic should be simplistic; it should, however, be easy enough to follow. Pure understanding is essential to an informative speech. If the members of your audience cannot understand a point, they are apt to stop listening. When that happens, the relevance of your speech vanishes.

An informative speech with clear, easily understood ideas is made even better by the use of *appropriate language.* To a large degree, whether or not ideas are understood depends on the words you use. Concrete, descriptive terms help any audience to understand new ideas. It is therefore wise to limit the use of abstract language.

The remainder of this chapter is divided into three sections: (1) informative speech topics, (2) organizing the informative speech, and (3) methods for presenting an informative speech. At the end of the chapter you will find a sample informative speech, complete with commentary.

INFORMATIVE SPEECH TOPICS

As a speaker, you have the luxury of drawing from a vast body of potential topics for an informative speech. What you *do* with that topic determines whether or not your speech will be successful or unsuccessful. The key ingredient is discovering how to develop the topic to make it relevant to your audience. For example, a high-school football team needs to listen to the coach's detailed strategy for Friday night's game, yet high-school faculty interest would be limited. Similarly, an instructor would present different speeches about seeing-eye dogs to a blind audience and an audience with sight. For the first audience, the focus might be on instructing students how to use a guide dog; for the second audience, the focus might shift to working with blind students who use guide dogs. Whatever the topic, it must be adapted to the audience.

The bulk of informative speech topics fall into one of the following categories: recreation, concepts, places, objects, and people.

Recreation

One area that offers several topics for the informative speech is recreation. Activities such as sports, exercise, hobbies, and moviegoing have a broad appeal. You can easily develop speeches that take a "how to" approach, such as how to play handball or croquet, how to

An informative speech about wind surfing can be both exciting and useful.

carve a watermelon into a whale, or how to plan a cross-country biking trip. There are also all sorts of prospects for pointing out the benefits of recreational activities, as in this example:

> Cathleen believes in the value of aerobic exercise for a healthy cardiovascular system. She wants her audience to know about the steps involved in getting started with a dance aerobics program. She also discusses some of the specific exercises designed for beginners. She feels that her speech will meet the audience's need to stay fit.

Cathleen's effort to give her audience information that was related to their well-being helped reinforce the relevance of her speech.

Concepts

Topics for informative speeches can be drawn from **concepts,** that is, ideas, theories, or thoughts generally used to explain abstract subjects, such as dream interpretation, supply-side economics, or bigotry. Because concepts are often abstract, your purpose will be, in part, to explain in more concrete language the ideas inherent in the topic. Your goal is to have the audience arrive at a better understanding of the concept by the speech's conclusion.

Places

As the subject of informative speeches, places can include such things as institutions, historical sites, cities, geologic landforms, and buildings. Specific examples are Wrigley Field, the Lincoln Memorial, Kilimanjaro. Consider the following:

> Nels is a student at a mid-sized Georgia college. He wants to tell a group of his fraternity brothers about the excitement of Chicago, where he recently visited some cousins. In order to give them a flavor of what Chicago has to offer, he decides to talk about Rush Street—the fast pace, the dozens of restaurants and nightclubs, and the atmosphere of sexuality that pervades the area. By the time he has completed this description, his friends are more than a little intrigued by this street in the Windy City.

When you give a speech about a place you have visited, you have the opportunity to bring some of your own experiences to the topic. Your efforts are likely to maintain the audience's interest.

Objects

Our environment is filled with thousands of unique and interesting objects; many make ideal subjects for an informative speech. When speaking about an object, you might explain how its use has a special significance for your audience. A few objects you might choose to discuss include computers, video cameras, or antique cars.

When you speak about an object, your purpose might be to explain its use, its appeal to a particular segment of the population, or its impact on society. For example,

Terri is a market research analyst for General Motors. She is scheduled to speak to a group of design engineers about the relationship between cars and cul-

An informative speech about a beautiful place, such as the canyon being painted by this artist, can open up a whole new area of experience for your audience.

ture. Specifically, she plans to focus her comments on the car-buying trends of baby boomers, those individuals born between 1946 and 1964, because they represent the largest group of consumers in the United States. She also makes some predictions about what features will appeal to this consumer group in the future and projects the average price they will be able to afford. Terri's information is invaluable to the engineers because it gives them ideas concerning additional features to include in the cars they produce over the next few years.

Terri's success in this example can be attributed to her efforts to tailor the information to the needs of her audience.

People

People represent a tremendous source for speech topics. You can easily develop a fascinating informative speech about an individual or a group of people, such as political leaders, steelworkers, or professional boxers. If you decide to speak about a person or group of people, try highlighting their unique qualities, contributions, or importance. For example, you might focus on the impact Steven Spielberg has had on the motion picture industry, the contributions of Martin Luther King, Jr., to the Civil Rights Movement, or the role played by Oliver North in the Iran-*contra* scandal. Table 14.1 provides a summary of informative speech topics.

Application Activity

WRITING AN INFORMATIVE SPEECH OBJECTIVE

1. Pick three speech topics, each one from a different category just described (for example, one topic about a concept, one topic about a place, and so on).

2. Write a clear informative speech objective for each topic you choose. Refer to Chapter 10 for assistance with this task.

3. Consider the factors of triggering the audience's needs and the topic's relevance to the audience as you do this activity.

TABLE 14.1　Informative Speech Topics

RECREATION	CONCEPTS	PLACES
Ballroom dancing	Altruism	Colonial Williamsburg
Baseball	Buying on margin	Epcot
Gardening	Feminism	The Everglades
Movies	Preparing a will	Moscow
Shopping	Totalitarianism	Niagara Falls

OBJECTS	PEOPLE
Clocks	Artists
Microwave ovens	The Beatles
Pianos	David Letterman
Shaker furniture	Presidential candidates
Skiing equipment	Gloria Steinem

ORGANIZING THE INFORMATIVE SPEECH

It may be helpful to review the material in Chapter 12 as you begin to structure your informative speech. There you will find a discussion about organizational patterns for the ideas in your topic; suggestions for developing the body, introduction, conclusion, and transitions; and outlining principles. Because you are working on an informative speech, you must always bear in mind that your purpose is to fill an information need of your audience. Your speech should first engage the audience's interest and then strive to present ideas that can be easily understood, always with the intent to maintain the relevance of your topic.

In the body of the speech, where you will focus your attention first, make sure to use an organizational structure that best fits the purpose of your speech. For instance, if your purpose is to explain the decline of the Chicago Bears in the 1986 National Football Conference playoffs, you may wish to organize your ideas in terms of causal order. After identifying the reasons for the Bears' dismal performance in the game against the Washington Redskins, you might discuss the long-term effects on the team for the season that followed. Similarly, if you want to explain how to bake lasagna, you could follow a chronological order which would take the audience

Application Activity

DEVELOPING AN INFORMATIVE SPEECH

1. Select a subject from the list of informative speech topics identified earlier in this chapter or one of your own to develop a five- to seven-minute informative speech.

2. Organize the presentation in a pattern that best reflects the purpose of the speech.

3. Develop a full-sentence speech outline using the outlining principles discussed in Chapter 12.

step by step through the process. The key is to identify the organizational pattern that best relates to the purpose of your speech.

As mentioned in Chapter 12, it is advisable to limit the number of points you plan to present in the body of an informative speech. The audience will have an easier time absorbing the information in a speech that has a well-developed theme rather than one that is overburdened with minute facts. While facts are essential to the development of a topic, it is counterproductive to overwhelm the audience with excessive details.

When you construct an introduction, remember that your intent is to trigger a need in the audience. You want to demonstrate why it is important for them to listen to your presentation. Try to do this by highlighting ways in which the information is relevant to them. For instance, if you plan to inform the audience about ways to improve relationships, you might point out how this information will benefit their relationships. It is critical to encourage the audience to listen to you as you develop your ideas.

In the conclusion, summarize your ideas and suggest to the audience what it is you want them to walk away with after listening to your speech. If you have explained a new procedure to the audience, you will want to encourage them to be patient as they attempt this new task. Furthermore, you might suggest sources where they can gain additional information on the process you have just explained.

Finally, transitions should be used as a bridge between the major parts of the speech and to reinforce the points you present in the body. These transitions help your audience to retain the information you impart.

This speaker is using a diagram to demonstrate his point.

METHODS FOR PRESENTING AN INFORMATIVE SPEECH

The effectiveness of an informative speech depends on the development of the topic and on your ability to narrate, describe, define, and demonstrate the ideas in your speech. These skills are discussed in the following section.

Narration

One way to present material in an informative speech is with a narrative. A **narrative** is a story or an account of an event told orally. The speaker can use a narrative to introduce a speech or to illustrate or clarify a point within a speech. In order to be effective, a narrative should evoke a feeling of "being there." When the members of an audience are able to visualize a point the speaker is trying to make, they develop a better understanding of the topic.

Narratives should use vivid language, should be easy to follow, and should avoid being too lengthy. You can create your own narrative for an informative speech, or you can quote the written or oral narratives of others. For example, to illustrate her point about the benefit of sharing feelings, Janet decided to quote some dialogue between Conrad and Dr. Berger, two characters from Judith Guest's book, *Ordinary People*:

> "That box," he says. "I feel like I've been in it for-ever. Everybody looking in, to see how you're doing. Even when they're on your side, they're still looking in. Like, nobody can get in there with you."
> "Yeah. Not much fun, is it?"
> "No. But sometimes I can get out of it, now. And then, there's you." He clears his throat nervously. "I never saw you out there, you know? You, I always saw inside the box. With me." He laughs, suddenly embarrassed. His face is hot. He brings his gaze to the opposite wall, glaring at the books, daring them to move from the shelves, daring the windows to shatter. "What I'm saying . . . I guess I think of you as a friend."[3]

The narrative here is effective because it successfully transports the audience to the room where Conrad and Dr. Berger are speaking and it allows the audience to feel the emotions being shared by these two men.

In a narrative, the speaker also can use personal experience as the basis for a story. In this example, Nancy Reagan tells her audience about her awakening to the widespread problem of drug abuse:

> Let me begin by taking you back, if I may, and telling you of my personal journey of awareness and commitment in regard to drug abuse . . . because in many ways my journey reflects that of the nation as a whole.
> I first became aware of the problem in the '60s in Sacramento when my husband was Governor. To be honest, I really didn't understand the scope or the intensity of the problem then. Few of us did. But I knew something was happening to our children, something very tragic—even deadly.
> I began getting calls from friends—calls of hurt and embarrassment and self-consciousness that their child could be on drugs—calls of confusion and ig-norance about what was happening to their family,

Application Activity

NARRATION

1. Select a topic to share with an audience.

2. First, write down a personal experience that helps communicate your feelings about this subject.

3. Next, gather outside resources to help illustrate your feelings about the topic. Write down the information as a narrative.

4. Share both narratives with a classmate.

5. Use the feedback from your classmate to improve one of the narratives for your next speech.

> and on occasion calls of great pain at the loss of a son
> or daughter.
> We were all so naive then.[4]

An audience is often drawn to a personalized account related to the speech topic, as illustrated in this example.

Description

A **description** is an image that is created verbally. In an informative speech, a description can be used to effectively communicate a speaker's ideas. *How* effectively depends on the language used. Descriptions that use **concrete terms**, where the language is detailed and specific, are easier for an audience to visualize than descriptions that use **abstract terms**, where the language is general or vague. A speaker might describe an object by telling about its shape, size, color, or texture. He or she uses words to paint a picture that the audience can visualize. Adjectives generally work best for this purpose, since by definition they act as descriptors. The following is a very effective description of Alzheimer's disease:

> Of all the incurable diseases, the degenerative brain
> disorder known as Alzheimer's may be the cruelest,
> because it kills its victims twice. In Alzheimer's, the
> mind dies first: names, dates, places—the interior
> scrapbook of an entire life—fade into mists of nonrec-
> ognition. The simplest tasks—tying a shoelace, cut-

Application Activity

DESCRIPTION

1. Take the topic of friendship and write a description of what it means to you.

2. Be sure to use concrete language, as shown in the first example describing Alzheimer's disease.

3. After you have completed describing the concept of friendship, share it with another member of the class.

ting meat with a knife, telling time—become insurmountable. Then, the body dies. No longer able to walk or control elemental functions, the victim lies curled in a fetal position, gradually sinking into coma and death.[5]

The following description of Alzheimer's disease pales by comparison: "Alzheimer's disease is a tragic disease that affects both its victims and their families." An audience, after hearing this description, would have little sense of how this disease affects its victims. The vague language used here fails to promote understanding.

Definition

Definition is a valuable form of support in the informative speech (see Chapter 11). Terms that are generally unfamiliar to an audience, however, need to be defined in language that the audience can easily understand. There are a number of ways to accomplish this, including the use of synonyms, antonyms, comparisons, and etymology.

One way to define a term is by using synonyms. **Synonyms** are different words that have the same or nearly the same meaning. Substituting the word *customs* for *mores* or *drunkenness* for *insobriety* can help to clarify the definition of an idea in your speech.

A speaker also can use **antonyms**, words that have opposite meanings, to define a concept for the audience. *Despair* is an antonym for *hope*. For instance, a speaker might use the word *despair* as an antonym for *hope* and talk in terms of a "hopeful future in light of a despairing past."

Application Activity

DEFINING

1. Define the concept of peace by

  a. Using synonyms

  b. Using antonyms

  c. Making a comparison

2. Use the preceding definitions to organize a speech on peace.

3. How can the use of definitions help add clarity to your presentation?

It is sometimes desirable to define a concept or an idea by making **comparisons.** In his acceptance address at the 1984 Republican National Convention, Ronald Reagan attempted to illustrate the differences between the Democratic and Republican parties' views of America:

> The choices this year are not just between two different personalities, or between two political parties. They are between two different visions of the future, two fundamentally different ways of governing—their government of pessimism, fear, and limits, or ours of hope, confidence, and growth.
>
> Their government sees people only as members of groups. Ours serves all the people of America as individuals. Theirs lives in the past, seeking to apply the old and failed policies to an era that has passed them by. Ours learns from the past and strives to change by boldly charting a new course for the future.[6]

In this statement, Reagan attempted to define the differences between the two parties by characterizing his party as one of the future and the Democratic Party as one plagued by the past. His proffered future of hope, confidence, and growth was contrasted with a past defined by pessimism, fear, and limits.

Still another way to define a term is to refer to its etymology, or origin. The **etymology** of a word is the history of its development

Application Activity

DEMONSTRATION

1. Select an activity that can be demonstrated to an audience, such as origami, balloon sculpture, or karate.

2. Outline the necessary steps involved in teaching this skill to someone else.

3. Ask a classmate to watch your demonstration.

4. Ask your classmate to give you feedback concerning how well you presented your ideas. Were you thorough? Did your demonstration proceed logically? Did you go through the steps slowly enough?

or use in the language where it is found. For example, in a speech about three mayoral candidates, you might characterize one candidate as a liberal. To clarify what you mean by the term *liberal*, you refer to the word's etymology: *liberal* comes from the Latin *liber*, meaning "free, or liberates, befitting a free man, generous."[7] One of the best reference sources for the etymology of words in the English language is the *Oxford English Dictionary*.

Demonstration

Demonstration is often an effective method for explaining a point or idea to an audience. In an effort to clearly explain a particular activity, such as cake decorating or operation of a video camera, you might show the audience the steps involved in the process. For example, Bill wants to explain the differences among various baseball pitches. To him the most logical and effective way to accomplish his goal is to demonstrate the different ways to grip the baseball for each type of pitch and to show the "follow through" motion for each pitch. His demonstration is accompanied by a verbal explanation.

SAMPLE INFORMATIVE SPEECH

In the following speech, prepared and delivered by a student, the speaker attempts to apply several techniques designed to provide an effective, informative speech.[8]

You've Come a Long Way, Baby!

The speaker's reference to a Virginia Slims ad captures the audience's attention.

The speaker establishes her credibility by mentioning previous speeches on sexism.

The speaker describes sexism in an effort to establish the relevancy of her subject, for both a male and female audience.

The speaker previews the major points that will be discussed in the body of her speech.

The speaker uses another tactic to familiarize her audience with the subject. Here she compares the status of men and women.

One of the most clever advertisements I've come across in magazines is the Virginia Slims cigarette ad, with its slogan—"You've come a long way, baby!" Now let me make myself clear from the start—I am *not* promoting cigarette smoking in this speech. I simply want to point out that the Virginia Slims ads do a good job of stating that only recently have women begun to change their image.

Historically, women have been seen in a very sexist light. This, coincidentally, is the topic of my speech this evening—Sexism and Its Historical Foundation.

Sexism, as I have stated in previous speeches, is a prejudice we learn at a young age. Further, sexism causes *human* suffering; it does so by limiting *human* achievement. Sexism prevents growth and development in *all* humans, male and female. You see, when one person, male or female, oppresses the ideas, capabilities, and spirit of another human being, male or female, then neither of the two grow, achieve, or release new energy (in the form of discoveries, cures, or solutions). Sexism does oppress ideas, capabilities, and the spirit of the female. But in the long run, it stunts the growth of males as well.

Under what I call the main cause of sexism—the perceived role of women throughout history—there are "subcauses." I'd like to explore for you this evening (1) the level and type of education afforded women and (2) the treatment of women by the media (television).

Stop and reflect, if you will, about the status of women throughout human civilization. What comes to mind? Childbearer or heir provider? Servant or owner? That's what comes to my mind. Generally, despite the few exceptions that could be the subject of another speech, women have had a submissive, less elaborate, less powerful status than men throughout the history of civilization.

When you compare the advances made by women in this century alone—gaining the right to vote in the 1920s, the role women played in the 1940s (working in munition factories), and the Feminist Movement of the 1970s (just

The speaker asks the members of the audience to consider their own attitudes about sexism, which provides a smooth transition into her first subcause—education.

The speaker includes examples that illustrate how education is male-dominated.

The speaker supports her contention about education by describing the difference between the curricula of men and women.

Here is a transition to the speaker's next subpoint (subcause)—treatment of women by the media.

The speaker describes, through examples, how women were portrayed in early television programs. The descriptions point to the biases shown women.

to name a *few*)—with the accomplishments women made before this century, you have a very uneven scale.

Sexism is the result of people (1) not accepting the rapid growth and development women have made in this century as *positive* growth for all humans and (2) not accepting history for what it is—something out of the past which can't be changed, only accepted. Why, you might ask, do people still harbor sexist attitudes when they're living with many of the changes made in recent history and have little direct experience with the roles women played in the past. This question brings me to my first "subcause"—the education of and about women.

History courses, unless you've done some specific studying (which the average person does not), almost always focus on wars, kings, and presidents. Wars are the starting and stopping points of different eras in history, and the kings and presidents are the key players. When we are taught this kind of historical perspective, it's easy to see how we grow up assuming we live in a "male dominated" world. People, other than the most powerful and influential, are seldom remembered in our history courses, and those who are mentioned are nearly all men.

Until recently, the education of men and women was vastly different. Women needed to know how to sew, cook, keep house, and take care of children. Men needed to be trained in math, foreign languages, science, and of course—history. These were the subjects and way of life men and women learned generation after generation. Sexism is a result of believing in the educational patterns dictated to us.

It's only been in the last century that women have crossed over the educational boundaries into those of men. Why, you might ask once more, has it taken women so long to become professionals in fields mainly dominated by men? This question brings me to my next "subcause" of sexism—the treatment of women on television.

Let me ask you to stop and reminisce about the early TV shows like *Leave It To Beaver*, *Rawhide*, and *The Lone Ranger*. If you didn't see them first-hand, perhaps you've seen the reruns. These old shows were for the most part very entertaining. But if you observe very closely the roles of women in most early TV shows, they usually fit into one of four roles. They're either the very supporting housewife, the evil villainess who seduces the male character into doing something wrong or illegal, the prize of

The speaker offers a comparison between the weaker roles given to women in TV with those written for men.

The speaker explains how our attitudes are gradually changing, due in part to the portrayal of women in today's programs.

Here the speaker recaps the major points developed in the body of her speech. This is a transitional summary.

In the conclusion the speaker returns to the central theme that the perception of women throughout history played a primary role in creating sexism.

The speaker cleverly uses the same slogan as in the introduction to leave the audience with something to think about.

an ongoing feud between the good guy and the bad guy, or finally, the beautiful but weak type who plays no other active role than to interfere with the great escape or wild chase.

As we all know, the media is very successful at molding or changing our perceptions, attitudes, and values. In early TV, these were the perceptions of women that molded our attitudes and values. Now surely, someone had to play these roles, but these were the *only* roles women got. Men were portrayed in much stronger, more adventurous, and more intelligent roles.

Sexist attitudes came from seeing women in only these weaker roles, thus forming attitudes about how women act or what they should be in real life. Fortunately, today's TV shows like *The Cosby Show*, *Cagney and Lacey*, and *Hill Street Blues* are depicting women in more substantial, meaningful roles. Hopefully, kids watching these shows today will grow up with more realistic perceptions of women, and their attitudes will reflect these perceptions when they are adults.

In essence, when I say that the status of women throughout history is the main cause of sexism, I'm talking about the "subcauses" that I have explored this evening: education (what is systematically taught in the schools) and the treatment of women by the television media (where women's roles have changed over the years from the helpless, submissive, less intelligent types to roles that are equally powerful, equally influential, and equally substantial as those given to men). These two "subcauses," and others not developed in this speech, instill sexism in the minds of young people today, just as they have done for years.

The only way these "histories" can be attacked, and sexism put out of its misery, is for people to accept them for what they are—history. Old educational traditions are fading, and television shows are starting to give women more powerful and meaningful roles. What people need to do is build new attitudes from the changing images education and television now provide. From the very forces that at one time caused sexism, we need to learn to create new histories that condemn sexism.

I'm feeling pretty good about being a woman today. I think it's safe to say that there is no better time for a woman to live than the present. I hope twenty years from now I can say that very same thing. We have come a long way—but we're far from home.

SUMMARY

The purpose of an informative speech is to educate an audience. From the early stages of selecting a topic through the final stages of presenting that topic, the speaker must strive to make the information relevant to the audience. The speaker accomplishes this by engaging the audience's interest in the topic, by presenting ideas that can be easily digested, and by using appropriate language.

Informative speech topics generally fall into one of these categories: recreation, concepts, places, objects, or people. Whatever topic the speaker selects, it should be adapted to the audience in order to remain relevant. Determining what the audience wants to know is a major consideration for the speaker.

Once the topic is decided, work begins on developing the major and minor points. All this planning and outlining is done with one thing in mind—every step of the way, give the audience information that will make a difference. The audience must come away from the speech having learned something worthwhile.

Certain methods are especially effective in passing on new information. These include the narrative, education through a story or account; description, enlightenment through concrete, sharply focused language; definition, explanations of unfamiliar ideas by means of language that the audience already understands; and demonstration of a concept or process.

All these parts add up to the speaker being a teacher, and the members of the audience being eager listeners.

REVIEW QUESTIONS

1. What is the primary concern when developing an informative speech objective?
2. List the five major categories for informative speech topics, and give an example of each.
3. When concluding an informative speech, what do you want to reinforce?
4. What are some resources you can use to create a narrative?
5. Why is it best to use concrete language when attempting to describe something in an informative speech?
6. Differentiate between the use of antonyms and the use of synonyms to define ideas in an informative speech.
7. When demonstrating something, why is it important to proceed slowly?

NOTES

1. Matt Clark et al., "AIDS," *Newsweek*, August 12, 1985, p. 20.

2. Tom Morganthau et al., "Future Shock," *Newsweek*, November 24, 1986, p. 31.

3. Judith Guest, *Ordinary People* (New York: Viking Press, 1976), p. 111.

4. Nancy Reagan, "The Battle Against Drugs: What Can You Do?" *Vital Speeches of the Day*, August 15, 1986, p. 645.

5. Matt Clark et al., " A Slow Death of the Mind," *Newsweek*, December 3, 1984, p. 56.

6. Ronald Reagan, "Acceptance Speech," *Vital Speeches of the Day*, September 15, 1984, p. 706.

7. Walter W. Skeat, *A Concise Etymological Dictionary of the English Language* (Oxford: Clarendon Press, 1958), p. 293.

8. Adapted from a speech manuscript prepared by Kelly Wimmer. Used with permission.

ADDITIONAL READINGS

An asterisk indicates an advanced reading.

*Frandsen, K. D., and Clement, D. A. "The Functions of Human Communication in Informing: Communicating and Processing Information." In C. C. Arnold and J. W. Bowers (Eds.), *Handbook of Rhetorical and Communication Theory*. Boston: Allyn and Bacon, 1984. Pp. 338–99.
> This article provides a comprehensive overview on information theory.

*Petrie, C. R., Jr. "Information Speaking: A Summary and Bibliography of Related Research." *Speech Monographs* 30: 79–91, 1963.
> This article summarizes early research on speech organization and retention.

Steinaker, N. W., and Bell, M. R. *The Experiential Taxonomy: A New Approach to Teaching and Learning* (Educational Psychology Series). New York: Academic Press, 1979.
> This book presents material on instructional strategies that may be of interest to those preparing an informative speech.

15

The Persuasive Speech

Learning Objectives

At the conclusion of this chapter you should be able to

1.   Write a clear persuasive speech objective.

2.   Organize an effective persuasive speech.

3.   Understand how to increase your credibility.

4.   Be aware of the importance of making ethical statements.

5.   Develop logical and emotional appeals in your speech.

Anita is sitting in her chair getting ready to speak. She is a candidate for county commissioner in Brown County, Indiana. As she waits to be introduced, she looks out at those assembled in the high-school gymnasium and hopes that her remarks will be both effective and persuasive enough to motivate the members of the audience to vote for her.

Although many of us may never seek election to a political office, we all participate in the persuasive process. We may try to persuade our employer that we deserve a raise, our children that we know what is best for them, our spouse that the expensive sofa would be perfect in the living room. In addition, we also encounter persuasive appeals on a daily basis—we read newspaper articles, watch television commercials, and listen to the appeals of salespeople and candidates running for office.

Persuasion is the act of convincing an audience, through verbal and nonverbal communication, to adopt or change an attitude, belief, or value. For example, a minister may try to persuade his congregants that they should annually contribute a certain percentage of their income to the church; a salesperson may try to persuade a customer that the red Chevrolet Beretta is the perfect car for her; or a sports celebrity may try to persuade junior high-school students that drugs are not "cool." In each of these cases, the speaker hopes that audience members will experience a change in their thinking as a result of his or her message. Persuasion is often a complex process, because the speaker must appeal to a group of unique individuals who each possess a special frame of reference.

DEVELOPING A PERSUASIVE SPEECH OBJECTIVE

When developing a persuasive speech, it is essential that you define your goal. What do you want the audience to do after listening to your speech? For example, do you want them to change their attitudes about allowing a tax credit to families whose children attend private schools, or do you want them to sign a petition to recall the mayor? In a persuasive speech, the speaker either calls for the audience to modify their beliefs or asks them to act on behalf of an issue or belief. As indicated in Chapter 10, developing a clear speech objective is essential in carrying out this process.

When calling on an audience to change a belief, use evidence to argue for or against a position. You are attempting to convince the members of your audience to alter their beliefs or behavior on a specific issue. To do this, you should rely on facts to convince the audience of the value, morality, or advantage of your position.

Sometimes persuading your audience to alter an attitude is a question of degree. For example, if you wish to bring about a dramatic change in the audience's opinion, you might try to create a conflict for audience members to contemplate. After presenting your arguments, you hope the audience members will change their opinions. On the other hand, perhaps an audience is already sympathetic to a particular issue or policy; if so, you might try to reinforce or strengthen the audience's already positive feelings about the topic.

A second type of persuasive speech objective attempts to move the audience to immediate action. The speaker calls on audience members to adopt a specific behavior or to discontinue their present actions. For instance, you might call on audience members to fulfill their civic responsibility and vote in the next election, or you might call for a halt to the picketing of abortion clinics and harassment of those women who seek counseling there. In both these cases you are calling on the audience to act.

TOPICS FOR A PERSUASIVE SPEECH

How do you decide what would make a good topic for a persuasive speech? The first thing you need to think about is your speech objective which, as indicated earlier, grows out of what you are trying to accomplish with the audience. Obviously, some topics lend themselves to a persuasive speech better than others. Topics that are controversial or current are more appropriate for persuasive speeches than topics that are dated and no longer socially relevant. Likewise, topics that place the speaker in a conflict with the audience are better for persuasive speeches than topics that are perceived as neutral or unemotional.

The different types of discussion questions—those based on fact, values, or policy (discussed in Chapter 9)—can help you determine possible persuasive speech topics. When constructing a persuasive speech based on *fact*, the speaker argues for the truth of a position or challenges its validity. For instance, a speaker might argue that the 1986 tax reform laws do not really benefit middle-class Americans.

When constructing a persuasive speech based on *values*, the speaker advocates a position based on what he or she perceives as the rightness or wrongness of an issue. The speaker's personal and cultural background can play a major role in the selection of a topic. For example, if the speaker believes that a child's biological mother is the only rightful mother, he or she might argue that a surrogate mother should not be legally bound to give up her baby. The speaker's values play a role in how he or she approaches a topic.

When constructing a persuasive speech based on *policy*, the speaker argues that a change is necessary in the future. For instance, a speaker might advocate that companies should not have the right to enforce employee drug testing programs. Such a speaker is trying to persuade the audience that the current policy is wrong.

. . . .

In the kind of persuasive speech shown here, the speaker calls upon the audience to act.

Application Activity

SELECTING A TOPIC AND DEVELOPING A PERSUASIVE SPEECH OBJECTIVE

1. Make a list of three topics (one dealing with fact, one with values, and one with policy) designed to change an audience's belief.

2. Use the guidelines identified in Chapter 10 to help you construct these objectives.

3. Make another list of three topics (one dealing with fact, one with values, and one with policy) designed to make an audience act.

4. Share these lists with your classmates to gain feedback on the viability of your objectives.

ORGANIZING YOUR PERSUASIVE SPEECH

In many ways, the organization of a persuasive speech follows the structure of an informative speech. First, you must engage the audience's attention; next, you attempt to appeal to a specific need or interest. The difference between persuasive and informative speeches, however, must be addressed at this point in the preparation process. As a speaker, you must decide whether you wish to educate your audience (the goal of an informative speech) or you wish to do more, that is, change an attitude, belief, or value (the goal of a persuasive speech). If you choose the latter, the development of your speech body takes a slightly different focus. You must set out to "prove your case," or offer a solution to a problem. This section examines two organizational plans for doing just that: Monroe's motivated sequence and refutation.

Motivated Sequence

The **motivated sequence** design, advanced by Alan H. Monroe, focuses on creating a sense of need and then explaining how that need can be satisfied.[1] If this sounds familiar to you, there is a good reason—the basic organizational pattern is that of problem solution, a concept discussed in Chapter 12. There are five steps in this plan: (1) arousing attention, (2) showing a need, (3) satisfying the need, (4) visualizing the results, and (5) calling for action (see Table 15.1).

TABLE 15.1   Monroe's Motivated Sequence

1. Arousing attention   We attempt to capture the audience's attention with our opening remarks.

2. Showing a need   We determine the need or problem our topic suggests.

3. Satisfying the need   We argue how our proposal will meet the need or resolve the problem described earlier.

4. Visualizing the results   We create a visual image that projects what will happen if our proposal is embraced or rejected.

5. Calling for action   We urge the audience to demonstrate its support.

The first step in Monroe's motivated sequence—arousing the audience's interest in your subject—is basic to all types of public speeches, whether they are informative, entertaining, or persuasive. You cannot expect an audience to listen attentively if you have not captured its attention. The techniques for drawing the audience's attention discussed in Chapter 12—using a narrative, a startling statement, a rhetorical question, or a quotation—apply to the persuasive speech. For instance, this opening statement is aimed at capturing the audience's interest: "The federal government has estimated that between 300,000 and two million people across the United States are homeless, as many as a third or half of them mentally ill."[2]

Step two—demonstrating a need—requires that you look closely at your topic in order to determine the need or problem that your topic suggests. For example, with the topic "Homeless Americans," you might appeal to the audience's need for safety/shelter (refer to the discussion of Maslow's hierarchy of needs in Chapter 10) or establish the nature of the problem and its relevance to the audience. For example: "Our country is faced with a perplexing problem. A nation that takes pride in its high standard of living and considerable wealth must confront the mounting evidence that increasing numbers live without a roof over their heads and that the ranks of those who live in poverty are also on the rise."

In step three you begin to argue your case, to show how your proposal will either meet the need or solve the problem described earlier. This is the body of your speech, the place where you develop a well-reasoned logical appeal, a solid emotional appeal, or a combination of the two (discussed later in this chapter). You might propose, for instance, that "additional low-cost shelter must be made available for this growing segment of our population. In fact, this is in contrast to what is actually happening in our large cities, where low-cost housing is disappearing."

The purpose of the next step—visualizing the results—is to create a visual image that projects what will happen if your proposal is embraced or what will happen if it is rejected. It is also possible to show your audience both sides of the picture. In fact, by presenting the negative aspects first, followed by the positive, you can build a strong case for having your audience support the action you have proposed. In this part of your presentation you want to increase your audience's identification with the problem. One of the most effective ways to do this is by describing the projected outcome in vivid language; the better your description, the better is the audience's conceptualization of the situation. If you choose to present a scenario that depicts the dangers the future holds should your proposal for increased low-cost housing be rejected, you might include this warning:

> Thousands of middle-class Americans are inching closer to joining the ranks of poor America. I've described what happens when unemployment becomes a way of life, when homes are repossessed by banks, when dejected individuals give up all hope and "check out" of life as they've known it. Expect to see more of these people on the streets in the future. They won't be able to afford a place to live if low-cost housing is replaced by parking lots, high-rise office buildings, and high-rent housing meant to lure prosperous people back to our cities. It's not only their sad plight—it's all of ours.

If the intent of your speech is to alter the audience's attitude, you can end on this note. If, however, you want your audience to actually demonstrate its support for your proposal, you would go one step further.

The call for action is the final step of the motivated sequence. In it you want to capitalize on the support you have attempted to win during the visualization step. For example, you might ask everyone to write their senators and representatives to urge them to vote for additional funds for housing for the poor and homeless.

Refutation

Refutation is the process of disputing the arguments of another person. This approach to persuasion is different from other approaches, because the speaker's argument rests on building a sound *response* to an argument already presented by someone else. You begin by looking at an established position and then proceed to develop your own arguments to systematically point out the flaws in the estab-

To be successful, a persuasive speech must be well organized.

lished view. A defense attorney, for example, might attempt to refute the statements made by the district attorney's key witness by
pointing out the weaknesses in that testimony. The two primary
ways to refute the ideas of others are to challenge the quality of the
evidence and to point out the flaws in the logic of the other person's
reasoning.

There are several ways to refute arguments when the quality
of the evidence is in question. Specifically, you can use refutation
(1) when the evidence is not based on facts, (2) when the evidence
is not recent, and (3) when the evidence comes from a biased
source.

When another person's argument is built on questionable
"facts," there is ample reason for disputing it. How do you determine whether or not your opponent's facts are shaky? If you can
answer "no" to the following questions, then the speaker's evidence
is open to attack: First, are the statistics used drawn from a large
enough sample? (Refer to Chapter 11 for a thorough explanation.)

Second, are there authoritative sources to support the testimony? (Failure to mention authoritative sources can lead the audience to doubt or question a speaker's claims.) Third, is the speaker's personal experience believable? For example, can Jan substantiate her claim that the diet she's been describing to her audience will provide results without any medical complications?

Equally damaging to a speaker's argument is the use of outdated evidence. For example, you would want to challenge your opponent's reference to a fifteen-year-old study if that speaker did not show that the findings are just as valid today as they were at the time the research was published.

Use of sources that might be considered biased, or lacking in objectivity, also leaves an argument open to attack. People who are associated with a particular political party, economic group, or stand on an issue will not be seen as objective sources, which can diminish the persuasive impact of their comments. In this example Leon attacks the objectivity of a source:

> Leon decided to respond to a previous speech that claimed that the government is still experiencing a "red scare." To support this argument, the previous speaker had quoted from *The New American*, a periodical known as the "voice" of the ultraconservative John Birch Society. Leon attacked the argument of his opponent by maintaining that *The New American* did not represent an objective source. Leon suggested that a more representative sample of America's political beliefs would have made the argument more plausible.

Refutation also can be done effectively by highlighting the fallacies in other speakers' reasoning. What are these fallacies? Persuasive speeches can be weakened by such flaws as arguments ad hominem, assumptions of cause and effect, non-sequiturs, and faulty analogies. When your opponents base their arguments on these fallacies, seize the opportunity to point out the defects in their arguments.

No doubt you have heard speakers attack the character of another person. This is called the fallacy of **argument ad hominem.** Ronald Reagan, in his derogatory comments about Libyan leader Muammar Kaddafi, made the mistake of using an argument ad hominem. Instead of constructing a well-reasoned argument that protested Kaddafi's terrorist policies, Reagan resorted to name calling: "I find he's not only a barbarian, but he's flaky."[3] Uppermost in Reagan's mind was to present a negative image of Kaddafi to his audience. However, in the process of name calling, little was said about the issue of terrorism. By refuting this type of argument or strategy, you can make your audience aware of a speaker's lack of sound reasoning.

A second approach to refuting a speaker's reasoning is to point out a faulty **cause-and-effect argument.** For example, the speaker who blames children's poor test scores on the teachers' strike earlier in the school year invites a challenge to his or her argument. There is no proof offered to show that one event caused the other to happen. Your effort to refute this argument could focus on establishing the true cause or causes of these poor test scores.

In a **non-sequitur**, the minor points are not related to the major points, or the conclusion does not logically follow the points that precede it. Look at this persuasive argument:

A. We need to reverse the trend of violent crimes in the United States.
B. Television programs depict too much violence.
C. Less violent television programs will help reduce the number of violent crimes annually.

The conclusion drawn by this speaker does not logically follow the earlier points. It is this flaw that allows you to refute the speaker's reasoning.

Finally, a faulty analogy invites refutation. In Chapter 11 **analogy** was defined as a form of support that compares the similar features in two seemingly different objects or situations. This definition implies that the comparison must be a valid one; when it is not, the analogy is flawed. The perceptive listener will be able to detect a faulty analogy, as in the following:

> Hans, in presenting his arguments for overturning the *Roe* v. *Wade* decision, which legalized abortion, compared the abortion of unborn human embryos and fetuses to Hitler's annihilation of millions in the gas chambers during World War II.

As an opposing speaker, you would attack the very comparison of these two events. They are simply not similar enough to justify comparison.

PRESENTING YOUR PERSUASIVE SPEECH

Presentation of an effective persuasive speech rests on your ability to establish or enhance your credibility as a speaker, as well as on your ability to develop sound logical or emotional appeals. Consider this point: If a speaker is not perceived by the audience to be a credible source, then even a well-constructed appeal will have little impact. Conversely, a well-reasoned argument can increase a speaker's credibility. The importance of each of these factors is discussed in the following section.

Speaker Credibility

A variable that plays a significant role in the persuasion process is the *credibility* of the speaker; does the audience perceive the speaker as someone who is qualified to speak on a particular topic? For example, your experience as a swimming instructor would likely make you qualified to speak on the subject of water safety, yet it is unlikely that the same audience would perceive you as someone qualified to speak about the benefits of tax-deferred annuities. To a large degree, perception is a strong determinant in establishing your credibility as a speaker.

Some audiences may see you as more qualified than other audiences. For example, an audience of persons who possess little information about a subject may see you as a credible speaker, whereas an audience of people whose background or experience is extensive may see you as less qualified. In addition to audience reaction, several other variables contribute to a speaker's credibility, including competence, dynamism, trustworthiness, and ethics (see Table 15.2).

Competence   **Competence** is a demonstrated ability or quality. In persuasion, competence is often a measure of a speaker's knowledge concerning a topic. Speakers may possess a special ability that qualifies them as experts. For example, CBS news anchor Dan Rather would be considered an expert on the subject of broadcast journalism. Classroom speakers, too, can achieve a degree of expertness because of the knowledge gained from personal experience.

> Luanne is very committed to M.A.D.D.—Mothers Against Drunk Drivers. She became involved in the

TABLE 15.2   Speaker Credibility at a Glance

Competence	A demonstrated ability or quality
Dynamism	Degree of excitement, energy, involvement in topic
Trustworthiness	The kind of "character" we communicate to our audience
Ethics	The integrity we bring to our message

organization six years ago when her son was killed by a drunk driver. That experience changed her life dramatically, but it gave her a special competence in mobilizing others to support the work of M.A.D.D. She now travels extensively speaking about the goals and benefits of M.A.D.D. When she addressed her speech class about her counseling experiences, her fellow students listened attentively.

One of the best ways to demonstrate your knowledge or competence is to incorporate evidence in your speech. The use of supporting material can add substance to your ideas. For example, reference to a study by a leading cardiologist as reported in the *Journal of the American Medical Association (JAMA)* would add credibility to your speech's goal: "To persuade your audience that exercise should be a part of everyone's daily routine." A thorough discussion of supporting materials can be found in Chapter 11. Being able to demonstrate your credibility increases the likelihood that your audience will listen to your presentation and support the position you are promoting.

Dynamism   Another dimension of credibility is dynamism. **Dynamism** is the degree of excitement that you bring to your presenta-

. . . .

Gospel preachers are noted for their dynamism.

tion, often accomplished by demonstrating concern for and involvement in your topic. The dynamic speaker communicates that he or she is excited about the presentation, which in turn can elicit excitement on the part of the audience.

There are different levels of energy that can be demonstrated during a presentation. It is not necessary to scream and shout to show that you are a dynamic speaker; you can demonstrate involvement by being forceful, energetic, or sensitive—whatever is appropriate for your selected topic. How do you exhibit these qualities? By incorporating facial expressions, gestures, movement, and variety of vocal inflection into your speech. These behaviors were discussed in detail in Chapter 13.

Trustworthiness   **Trustworthiness** refers to the kind of "character" you communicate to your audience. People want to put their faith in someone of high moral character, someone who they believe is honest and reliable. Looking back at former national leaders, we see that Richard Nixon suffered substantially because he was perceived as an untrustworthy individual.

How do you convey your trustworthiness to an audience? If you are already familiar to an audience, your past behavior may speak for itself. However, how do you establish trust with an audience who has never heard or seen you before? You might try revealing a bit of your background as a way of introducing yourself. Often mentioning how you are directly involved in your speech topic leads your audience to perceive you as sincere or committed, that is, trustworthy.

Ethics   **Ethics,** the rules that govern moral behavior, must be considered as you develop your persuasive speech. The integrity you bring to your message affects both the way you interact with your audience and the way the audience assesses your credibility. Senator Joseph Biden, for example, was forced to abandon his 1988 bid for the presidency because of his questionable ethics during the early stages of the campaign. His failure to acknowledge that he had "borrowed" excerpts from the speeches of other politicians and the misrepresentation of his academic standing in law school stood out as glaring examples of unethical behavior. His candidacy ended abruptly, a direct result of his dishonesty. As shown in this example, a perception of the audience that you lack ethics can greatly diminish your credibility and decrease the believability of your propositions.

Because ethics are such an integral part of the persuasion process, extreme care should be taken not to compromise your integrity in order to reach your speech goals. To ensure that this does not

This speaker's credibility is enhanced by his common ground with his audience.

happen, practice the following principles: (1) be honest with your audience, (2) do not engage in name-calling, and (3) give credit to outside source materials.

Any argument you construct should be based on facts. Part of your responsibility as a speaker is to present accurate information to your audience. The use of evidence or supporting materials helps you to achieve this goal. Exaggerated claims, fabricated stories, and misuse of statistics all represent deliberate efforts to distort information.

The ideas in your speech should be strong enough to stand on their own merit. Verbal attacks directed at others are an inappropriate way to gain support for your cause. Besides, an audience is apt to question the ethics of a speaker who resorts to name calling.

Outside sources that support the ideas in your persuasive speech should receive proper credit. The accepted way to do this is by using oral footnotes, a concept discussed in Chapter 11. Bear in mind that quotations should be accurate and that the information you cite should not be taken out of context or fabricated.

Techniques for Enhancing Your Credibility

While the ability to persuade an audience depends on a speaker's competence, dynamism, trustworthiness, and ethics, there are specific techniques that you can employ to enhance your credibility as a speaker.

Establish Common Ground with the Audience One way to enhance your credibility is to establish a common ground with the audience. You might try to share information about yourself that reflects a value system similar to the audience's. Another way to establish common ground is to include supporting material that your audience can identify with, preferably early in the speech. Consider the following:

> Pauline, a psychologist, was invited to speak at a gathering of Overeaters Anonymous, a group designed to help individuals control their eating. At the beginning of her speech she related a story about her-

This photo shows a 1960s civil rights rally led by Martin Luther King, Jr., one of the most dynamic speakers of his day.

self and made reference to the fact she had once weighed 250 pounds. After hearing this story, her audience was "with" her. Her effort to "declare war on food" was successful, in part, because of the shared experience she had with the audience.

Indicate Your Special Knowledge   Another technique that increases your credibility is to indicate that you have special credentials or knowledge that makes you uniquely qualified to speak on a topic. Without appearing to brag, tell the audience about your background and its special relationship to your topic. For example,

> The Board of Trustees of a local church called a special meeting to respond to the community's outcry over the firing of a popular nursery school teacher. In an effort to justify the teacher's firing, the board members prefaced their remarks to the assembled parents by stating their qualifications as educators. Dave, a concerned parent, was angered by what he considered to be their inept handling of the issue. He offered his own credentials, a Ph.D. in communication, and then spoke about the interpersonal communication problems of the organization and the poor public image they had created in the community. The effectiveness of his insightful remarks were reinforced by the positive response he received from the audience.

The person who introduces you to an audience can help reinforce your expertise. For example, the emcee at an American Association of Retired Persons (AARP) luncheon introduced the keynote speaker in the following way:

It is my sincere pleasure to introduce Dr. Clarice Fernandez to you. She is a clinical psychologist with an extensive background in the area of human sexuality. She is the author of two books, one which deals with sex after sixty. Please join me in welcoming Dr. Fernandez, who will speak to you on improving intimate relationships after the age of sixty.

In this example, the introduction served to enhance the credibility of Dr. Fernandez. By highlighting her achievements, the emcee showed how Dr. Fernandez was uniquely qualified to speak on her topic.

Application Activity

INCREASING CREDIBILITY

1. Name a public speaker who possesses each of the dimensions of credibility discussed in this section:

    a. Competence

    b. Dynamism

    c. Trustworthiness

    d. Ethics

2. Why does each of these speakers possess credibility in your mind?

3. What can you do to increase your own credibility based on the behavior of these speakers?

Developing a Persuasive Argument

The heart of a persuasive speech lies in the argument that the speaker constructs. There are a few ways to approach this argument; choosing the best one depends on such factors as (1) your speech objective, (2) the topic that you have selected, (3) the audience to be addressed, and (4) how successfully you have established your credibility. Your assessment of these factors will help you to determine whether you wish to build a logical argument or charge a logical appeal with emotion.

Logical Appeals   A **logical argument** helps your audience understand your ideas, thereby increasing the likelihood that members will be persuaded by what you say. Two ways to develop logical appeals are through deductive reasoning and inductive reasoning.

    Deductive reasoning follows a simple formula: It starts with a general premise, is followed by a minor premise, and ends by drawing a conclusion. In a persuasive speech, deductive reasoning can provide a clear development of your ideas and at the same time can assist the audience in following your thoughts. With deductive reasoning it is imperative that your **premise,** the proposition that serves as the basis for your argument, warrants the conclusion you are advocating. In the following example, your audience would probably accept the claims you are making because they are based on fact:

"Is THAT ALL, SENATOR? JUST, "OH, YEAH!"?"

General premise: One cause of skin cancer is exposure to the sun's ultraviolet rays.

Minor premise: Those who sunbathe regularly expose themselves to ultraviolet rays.

Conclusion: As a group, sunbathers are at a higher than normal risk for getting skin cancer.[4]

Before constructing a persuasive speech using the deductive reasoning just provided, you should establish the relationship between your argument and your speech objective. In this case your speech objective might be "To persuade the classroom audience that sunbathing poses a risk to everyone's health." Beginning with your general premise, ask yourself whether or not the audience is likely to accept your statement without questioning its truthfulness. If you are in doubt, offer supporting evidence.

As a speaker, you need to realize the importance of building your arguments on a sound foundation. Lack of a sound premise spells disaster for the persuasive speech. Consider the following:

General premise: All college students watch MTV.

Minor premise: Catherine is a college student.

Conclusion: Catherine watches MTV.

The general premise in this example is faulty. Not all college students watch MTV; consequently, the incorrect premise means the conclusion is faulty.

Another type of reasoning you can use when developing a persuasive speech is **inductive reasoning,** in which one moves from specific instances to generalizations. For example,

A. Child abuse has increased over the past five years.
B. Spousal abuse has increased over the past five years.
C. Abuse against the elderly has increased over the past five years.

Conclusion: Family violence is on the rise.

Speakers who use inductive reasoning need to be sure about the soundness of their ideas before making a generalization. Faulty logic can trip you up if you are not careful, as in the following example:

A. Susan had mechanical problems with her Pontiac after 25,000 miles.
B. George had his Ford in for repairs at 23,000 miles.
C. Valerie's Toyota has not required repairs. It now has 45,000 miles.

Conclusion: Toyotas are superior cars.

Application Activity

CREATING INDUCTIVE AND DEDUCTIVE ARGUMENTS

1. Choose one of the speech objective topics you developed earlier in this chapter.

2. Develop an outline for an inductive and deductive argument for that topic (refer to Chapter 12 for help with outlining skills).

3. Be sure to include supporting material for both arguments you construct.

In this example, the audience should be suspicious because the generalization is unwarranted. A larger and more representative sample is necessary to convince the careful listener of the validity of the generalization.

Supporting material in the form of statistics, research findings, or authoritative opinion can bring an added dimension to the logical appeal and can strengthen your argument, whether you have chosen to use deductive or inductive reasoning. For example, in the speech on family violence, the citing of statistics (the number of reported cases of child abuse and spousal abuse for each of the last five years) or research findings would lend strength and credibility to the argument.

Emotional Appeals   **Emotional appeals** are used to trigger the emotions or feelings of an audience: anger, fear, and pride. For instance, photographs of starving children in Third World countries can effectively stir our emotions. However, emotion should not be a substitute for reasoning; rather, the emotional appeal can serve as a foundation for building a well-reasoned argument.

In constructing an emotional appeal, you can attempt to stir a wide variety of feelings. To a great extent your topic will dictate the type of emotional response you want your audience to exhibit. Do you want to anger them so they will be moved to take action? Do you want to appeal to their sense of pride or compassion? Or do you want to trigger their fears? Whatever your decision, there are specific ways to achieve the desired response.

One technique is to use emotionally charged language. This also serves as an indicator of your own involvement in the topic. The following examples help illustrate how language can play a significant role in generating an emotional appeal. This introductory statement is void of emotional language: "Statistics point to an alarming trend in this country. The rise in teenage suicides needs to be stopped." Now consider the treatment of the same topic using more powerful language:

Your first reaction is to cry when you learn how this deadly disease is sweeping our society. It is like a cancer, spreading at a rapid pace, touching people from all walks of life. This cancer touches individuals in our rat-infested ghettos, as well as those in upper-middle-class suburban ghettos. I am speaking about the epidemic of teenage suicides; the thousands of time bombs ticking away in today's adolescents.

In the second example note how much more of an impact the speaker's message has on the audience. The language used by this speaker dramatically builds the case.

Another way to use the emotional appeal is to personalize your speech. New York Governor Mario Cuomo shared part of his background in his Keynote Address at the 1984 Democratic National Convention. His words are intended to stir our national pride:

> That struggle to live with dignity is the real story of the shining city. It's a story I didn't read in a book, or learn in a classroom. I saw it, and lived it. Like many of you.
>
> I watched a small man with thick calluses on both hands work fifteen and sixteen hours a day. I saw him once literally bleed from the bottoms of his feet, a man who came here uneducated, alone, unable to speak the language, who taught me all I needed to know about faith and hard work by the simple eloquence of his example. I learned about our kind of democracy from my father; I learned about our obligation to each other from him and from my mother. They asked only for a chance to work and to make the world better for their children and to be protected in those moments when they would not be able to protect themselves. This nation and its government did that for them.
>
> And that they were able to build a family and live in dignity and see one of their children go from behind their little grocery store on the other side of the tracks in south Jamaica where he was born, to occupy the highest seat in the greatest state of the greatest nation in the only world we know, is an ineffably beautiful tribute to the democratic process.[5]

The success of Cuomo's appeal rests on his ability to make the audience feel as much gratitude toward his parents and as much pride in this country as he feels.

You also can draw the audience into your speech with the overall tone of the presentation. Tone, along with your sincerity, can tug at the audience's emotions. Dawn wanted to persuade her fellow nurses not to talk openly about the condition of patients. To draw the attention of her audience, she related the following story about Tom, a victim of a motorcycle accident:

Application Activity

DEVELOPING AN EMOTIONAL APPEAL

1. Choose one of the topics from your persuasive speech objectives list.

2. Make up a story that supports the topic.

3. Embellish the story with vivid language and an appeal to a specific emotion.

4. Share this story with one of your peers to see if it triggers an emotional response.

Tom was given little chance of surviving, and in fact remained in a coma for three months. During that time, the nurses who cared for him spoke openly of his "hopeless" condition. When Tom was transferred from the fourth floor, Dawn assumed that he had died, and after several months, she forgot about him. Nine months later she was asked to attend a meeting with the other nurses who had treated this man. Tom was at that meeting. He recounted his stay in the hospital and how angry he was about the way the nurses had discussed his condition *in his presence.* He told them how painful and discouraging it was to overhear their remarks. Dawn was visibly shaken by his account and felt overwhelmed with shame. Likewise, the audience was moved by this story.

SAMPLE PERSUASIVE SPEECH

In the following speech, prepared and delivered by a student, the speaker attempts to provide a well-reasoned persuasive speech. (*Note:* This speech was developed as part of a classroom activity. Specifically, the assignment directed students to develop a proposal, aimed at management, to implement a new policy.[6])

The Benefits of a Corporate Psychologist

The speaker attempts to arouse the audience's attention by introducing a short quiz.

The speaker attempts to establish common ground with her audience and at the same time display her special knowledge of the problem.

This is an additional reference to the speaker's special knowledge of the problem—that executives' physical and mental health are at risk in this company.

The speaker offers a solution to the problem.

The speaker explains how the proposal would work.

The speaker explains how the proposal would be paid for with existing funds.

To make the grade in the business world, many executives like yourselves strive for straight As—even if it's at the risk of your own physical or mental health. Before I present my proposal, I would like to first give you a short quiz which may reveal characteristics of your personality you may not have been aware of. On a scale from one through eight, rate yourselves on the following traits.

(List traits from test)

At this point, I would like to ask you to cover or put away your answer sheets and leave them alone until I ask you to take them out again.

Now, all of you, I know, are familiar with long hours, long days, and long weeks—I know from being a part of this company for several years that many of the executives here sometimes have trouble knowing when to call it a day. I feel good being a part of the hard-working team that you make up, but at the same time I worry that the strain of the long hours and long days may ultimately shorten your lives. As shown by the records kept in the personnel office, executives here have had their share of sick days. Thousands of dollars have been spent on these employees who stay at home, while additional sums go to pay their doctors. More of that money should have gone to pay for productive days spent on the job. That's money that I feel could instead be spent in a more "healthy" manner—one beneficial to the company—and more important, one beneficial to the physical and mental health of the members of our team.

For these reasons, I suggest establishing some help from within—establishing a resident part-time psychologist for the company. Under my proposal, this psychologist would work in the building three days a week, as well as be on call at least one evening a week. This psychologist would be properly compensated for being away from his or her office. Further, I propose that he or she be paid with the same money currently being spent on sick days

The speaker offers evidence that her proposal has been tried elsewhere.

The speaker outlines some of the benefits of this program.

The speaker focuses on a second benefit of this program—learning how to relax.

The speaker offers a third benefit of the proposal—executives can improve their decision-making abilities.

The speaker attempts to help her audience visualize the dangers posed by type A personality traits.

The speaker uses an effective analogy to demonstrate the dangerous side effects of these personality traits.

This is the speaker's transitional summary. In it she reiterates the benefits of her proposed solution.

Conclusion: the speaker calls for action here, urging management to adopt her proposal.

and insurance claims. Am I saying, then, that our executives would spend three days a week on the "couch"—spilling their deepest thoughts to an inhouse "shrink"? *No*—and to illustrate, I would like to tell you about a service that's being used by some of this country's largest corporations. Psychologists from major institutions have been teaching executives some important principles of psychology. This service gives managers insights into themselves and others while helping them solve the varied problems of corporate life. Executives examine such themes as leadership, motivation, and change.

We have executives here who are wearing themselves out because of long hours and taxing responsibilities. I feel that management needs to take some time out to discover *what* makes them tick—perhaps even learn how to relax somewhat amidst the pressures of their positions. I feel this type of resident counseling will help the executives take the time to weigh issues carefully, explore a wide range of alternatives, and make well-thought-out decisions.

In the introduction I alluded to the type A personality. Type As react more strongly to both physical and psychological stress and experience a much higher incidence of serious heart disease. Several of you here, in fact, are undoubtedly type A personalities. Type As are like machines running at high speed for long periods of time without sufficient rest. While these machines are *very effective while operating,* they are much more likely to suffer a catastrophic failure than machines operated at more reasonable rates. In the long run, obtaining a resident psychologist will not only save this institution money, but it just may preserve the mental and physical health of our corporate team.

Now—before I leave, I'll ask you to take out those answer sheets from the quiz I gave you earlier. Total your scores—then multiply them by 3. Although this quiz is hardly a definitive indicator of the type As (and the more relaxed type Bs) in this group, it may help you decide to take my proposal to heart. I urge you to examine my proposal thoroughly. If you need any additional information, I will obtain it for you.

SUMMARY

Persuasion is the act of convincing an audience to alter or change an attitude, belief, or value. In this chapter we treated the subject of the speech objective first. In a persuasive speech your objective is either to modify a belief or ask your audience to act on behalf of an issue or belief. With the speech objective and audience in mind, you begin to consider what would make a suitable topic. We discussed the fact that certain topics lend themselves to persuasive speeches, namely, those which are controversial, current, or that place the speaker and audience in a position of conflict.

Once you have decided on your topic, your next decision involves choosing an effective organizational design. Two patterns were described in this chapter: Monroe's motivated sequence, and refutation. With the motivated sequence, the focus is on creating a sense of need and then explaining how that need can be satisfied. Each of the five steps in the motivated sequence was described: (1) arousing attention, (2) showing a need, (3) satisfying a need, (4) visualizing the results, and (5) calling for action. Refutation is the process of disputing the arguments of another person. This is accomplished by first studying the established position and then by developing your own arguments which systematically point out the flaws in that view. Two primary ways to refute the ideas of others are to challenge the quality of the evidence and to point out the flaws in the logic of the other person's reasoning.

There are several factors to consider when presenting a persuasive speech. One of these is speaker credibility. The issues of competence, dynamism, trustworthiness and ethics come into play. Also discussed were techniques for increasing your credibility, such as establishing common ground with the audience and demonstrating to the audience that you have special knowledge regarding your topic. Your efforts in both these areas will help convince your audience—and yourself—that you are a credible speaker.

It is in the body of the speech that you develop your persuasive argument—either a logical appeal or an emotional appeal. In this chapter we discussed how to develop a logical appeal by using either deductive or inductive reasoning. Deductive reasoning starts with a general premise, is followed by a minor premise, and ends by drawing a conclusion. Conversely, with inductive reasoning you move from specific instances to generalizations. While an argument should always be built on a strong logical base, it is sometimes appropriate to trigger the emotions of an audience. In an emotional appeal you can use emotionally charged language or attempt to personalize your speech in order to achieve the desired response from your audience. As your ability to develop convincing arguments increases, so too will your confidence as a public speaker.

REVIEW QUESTIONS

1. Identify the two different types of persuasive speech objectives.
2. How is a persuasive speech on policy different from a persuasive speech on values?
3. Briefly describe the five steps in Monroe's motivated sequence.
4. What steps can a speaker take to increase his credibility?
5. How does the issue of ethics enter into the development of a persuasive speech?
6. Differentiate between inductive and deductive reasoning. How can you use both types of reasoning in a persuasive speech?
7. What role does language play in a speaker's attempt to trigger the emotions of the audience?
8. Why does a speaker attempt to introduce conflict in a persuasive speech?

NOTES

1. For further discussion of Monroe's motivated sequence, see Bruce E. Gronbeck et al., *Principles of Speech Communication*, 10th Ed. (Glenview, Ill.: Scott, Foresman, 1988), Chap. 12.

2. Josh Barbanel, "Societies and Their Homeless: Cycles of Concern," *New York Times*, November 29, 1987, sec. 4, p. E1.

3. Russell Watson, Michael A. Lerner, and Theodore Stanger, "Flake or Fox?" *Newsweek*, January 20, 1986, p. 14.

4. Jerry Adler and Nikki Finke Greenberg, "The Dark Side of the Sun," *Newsweek*, June 9, 1986, pp. 60–4.

5. Mario Cuomo, "Keynote Address," *Vital Speechs of the Day*, August 15, 1984, p. 649.

6. Adapted from a speech manuscript prepared by Laura Waluszko. Used with permission.

ADDITIONAL READINGS

An asterisk indicates an advanced reading.

Bostrom, R. N. *Persuasion*. Englewood Cliffs, N.J.: Prentice-Hall, 1983.
    This is an impressive overview of persuasion.

Johannesen, R. L. *Ethics in Human Communication*. Prospect Heights, Ill.: Waveland Press, 1978.
    This book provides an important discussion on the issue of ethics.

Larson, C. U. *Persuasion: Perception and Responsibility*, 4th Ed. Belmont, Calif.: Wadsworth, 1986.

> Chapter 7 offers an illuminating discussion on the application of persuasion to political campaigns and social movements.

*Reardon, K. K. *Persuasion: Theory and Context* (Foreword by Gerald R. Miller. Sage Library of Social Research, Vol. 122). Beverly Hills, Calif.: Sage, 1981.

> This book provides a thorough discussion of persuasion and includes an impressive bibliography.

Glossary

abdicrat: according to William Schutz, an individual who retreats from the decision-making process.

abstract: words or phrases that are general or vague.

abstraction: the use of broad terms to explain ideas or concepts.

active listening: listening with a sense of purpose and involvement.

adaptors: nonverbal behaviors individuals use to adjust to or cope with uncomfortable communication situations.

affect displays: nonverbal signs of our emotional state.

affection needs: one of three categories of interpersonal needs identified by William Schutz; a desire for intimacy.

agenda: an outline of the points to be included in a discussion.

aggression: in conflicts, hostile or intimidating behavior displayed toward another party in an effort to get the better of that party.

allness stereotyping: attributing a particular characteristic to a group of people without regard for the unique qualities of individuals.

analogy: a form of support that compares the similar feature(s) in two seemingly different objects or situations.

argument ad hominem: a false statement that attacks the character of another person.

arrangement: the physical placement of individuals within a group.

articulation: the clear or distinct pronunciation of words.

attitude: a predetermined position that affects the way we interpret data about a person, event, concept, or object.

authoritative opinion: the words or ideas of individuals knowledgeable about a topic.

autocrat: according to William Schutz, an individual who attempts to dominate the decision-making process.

autocratic leader: an individual who attempts to dominate group interactions.

avoidance: a defense mechanism used when an individual wishes to retreat from a problem in a relationship.

belonging needs: on Maslow's hierarchy, the desire to be part of a group.

blind area: the quadrant of the Johari window that represents that part of oneself that one is unaware of, but that one unconsciously reveals to others.

body: the main part of an interview or speech in which the majority of questions and answers occur or major ideas are developed.

brainstorming: a spontaneous method for generating ideas.

causal order: in a cause-and-effect format, the speaker first defines the cause, then follows up by discussing effect.

certainty: in a defensive communication climate, the belief that others cannot contribute new knowledge.

channel: the vehicle by which a message is communicated from the source to the receiver.

clichés: worn-out phrases that have lost their effectiveness.

closed questionnaire: a questionnaire that directs the respondent to select an answer from two or more choices.

closed questions: interview questions designed to elicit specific feedback from respondents.

closure: the process of filling in missing information to make one's perceptions complete.

cohesiveness: a demonstrated sense of purpose within a group.

commitment: the motivation of members to meet the goals of the group.

committee: a group with an assigned task or responsibility.

communicaton: the interdependent process of sending, receiving, and understanding messages.

communication climate: the emotional atmosphere surrounding our communication with others; includes our feelings about ourselves and others and our attitude about the subject being discussed.

competence: one aspect of credibility; a measure of a speaker's knowledge concerning a topic.

concepts: ideas, theories, or thoughts generally used to explain abstract subjects; topics for informative speeches can be drawn from concepts.

conclusion: the last part of a speech; a time to summarize the central points or ask the audience to take some action.

concrete: language that is detailed and specific; to be concrete is to break down or dissect an abstract concept into parts that are easier to explain and to understand.

conflict phase: as defined by B. Aubrey Fisher, one phase of small-group decision-making; it is characterized by disagreement and tension over opposing ideas.

connotation: a personalized meaning of a word attributable to one's experiences, values, and culture.

consensus: genuine agreement among group members that an appropriate decision has been reached.

context: environment or conditions surrounding our communication with others.

control needs: one of three categories of interpersonal needs identified by William Schutz; a desire for power over, influence in, or responsibility for our social environment.

control orientation: in a defensive communication climate, the effort of one party to have the other party conform to his or her way of thinking.

coordinate points: the major ideas in a speech that grow out of the thesis statement.

cost-benefit theory: a theory developed by John Thibaut and Harold Kelley that individuals choose to maintain or leave relationships based upon the rewards they receive within those relationships.

cover letter: a short letter in which one introduces oneself to a prospective employer.

culture: the customary beliefs and attitudes of a racial, religious, or social group.

dating: the use of a specific time reference to clarify a message.

decoding: the process of interpreting or attaching meaning to the sender's message.

deductive reasoning: a logical argument consisting of a general premise followed by a minor premise and ending with a conclusion.

defense mechanisms: the defensive communication behaviors we exhibit when we feel threatened or uncomfortable (e.g., avoidance, psychological withdrawal, distancing).

defensive climate: a climate that inhibits interaction between individuals.

defensive communication: a reaction, either verbal or nonverbal, to a communication situation in which one feels personally threatened or uncomfortable.

democrat: according to William Schutz, one who can cope with the responsibilities of decision-making.

democratic leader: one who demonstrates confidence in the group by involving group members in decision-making matters.

denial: refusal to acknowledge that a problem exists.

denotation: a definition shared or understood within a given culture.

description: in an informative speech, an image that is created verbally.

descriptive language: specific words used to represent observable behavior or phenomena.

descriptiveness: in a supportive communication climate, the ability to focus on observable behavior.

discreteness: the ability to stand alone; in a speech outline, each idea should be able to stand on its own.

distancing: a defense mechanism used to shield or hide one's perceived weaknesses from others; distancing communicates that one does not wish to be approached.

dyadic communication: the interaction between two people.

dynamism: one dimension of speaker credibility; the degree of excitement one brings to a presentation.

emblems: nonverbal behaviors that take the place of words.

emergence phase: as defined by B. Aubrey Fisher, the stage in small-group decision-making when members are anxious to reach a consensus.

empathy: the ability to look at a situation from another person's perspective and understand what that person is feeling.

encoding: the process of putting thoughts, ideas, or feelings into meaningful symbols that another person can understand.

equality: in a supportive communication climate, the state of treating others on a par with oneself.

esteem needs: on Maslow's hierarchy, the desire for influence or status within the social structure.

ethics: rules that govern moral behavior.

evaluative behavior: in a defensive communication climate, judgmental behavior that attacks an individual rather than the individual's actions.

examples: as a form of support, statements that attempt to illuminate facts.

extemporaneous delivery: a thoroughly prepared and practiced speech delivered in a spontaneous, conversational style.

external noise: sounds or visual stimuli that draw our attention away from the intended message.

factual example: an example taken from one's own experience; something one has observed.

feedback: the receiver's response to the sender's message.

flexibility: the ability to adapt to a variety of situations; an important ingredient in resolving conflicts.

formula communication: defense mechanism used by individuals who are hesitant to share their feelings; superficial, nonthreatening communication that involves little or no risk to the communicator.

forum: a small-group presentation in which the audience is invited to join the discussion.

functional perspective: a leadership perspective that focuses on the kinds of behaviors members can exhibit to help the group solve a problem.

gatekeeper: one who attempts to regulate the flow of communication within a group.

general purpose: the overriding goal of a speech—to inform, to persuade, or to entertain; these frequently overlap.

generalization: the use of nonspecific language to describe objects, events, feelings, and so on.

graduated scale: a questionnaire in which answers are ranked on a continuum.

halo and horns stereotyping: allowing our initial perceptions of an individual, either positive or negative, to transfer to other situations.

hearing: one's physical ability to perceive sounds.

hidden area: the quadrant of the Johari window that represents that part of oneself that one is aware of but has not shared with others.

hypothetical example: an example created expressly for the speech being presented.

illustrators: nonverbal symbols that reinforce a verbal message.

impromptu delivery: a speech delivered without advance preparation or practice.

inclusion needs: according to William Schutz, a desire to be part of a group.

indexing: a technique that takes into account differences among people, objects, places, and so on.

inductive reasoning: a type of reasoning that moves from specific instances to generalizations.

inflection: changes in the loudness or tone of your voice.

internal noise: one's own thoughts or feelings that prevent one from processing a sender's message.

interpersonal communication: an informal exchange between two or more persons.

interpersonal conflict: according to Frost and Wilmot, an expressed struggle between at least two interdependent parties who perceive incompatible goals, scarce rewards, and interference from each other.

interview: a planned interaction between two parties in which questions are asked and answers given.

interviewee: the party who responds in an interview.

interviewer: the party who asks the questions in an interview.

intimate distance: that distance at which it is appropriate for highly personal communication encounters to occur; the area ranges from actual touching to a distance of approximately 18 inches.

intrapersonal communication: ongoing communication with oneself; includes such activities as evaluating oneself and one's relationships with others, planning for the future, internal problem-solving, and so on.

introduction: the initial part of a speech in which one strives to create a "need to know" on the audience's part.

jargon: highly specialized words used and understood by specific groups of people.

Johari window: a visual model composed of four quadrants (open, blind, hidden, and unknown) that illustrates degrees of awareness and self-disclosure in interpersonal relations.

journals: publications that contain research findings.

laissez-faire leader: a leader who gives minimal direction or instruction to group members.

leadership: the ability to exert influence on a group by providing a sense of direction or vision.

leading questions: questions designed to move an interview in a specific direction.

listening: the process of giving thoughtful attention to what we hear.

magazines: publications containing articles that frequently put into perspective the circumstances surrounding a particular event.

manuscript delivery: a speech delivered from a prepared script, read word for word.

Maslow's hierarchy of needs: a classification system used to explain people's basic needs, ranging from physiological, to safety, to belonging, to esteem, to self-actualization.

mean: a statistical method sometimes referred to as the average; to calculate, add all the values and divide the sum by the number of numerals in the set.

median: the middle point of a set of numbers; half the numbers are above the midpoint and half the numbers are below the midpoint.

memorized delivery: a type of speech in which the speaker develops a complete manuscript, then spends additional time memorizing it word for word.

message: the thought, feeling, or action sent from a source to a receiver.

mode: the number that occurs most frequently in a set of numbers.

Monroe's motivated sequence: an organizational plan helpful in the development of a persuasive speech; its five steps are arousing attention, showing a need, satisfying the need, visualizing the results, and calling for action.

narrative: a story or an account of an event told orally.

needs: physical or emotional desires that grow out of our immediate environment.

neutrality: in a defensive communication climate, indifference displayed toward another individual.

neutral questions: questions that reveal nothing of the interviewer's biases, preferences, or expectations.

noise: any unintended stimulus that affects the fidelity of the sender's message.

nonjudgmental: one quality of empathic listening; the ability to keep an open mind while another party is speaking and to avoid judging the statements of others.

non-sequitur: in an argument, minor points unrelated to the major points, or a conclusion that does not logically follow the points that precede it.

nonverbal communication: messages we send without verbalizing our thoughts or feelings; includes bodily movements, space, touch, clothing, and paralanguage.

norms: rules that dictate how group members ought to behave.

open area: the quadrant of the Johari window that represents that part of oneself that one knowingly shares with others and that others can readily determine about one.

open questionnaire: a questionnaire that gives respondents the opportunity to fully express their feelings.

open questions: nonrestrictive questions designed to give the respondent maximum latitude in formulating an answer.

orientation phase: as defined by B. Aubrey Fisher, the beginning of a group discussion in which members are chiefly concerned with establishing a comfortable social climate.

outdoing others: a defense mechanism displayed when one feels the need to top the achievements of others.

overly critical communication: a defense mechanism characterized by judgmental behavior.

overpersonal: according to William Schutz, the quality of compensating for anxiety in interpersonal relations by establishing many relationships.

oversocial: according to William Schutz, the quality of compensating for extreme discomfort in social interactions by actively seeking out such interactions.

panel: a public small-group discussion in which members attempt to solve problems or inform an audience about a topic.

paralanguage: the nonverbal aspects of speech, including pitch, volume, rate, and quality.

paraphrasing: restating another person's message in our own words.

passive listening: listening without providing feedback; watching television is an example of passive listening.

perception: the process of assigning meaning to stimuli.

perception checking: a verbal statement that reflects our understanding of a nonverbal message.

periodicals: publications published at regular intervals (e.g., weekly, monthly, quarterly, semi-annually).

personal: according to William Schutz, the quality of feeling comfortable with one's ability to handle close personal relationships.

personal distance: that distance most appropriate for interpersonal interactions dealing with personal matters; approximately 18 inches to 4 feet.

personal space: the physical area between oneself and others.

persuasion: the act of convincing an audience, through verbal and nonverbal communication, to alter or adopt an attitude, belief, or value.

physiological needs: on Maslow's hierarchy, the lowest level needs (e.g., food, water, air).

plagiarism: the use of someone else's ideas without proper credit.

power: control, authority, or influence over others.

premise: a proposition that serves as the basis for an argument.

primary questions: those questions that introduce a major area of discussion to be guided by the interviewer.

primary sources: documents, such as letters, manuscripts, and taped interviews.

problem orientation: in a supportive communication climate, the belief that more than one person contributes to a problem, and that solution of the problem necessitates adjustment of behavior on all fronts.

problem solution: a method of organizing a speech in which one identifies a conflict, then offers a potential course of action to correct the problem.

process-related leadership behaviors: those behaviors concerned with maintaining a positive climate within the group.

pronunciation: correct utterance of words.

provisionalism: in a supportive communication climate, a willingness to explore new ideas.

proxemics: the study of physical space as it relates to human interaction.

proximity: the psychological or physical closeness of stimuli to one another.

psychological withdrawal: a defense mechanism displayed when one feels uncomfortable in a situation but cannot physically withdraw from that situation.

public communication: sharing information with a large group; typically, a speaker presenting ideas to an audience.

public distance: that distance most appropriate for public communication; a distance exceeding 12 feet.

questioning: a communication skill designed to help us understand another person's message.

question of fact: a question that asks whether a statement is true or false.

question of policy: a question that asks whether any specific action is in order.

question of value: a question that asks whether something is good or bad, right or wrong.

rate: the number of words spoken in a given amount of time, usually 120 to 150 words per minute.

reaction formation: a defense mechanism in which one behaves contrary to the way one actually feels.

receiver: the person to whom a message is sent.

refutation: the process of disputing the arguments of another person.

regulators: nonverbal behaviors used to control, or regulate, communication between individuals.

reinforcement phase: as defined by B. Aubrey Fisher, the final phase of the decision-making process in which consensus is achieved and members reinforce their positive feelings concerning the decision.

responsive listening: a type of listening in which the listener provides the sender with feedback about the message.

résumé: a short written account of one's qualifications for a particular position.

safety needs: on Maslow's hierarchy, the desire to feel secure; safety needs function on two levels: physical security and personal security in social situations.

Sapir-Whorf hypothesis: the theory that our perception of reality is dependent on the language system that supports our thought processes.

sarcasm: a defense mechanism in which a biting sense of humor is used to keep people at a distance and to maintain control in a situation.

secondary questions: questions designed to gain additional information from the interviewee.

secondary sources: interpretations of primary material.

selective attention: the process of determining what we focus our attention on and what we ignore.

self-actualization: the highest level of needs on Maslow's hierarchy; the perception that one is at the highest level of what one believes to be his or her potential.

self-concept: one's total perception of oneself.

self-disclosure: the conscious decision to share information about oneself.

self-esteem: one's measure of self-worth; the evaluative dimension of self-concept.

self-fulfilling prophecy: fulfillment of someone's expectations about one's behavior due to those expectations.

self-image: the way one defines oneself.

significant other: an individual to whom one is emotionally close and whom one allows to influence one's life.

similarity: the organization into groups of stimuli that resemble one another.

situational perspective: a leadership perspective that recognizes that each group creates a new situation, which in turn dictates the style of leadership that is most appropriate.

small-group communication: according to Beebe and Masterson, interactions with three to eight people who share a common purpose or goal, feel a sense of belonging in the group, and exert influence on one another.

social distance: that distance most appropriate for communication of a nonpersonal nature; approximately 4 to 12 feet.

source: the individual who creates and sends a message.

spatial order: the organization of the parts of a topic according to the relationship of their positions.

specific purpose: a single sentence that states what one hopes to accomplish during a speech, which aspect of the topic one will cover, and who the intended audience is.

spontaneity: in a supportive interpersonal climate, an open discussion of feelings; in public communication, a speaker's apparently natural behavior at the time of delivery.

status: the relative standing of one party in relation to another.

stereotyping: placing or categorizing people, places, objects, or events into groups on the basis of generalized characteristics.

strategy: in a defensive communication climate, efforts to manipulate interactions among individuals.

subordinate points: in a speech outline, the minor points that grow out of and support the major ideas.

superiority: in a defensive communication climate, the attitude that one is better, more important, or more valuable than someone else.

supportive behavior: communication designed to assist or encourage speakers to express their feelings.

supportive climate: a climate that encourages free and open interaction between individuals.

suppression: in conflicts, acknowledging that a problem exists, but attempting to minimize its importance.

symbol: something that represents something else.

symposium: a small group of speakers who share a topic but who discuss it individually, often with each focusing on a specific aspect.

task-related leadership behavior: actions whose purpose is to keep the group focused on a problem or question.

technical language: the specialized terms associated with a particular discipline, skill, or career.

territory: the space one claims as his or her own.

thesis statement: a statement that includes the major ideas of a speech and at the same time refines the specific purpose.

time order: in a speech outline, the chronological arrangement of ideas.

topic order: in a speech outline, dissection of the main topic into smaller points that are pertinent to the main idea.

touch: a form of nonverbal communication that conveys a wide range of emotions.

trait perspective: a leadership perspective that suggests that certain individuals are "born leaders" because they possess special qualities.

trustworthiness: one dimension of speaker credibility; the type of "character" one communicates to an audience.

underpersonal: according to William Schutz, the quality of shying away from developing close, intimate relationships with others.

undersocial: according to William Schutz, the quality of finding it difficult to participate in groups, usually because of a belief that one is not capable of effective social interaction.

unknown area: the quadrant of the Johari window that represents that aspect of oneself that is unknown to both oneself and others.

vague language: language that lacks directness, specificity, and details.

verbal communication: the expression of thoughts, feelings, and attitudes through words.

visual aids: visual support for verbal messages (e.g., graphs, drawings, slides, movies, photographs, body language).

volume: the loudness of a speaker's voice.

words: symbols that represent things (e.g., feelings, objects, behaviors).

Acknowledgments

Literary Credits
Page 8: From Jonathan Alter, "The Great TV Shout-Out," *Newsweek,* February 8, 1988, p. 20. Copyright 1988, *Newsweek,* Inc. All rights reserved. Reprinted by permission.   Page 19: From Vincent Canby, "'Platoon' Finds New Life in the Old War Movie," *The New York Times,* January 11, 1987, Sec. 2, p. H21. Copyright © 1987 by The New York Times Company. Reprinted by permission.   Pages 19–20: From Pauline Kael, "The Current Cinema: Little Shocks, Big Shocks," *The New Yorker,* January 12, 1987, pp. 94 and 95. Reprinted by permission: © 1987 Pauline Kael. Originally in *The New Yorker.* Page 66: From *Vital Speeches of the Day,* September 15, 1984, p. 710.   Page 67: Figure, p. 11, from *The Meaning of Meaning* by C. K. Ogden and I. A. Richards reprinted by permission of Harcourt Brace Jovanovich, Inc.   Pages 68–70: From Stokely Carmichael, "Toward Black Liberation," *Massachusetts Review,* Autumn, 1966, pp. 639–651. Reprinted by permission of the authors, Stokely Carmichael and Mike Thelwell.   Page 73: From *Vital Speeches of the Day,* August 1, 1972, p. 612.   Page 73: From *Vital Speeches of the Day,* September 15, 1982, p. 707.   Page 80: From *Vital Speeches of the Day,* August 15, 1984, p. 646.   Page 109: Figure 6.1 from *Group Processes: An Introduction to Group Dynamics,* by Joseph Luft. By permission of Mayfield Publishing. Copyright © 1984, 1970, and 1963 by Joseph Luft.   Page 118: From *Ordinary People* by Judith Guest. Copyright © 1976 by Judith Guest. All rights reserved. Reprinted by permission of Viking Penguin, Inc.   Page 290: From Ralph Abernathy, "Martin Luther King's Dream," in Lynda Rosen Obst (Ed.), *The Sixties: The Decade Remembered Now, by the People Who Lived It Then,* 1977, p. 94. Copyright © 1977 Rolling Stone Press.   Page 317: From *Ordinary People* by Judith Guest. Copyright © 1976 by Judith Guest. All rights reserved. Reprinted by permission of Viking Penguin, Inc.   Pages 317–318: From *Vital Speeches of the Day,* August 15, 1987, p. 645.   Pages 318–319: From Matt Clark, et al., "A Slow Death of the Mind," *Newsweek,* December 3, 1984, p. 56. Copyright 1984, *Newsweek,* Inc. All rights reserved. Reprinted by permission.   Page 320: From *Vital Speeches of the Day,* September 15, 1984, p. 706.   Page 350: From *Vital Speeches of the Day,* August 15, 1984, p. 649.

Photo Credits
All photos not credited are the property of Scott, Foresman and Company.   Page 1: Charles Feil.   Page 4: Sidney Harris.   Page 12: Laimute Druskis/Taurus Photos.   Page 14: Bill Fitz-Patrick/The White House.   Page 25: Michael Weisbrot/Stock, Boston.   Page 28: R. Matusow/Monkmeyer Press Photo Service.   Page 32: Elizabeth Crews/The Image Works.   Page 36: Ellis Herwig/The Picture Cube.   Page 55: Mini Forsyth/Monkmeyer Press Photo Service.   Page 58: UPI/Bettmann Newsphotos.   Page 69: David Strickler/ Monkmeyer Press Photo Service.   Page 90: UPI/Bettmann Newsphotos.   Page 93: H. Koelbl/Leo de Wys, Inc.   Page 97: Michael Hayman/Stock, Boston.   Page 105: Ellis Herwig/Stock, Boston.   Page 108 and 123: Reprinted with special permission of NAS, Inc.   Page 133: Rhoda Sidney/Monkmeyer Press Photo Service.   Page 136: Mimi Forsyth/Monkmeyer Press Photo Service.   Page 138: Liamute Druskis/Stock, Boston.   Page 141: Elizabeth Crews.   Page 158: Ann Hagen Griffiths/Omni Photo Communications.   Page 160: © Allan S. Adler/Photoreporters.   Page 170: Sidney Harris.   Page 183: Spencer Grant/Taurus Photos.   Page 184: Paul Conklin/Monkmeyer Press Photo Service.   Page 195: Michal Heron.   Page 203: Constantine Manos/Magnum Photos.   Page 206: Ford Button.   Page 220: Ellis Herwig/Stock, Boston.   Page 221: Jean-Claude Lejeune.   Page 235: Hazel Hankin/Stock, Boston.   Page 240: Howard Dratch/Leo de Wys, Inc.   Page 252: Richard Wood/The Picture Cube.   Page 260: Howard Dratch/The Image Works.   Page 270: Sidney Harris.   Page 294: Peter Vandermark/Stock, Boston.   Page

296: UPI/Bettmann Newsphotos.   Page 301: Sidney Harris.   Page 303: Mark Chester/
Leo de Wys, Inc.   Page 308: Jeff Dunn/The Picture Cube.   Pages 310 and 312: Jean-
Claude Lejeune.   Page 316: Robert George Gaylord.   Page 333: Wide World Pho-
tos.   Pages 337 and 341: Alan Carey/The Image Works.   Page 343: Elizabeth
Crews.   Page 344: UPI/Bettmann Newsphotos.   Page 347: Sidney Harris.

Index